MONIKA WIESAK

Echoes of a Lost America

Unraveling the Murder of JFK

First edition

ISBN: 979-8-9865568-6-4

This book was professionally typeset on Reedsy.
Find out more at reedsy.com

To Every American

Contents

Preface   iii

 1 Cui Bono   1

 2 The Alleged Assassin   40

 3 The Lead Up to the Crime   53

 4 The Crime   83

 5 The Assassin of the Alleged Assassin   109

 6 The Initial Cover-Up   117

 7 The Little Brother   140

 8 New Investigations and Continuing Cover-ups   193

 9 The Son   211

10 Conclusion   229

11 Why JFK Still Matters   233

Notes   236

Preface

"It was the moment the innocent world ended." – filmmaker Wes Craven on John F. Kennedy's assassination

I felt the chilly morning air as I zipped up my jacket and stared ahead at the *X* marked in the center of the road, lost in my thoughts. I was in Dallas, standing in the infamous Dealey Plaza, where one or more gunmen had brutally murdered John F. Kennedy. The *X* was an eternal reminder of that horrific moment, frozen in time. As I stood there, images from the Zapruder film haunted me. It was an amateur film taken on the day of the assassination, capturing the awful moment at which Kennedy's head exploded.

I was not sure I wanted to see this dreadful place, but I was in the area and felt compelled to witness it. After all, this was the location where good and evil, light and darkness, had collided. Indeed, the street I was standing on had inspired the title of the horror film *Nightmare on Elm Street*. Filmmaker Wes Craven revealed that Kennedy's murder was the moment the innocent world ended for him.[1] That moment stole hope from the American people and the broader global public. I was standing where innocence and belief in government had shattered. I felt it in the air. It had been sixty years, but JFK's presence still lingered, crying out for justice, not only for himself but for all who suffered and continue to suffer as a result of that cruel and fateful day.

My entire childhood, I had heard stories about who killed John F. Kennedy, from the lone-nut thesis initially purported by the government to the various hypotheses pointing the finger at more sophisticated players. I had always felt an acute sadness for his untimely death, but I did not know what the heartache meant or if his death still mattered. The individual players had left the scene and were long gone. But I felt an inexorable pull to understand it and to understand the significance of that moment in history, so I embarked on studying Kennedy's presidency. In the process, I became aware of the depth of what had been lost on that grisly day. Realizing that loss was more than I could have ever imagined compelled me to write the book *America's Last President: What the World Lost When It Lost John F. Kennedy.*

Nevertheless, the numerous potential motives I had uncovered did not preclude that the crime could have simply been a coincidence, that the motives and timelines were mere happenstance. Motives and beneficiaries are a starting point, but it is still important to explore the details. What is the evidence? Do the pieces fit together? Who were the players that were involved? Who were they connected to? Was there ever a genuine attempt to investigate the crime? Were there attempts to cover it up? Is there a reason it remains unsolved? Or has it been solved, but it is just not widely reported? What about the murder of JFK's brother and closest confidant, Robert F. Kennedy? Is it just a coincidence that the two brothers were killed, or are their deaths related? What about the plane crash that killed his son and namesake, John F. Kennedy Jr.? Was it an accident or a Kennedy curse, or was foul play involved? Were these just random crimes and accidents, or is there more to it? And if these deaths are related, are vital clues missed when they are analyzed individually instead of collectively?

How did we go from having the most popular president in history, based on approval ratings,[2] and a potential dynasty in the making to sixty years later still having no resolution and no justice for his murder nor his brother's murder? Why is the truth not widely available today? After all, is this not a historical event long ago passed? Or do the entities on whose behalf the culprits acted still hold immense power today? If the crime was indeed a coup d'état, is the regime it installed still in place?

This book will try to shed light on these questions. It will not follow the approach typically taken in most books, i.e., it will not argue any thesis regarding the crime. Instead, it will lay out the available evidence, ask questions along the way, and let the reader decide. Some questions may be uncomfortable, and I do not pretend to know the answers; but when searching for truth and justice, no question should be left unasked.

I did not want to write this book. Indeed, I dreaded it. My interests lie in policy, not in murder scenes; in Kennedy's life, not in his death. But the truth matters, no matter how ugly, and my desire for truth and justice compelled me to put this together. John F. Kennedy deserves that much, as do America and the world. The violent removal of a head of state is an affront to the people. It is a gruesome message that votes do not matter and that democracy is merely an illusion.

In this author's view, the Kennedy assassinations are the Rosetta Stone of our modern world. It is only through understanding these murders that we can fully comprehend our current reality and how it came to be. Discovering the truth behind these crimes can not only bring justice to those callous moments, but also form a basis for creating a better world—a world closer to the one John F. Kennedy envisioned and worked and died for. As the saying goes, the truth shall set us free.

1

Cui Bono

[The president] must serve as ... the defender of the public good and the public interest against all the narrow private interests which operate in our society. –
John F. Kennedy

The first question to ask about any crime is cui bono—what did anyone have to gain from it? Thus, before delving into the details of John F. Kennedy's assassination, it is vital to understand who the beneficiaries of that crime were. It is imperative to note that just because a person or entity benefited from the assassination does not mean they were involved in it or had any prior knowledge. Happenstance does occur. Nonetheless, it is crucial to understand who the beneficiaries were so that when examining the details of the assassination, no stone is left unturned and no avenue is left unexplored. After all, if there is no awareness that a particular party benefited from the assassination, then details that link that party to the assassination may be easily overlooked and vital clues ignored. Understanding the beneficiaries gives the appropriate lens through which to explore the evidence. Today there is an excellent knowledge of Kennedy's policies as the result of declassification of files and extensive oral histories, as well as sixty years of aftereffects available to analyze the immediate, mid-term, and long-term beneficiaries properly. There is a broader picture at one's disposal now than was available to earlier researchers.

Various parties, both individual and collective, benefited from John F. Kennedy's removal from office. This chapter will do its best to list the major beneficiaries in no particular order. It is up to the reader to decide which individuals and parties had the most to gain from JFK's removal and the most to lose if Kennedy maintained his position of power and influence. Factors to keep in mind are who had the most urgent motives and who could not wait until the 1964 campaign, at which point more legitimate means of removal could have been pursued before resorting to violent methods. One can argue that assassination is the preferred removal method, for it leaves an indelible mark and serves as a stark warning to others. However, one can also contend that assassination is a last resort, for it forces the guilty party or parties to reveal their hand and turns the victim into a martyr so that even sixty years later, concerned citizens are still digging and fighting for the truth. While timelines are not definitive, it is worthwhile to keep them in mind. It is also paramount to consider the possibility of collusion between various interests and parties. The involvement of one party does not preclude the potential involvement of another. It is not uncommon for multiple entities to work together.

Five leading interests benefited from John F. Kennedy's removal from office: anti-Communist interests, pro-war interests, Central Intelligence Agency (CIA) interests, Israeli/Zionist interests, and powerful financial interests. Organized crime networks also benefited. The John F. Kennedy Administration was probably the only presidential administration to make a serious effort to reign in organized crime. From 1961 to 1962, convictions of organized criminals grew by 350 percent.[3] There is no doubt that Robert Kennedy's Justice Department was serious about cracking down on organized crime.

It is critical to note that these interests also considerably overlapped and that influential players were committed to several of these matters. Lastly, various individual actors also had personal reasons for wanting John F. Kennedy removed.

Anti-Communist Interests

John F. Kennedy assumed office at the height of the Cold War, an ideological battle between the West and East, capitalism and Communism. It would, at times, turn hot, resulting in military conflict. Kennedy was not a typical cold warrior, even though he has been portrayed as such by many. The nuance of his views is often lost. Ideologically, he believed a free-market system could better uplift the lives of a nation's people than a Communist system could. However, the Cold War, while on the surface being an ideological war, was much more than that. It was a tool for empire-building. It justified building a large American national security state with its enormous military and CIA budgets. It warranted military intervention in far-off lands. It rationalized various other forms of interference in foreign domains, ostensibly to stamp out Communism. However, the intent was often to secure access to vital resources across the globe.

Kennedy wanted to see a world of decentralized power where each country would retain its own independence. He did not believe that the nations of the globe needed to "side" with the United States. During the Cold War era, many prominent figures expected countries to align with the United States or the Soviet Union. Kennedy, however, supported those countries that chose to remain unaligned. When questioned on his willingness to aid such nations, Kennedy responded:

> We're not attempting to use our aid in order to secure agreement by these countries with all of our policies. Our view of the world crisis is that countries are entitled to national sovereignty and independence. That is all we have ever suggested. That is the purpose of our aid, to make it more possible. ... These people in the underdeveloped world are newly independent, they want to run their own affairs, they would rather not accept assistance if we have that kind of string attached to it.[4]

Kennedy, at his core, was an anti-imperialist. While many prominent Americans viewed the Cold War as a useful imperial tool, Kennedy, in many ways, used it as an anti-imperial tool. Rather than using it to push American imperialism, he used it to encourage third-world independence. In his remarks on the Foreign Assistance Act of 1961, he informed Americans that aiding poorer nations was vital to their own security:

> I cannot emphasize ... how important this [foreign aid] bill is. ... This is as important dollar for dollar as any expenditure for national defense itself. ... I recognize that many of our fellow citizens disapprove of it, but I really believe that that's because they do not recognize how closely tied in it is to our national interests. They support these large expenditures for defense in many cases and oppose this and yet I put the two side by side and in many areas, this is the most important because it assists those countries which are directly under the gun.[5]

Even JFK's own family did not always side with the president in his decisions to aid nations that did not align politically with the United States. After JFK decided to fund Ghana's Volta River Project, he stated, with his brother, Attorney General Robert Kennedy, sitting behind him, "The Attorney General has not yet spoken, but I can feel the hot breath of his disapproval on the back of my neck."[6] This decision, however, ultimately contributed to the peaceful resolution of the Cuban Missile Crisis, when Ghana refused to allow the Soviet Union to use it as a refueling base.[7]

So, while Kennedy was ideologically anti-Communist, he did not share the imperial mentality of many cold warriors. Nor did he think the United States needed to stamp out Communism at any cost. And while he was gravely concerned about Cuban leader Fidel Castro's affiliation with the Soviet Union, he was open at the end of his life to normalizing relations with Cuba on the condition that Cuba function as an independent state. US Ambassador William Attwood, who was helping Kennedy establish secret communications with Castro, reflected, "There is no doubt in my mind. If there had been no assassination, we probably would have moved into negotiations leading to a normalization of relations with Cuba."[8]

In Laos, Kennedy supported a policy of neutralization, whereby different factions, including Communist elements, share a government. He ultimately wanted to pursue the same solution for Vietnam. On May 9, 1963, Kennedy reached out to Roger Hilsman, the head of State Department intelligence, to prepare for the neutralization of Vietnam. Hilsman recalled in a later interview:

> [Kennedy] began to instruct me ... to position ourselves to do in Vietnam what we had done in Laos, i.e., to negotiate the neutralization of Vietnam. He had made a decision on this. He did not make it public of course, but he had certainly communicated it to me as I say, in four-letter words, good earthy Anglo-Saxon four-letter words, and every time that I failed to do something [in a way] he felt endangered this position, he let me know in very clear language.[9]

While Kennedy had increased the number of military advisors in Vietnam in November of 1961, after much pressure throughout the year to send combat troops, he soon after, in the spring of 1962, asked Secretary of Defense Robert McNamara to begin working on withdrawal plans.[10] In May 1963, the military proposed its initial withdrawal plans. However, McNamara immediately rejected the timeline, saying it was too slow. McNamara, on Kennedy's orders, requested that a plan be written up for withdrawal to begin in 1963, with one thousand advisors withdrawn by the end of the year.[11] On October 11, 1963, JFK signed National Security Action Memorandum 263, authorizing the withdrawal of one thousand US advisors from Vietnam by the end of 1963.[12] This memorandum came as a result of a McNamara and General Maxwell Taylor trip to Vietnam. The report that resulted from that trip called not only for the withdrawal of one thousand advisors by the end of 1963 but also for a "withdrawal of the bulk of US personnel by 1965."[13] In a September 2, 1963, TV interview with Walter Cronkite, JFK stated about the South Vietnamese, "In the final analysis, it's their war. They're the ones that have to win it or lose it. We can help them. We can give them equipment. We can send our men out there as advisors. But they have to win it, the people of Vietnam against the Communists."

In what may have been the most significant agitation to anti-Communist interests, on June 10, 1963, Kennedy gave a speech at American University where he essentially called for an end to the Cold War. He humanized the "other" side, stating, "We all breathe the same air. We all cherish our children's future. And we are all mortal."[14] He followed that up by suggesting at the United Nations in September 1963 a joint moon mission with the Soviets,[15] and in October 1963, he agreed, against much opposition, to sell wheat to the Soviets. He stated of the sale, "It shows that peaceful agreements with the United States which serve the interests of both sides are a far more worthwhile course than a course of isolation and hostility."[16] Kennedy had spoken of ending the Cold War and exploring space with the Soviets throughout his presidency; however, in 1963, the prospects that these wishes would come to fruition were brighter than ever.

After Kennedy's murder, the U.S. greatly intensified its involvement in Vietnam. JFK's wife, Jackie, stated about Vietnam in early 1964 that her husband "always said the political there was so much more important than the military."[17] Immediately after JFK's death, however, Lyndon Johnson approved Americanizing the war, something Kennedy never did during his entire presidency. In the early weeks of December 1963, plans began for American attacks on North Vietnam. These activities included "patrols" by US Navy patrollers in the Gulf of Tonkin. The first patrol began on February 28, 1964; the second patrol, which began July 31, 1964, led to the August 2 Gulf of Tonkin incident, which in turn led to the Gulf of Tonkin Resolution by Congress, and the eventual deployment of US combat troops into Vietnam in 1965.[18] It is inconceivable that JFK would have ever sent the five hundred thousand US combat troops to Vietnam that his successor, Lyndon Johnson, did. The war eventually spread into Cambodia and Laos as well. It took the lives of approximately 58,000 Americans and two million civilians.[19]

It was not only in Vietnam that Cold War interests benefited from Kennedy's assassination. In the Dominican Republic, Juan Bosch, the first democratically elected leader in thirty-eight years, was overthrown in a military coup on September 25, 1963, after less than one year in office. Kennedy immediately ordered the suspension of diplomatic relations and an end to economic aid to the Dominican Republic. He then announced the withdrawal of all military and economic assistance personnel from the country. Lyndon Johnson reversed this policy. In early 1965 Bosch supporters and other opponents of the military government organized to restore a constitutional government. In response, Johnson ordered a US invasion of the Dominican Republic. Hence, within a short period after Kennedy's assassination, the United States was using its military power against the forces that Kennedy had stood behind and considered democratic.[20]

In Indonesia, Kennedy supported its leader, Sukarno, a leading figure of the non-aligned movement. Kennedy had signed off on National Security Action Memorandum 179, calling for the U.S. to build better relations with Indonesia: "I would like to see us ... move toward a new and better relationship with Indonesia ... I have in mind the possibility of expanded civic action, military aid, and economic stabilization and development programs, as well as diplomatic initiatives."[21]

Within a few months of Kennedy's assassination, the US government cut off aid to Indonesia, except for military aid. The Indonesian army was under the control of General Suharto, who, with the covert support of the U.S., was preparing to overthrow Sukarno.[22] In fact, back on November 4, 1963, Sukarno told ambassador Howard Jones that "he had been given evidence of a CIA plan to topple him and his government." Jones reported to the State Department, "Sukarno acknowledged he was convinced that President Kennedy and the US ambassador were not working against him. However, he was aware from the past that CIA often participated in activities of which the ambassador was not aware and which even perhaps the White House was not aware."[23]

In October 1965, a military coup overthrew Sukarno. An estimated one-half million to more than one million PKI (Communist Party of Indonesia) peasants were slaughtered.[24] An observer from the CIA described it as "one of the worst mass murders of the [twentieth] century."[25] There is much evidence to indicate that the CIA instigated and supported this coup.[26] General Suharto became the new Indonesian president and remained in power for over thirty years, until 1998.

In the Congo, Kennedy put in great effort to establish a constitutional government, with centrist Cyrille Adoula as the prime minister and the left and right also represented.[27] The Congo gained its independence from Belgium in the summer of 1960. However, Western interests viewed its initial prime minister, Patrice Lumumba, unfavorably. After being denied aid by Kennedy's predecessor President Dwight Eisenhower, Lumumba reached out to the Soviet Union for assistance. According to some in attendance, this led to Eisenhower ordering Lumumba's assassination during a summer 1960 meeting.[28] Lumumba was removed from power by a CIA-supported military coup in the fall of 1960. He was ultimately murdered on January 17, 1961, three days before JFK's inauguration.[29] Lumumba's enemies perhaps sped up his assassination due to fears over what Kennedy would do once he took power. A photographer captured the moment Kennedy found out about Lumumba's death. The anguish was evident on Kennedy's face. No picture better conveys the difference in policy between Kennedy and the typical cold warriors of the era. While Eisenhower had ordered the assassination of Lumumba, Kennedy reacted in agony. Shortly after Kennedy's assassination, rebellions broke out in the

Congo, and the new Lyndon Johnson administration abandoned the support of the center and Prime Minister Adoula, whom Kennedy had supported, and moved its support to the right wing and Colonel Joseph Mobutu. Adlai Stevenson, the US ambassador to the United Nations, reflected, "A year before we were regarded as champions of Africa's cause. Now we are as reviled as the Belgians." In 1966, Mobutu installed himself as a military dictator.[30]

Thus, it is evident that, despite Kennedy's ideological opposition to Communism, he was willing to support various centrist and even Socialist leaders that the American Cold War establishment was not. After JFK's assassination, US policy changed drastically in Vietnam, Laos, Indonesia, Congo, and the Dominican Republic. Kennedy's détente with the Soviet Union stalled, and the Cold War continued for another twenty-five years.

Pro-War Interests

John F. Kennedy's push for ending the Cold War did not sit well with many military figures. He had avoided pressures to go to war throughout his presidency. The first push for a war that Kennedy faced was over the failed Bay of Pigs invasion. In early 1960, President Eisenhower authorized the training and arming of a force of Cuban exiles who would return to the island, meet up with dissidents, and establish an alternative government to Castro's. The CIA was to direct the plan and ready it for implementation by early 1961, just a few months after the new president, John F. Kennedy, was to take office.[31] Kennedy reluctantly allowed the plan to proceed but made it clear he would not offer military support beyond the basic assistance needed to get the approximately 1,400 exiles established back on the island.[32] After the plan went badly awry, Kennedy was pressured to offer US military support but refused. According to his wife, Jackie, the events deeply impacted him. She revealed, "He really looked awful. ... He came back over to the White House, to his bedroom, and he started to cry, just with me ... just put his head in his hands and sort of wept."[33] Kennedy

9

felt that a US invasion of Cuba would give the Soviet Union, occupying East Berlin at the time, the justification to take over West Berlin. Because of US obligations to protect West Berlin, Kennedy felt this would escalate into a world war.[34]

After the Bay of Pigs failure, the military pressured Kennedy to send combat troops to Laos. He resisted that pressure and instead agreed with Soviet Premier Nikita Khrushchev to mutually support a neutral and independent Laos under a government chosen by the Laotians.[35] After the military failed to convince Kennedy to send combat troops into Laos, they began to pressure him to send combat troops to Vietnam, as early as May 1961. Then on November 8, 1961, Defense Secretary Robert McNamara and the Joint Chiefs of Staff recommended sending an initial eight thousand combat troops to Vietnam and expanding to as many as 205,000 combat troops. Kennedy rejected this virtually unanimous recommendation of his advisors. General Maxwell Taylor expressed, "I don't recall anyone who was strongly against [sending combat troops], except one man and that was the president. The president just didn't want to be convinced that this was the right thing to do. ... It was really the president's personal conviction that the US ground troops shouldn't go in."[36] Kennedy did agree to expand the number of military advisors in South Vietnam and supply general military aid to support the South Vietnamese. However, as previously mentioned, shortly after this increase, he asked his defense secretary to draw up a withdrawal strategy for the advisors and issued the first order for withdrawal in October 1963.

In the summer of 1961, Kennedy faced great tension with the Soviet Union over Berlin. After World War II, Germany was divided into four zones, and wartime agreements established four-power control over Berlin: US, Soviet, French, and British. The U.S., French, and British allied with West Germany, and the Soviets with East Germany. However, Berlin, which was deep inside East German territory, was split between Western control and Soviet control, with West Berlin being occupied by the Americans,

British, and French. Khrushchev was threatening to take over West Berlin.[37] JFK's military advisers insisted at two summer meetings that they wanted his authorization to use nuclear weapons against the Soviet Union in a pre-emptive US first-strike scenario. JFK's response was to walk out of the meetings. After one of these walkouts, he threw his hands in the air, glanced back at the generals, and said, "These people are crazy."[38] After the other, he commented to his secretary of state, Dean Rusk, "And we call ourselves the human race."[39] JFK had to, on the one hand, hold back his military forces, who were itching for an attack and a head-to-head battle with the Soviet Union, and, at the same time, show enough resolve to Khrushchev to discourage him from invading West Berlin. The conflict ultimately dissipated when Khrushchev put up the Berlin Wall, which separated East and West Berlin for approximately thirty years. One of Khrushchev's primary reasons for threatening to take over West Berlin had been the exodus of citizens from East Berlin to West Berlin. The wall prevented that exodus. Kennedy, relieved, commented, "It's not a very nice solution, but a wall is a hell of a lot better than a war."[40]

The next major crisis that Kennedy faced was the Cuban Missile Crisis in October 1962. This crisis could have led to a catastrophic war had it not been handled correctly. Soviet Premier Nikita Khrushchev secretly placed nuclear missiles onto the island of Cuba after publicly swearing he had no plans to do so. Kennedy came under immense pressure from his military brass to invade the island. He instead chose to start with a naval quarantine. He felt this would send a message to the Soviets that the U.S. would not tolerate the placement of missiles in Cuba while giving time for Khrushchev to change his mind and reverse course. After almost two weeks of tension, Khrushchev ultimately agreed to remove his missiles in exchange for Kennedy publicly pledging never to invade Cuba. Privately, JFK also agreed to quietly withdraw obsolete US missiles from Turkey approximately six months after the crisis.[41]

Despite the good news about the settlement, the military still wanted to attack. General Curtis LeMay lamented, "We lost! We ought to just go in there today and knock 'em off!"[42] LeMay later said, "We had a chance to throw the Communists out of Cuba. But the administration was scared to death [the Russians] might shoot a missile at us."[43] Admiral George Anderson stated, "We have been had." Daniel Ellsberg, famous for leaking the Pentagon Papers, conveyed, "There was virtually a coup atmosphere in Pentagon circles ... not that I had fear there was about to be a coup—I just thought it was a mood of hatred and rage. That atmosphere was poisonous, poisonous."[44] JFK was aware of this; he commented, "The military are mad. They wanted to do this."[45] Later on, in 1971, while giving his oral history to the Lyndon Johnson Library, Curtis LeMay referred to Kennedy's loyal aides as "cockroaches." He further lamented, "Everyone that came in with the Kennedy Administration ... is [sic] the most egotistical people that I ever saw in my life. They had no faith in the military. They had no respect for the military at all."[46] There is no doubt that LeMay had great disdain for Kennedy.

Long before John F. Kennedy became president, he had been thinking about disarmament. According to his wife, "It started so long ago. ... It seemed so extraordinary, I never saw it in newspapers here, but you should sort of disarm or come to some agreement, and that would be possible without selling out. ... It started so long ago that he was thinking about that."[47] In September 1961, JFK signed into law a bill establishing the United States Arms Control and Disarmament Agency, the first full-scale, full-time research and planning agency of its kind in the world.[48]

Though it may seem contradictory, JFK did not see his increased defense spending and his simultaneous pursuit of disarmament as contradictory. He still had a responsibility to protect the security of the United States, and there was a very real threat of war with the Soviet Union. Aide Arthur Schlesinger Jr. explained JFK's outlook:

His view was that, unless we convinced the Russians we would stay in the arms race as long as they could, we would remove the incentive most likely to make them accept general disarmament; for obviously, if we let them win the arms race, they would see no reason to abandon their military superiority and expose their society to external inspection. Both the securing of a second-strike capacity and the diversification of the defense establishment seemed to him, moreover, vital parts for the strategy of deterrence and arms control.[49]

At the UN in September 1961, JFK outlined a broad plan that could serve as a basis for negotiations, of which the first step would be a nuclear test ban treaty.[50] He reiterated his desire for disarmament and a test ban treaty at his 1962 State of the Union address.[51] Despite his hopes for such a treaty, he was making little progress in this area. Then on May 6, 1963, he signed National Security Action Memorandum 239, reiterating his desire to pursue disarmament.[52] In what was the pivotal moment in progressing the treaty, JFK gave his "Peace Speech" at American University on June 10, 1963. In the speech, he declared:

> Our primary long-range interest ... is general and complete disarmament, designed to take place in stages. ... To make clear our good faith and solemn convictions on this matter, I now declare that the United States does not propose to conduct nuclear tests in the atmosphere so long as other states do not do so. ... Is not peace, in the last analysis, basically a matter of human rights, the right to live out our lives without fear of devastation, the right to breathe air as nature provided it, the right of future generations to a healthy existence? ... The United States ... will never start a war. We do not want a war. We do not now expect a war.[53]

This speech kicked off the negotiations needed to get the treaty over the finish line. On September 24, 1963, the Senate ratified the treaty. Aide Arthur Schlesinger Jr. stated, "I have the impression that we would not have had a test ban treaty if ... the president ... had not been so deeply committed and forced the issue."[54]   The treaty only banned atmospheric testing. Kennedy hoped to build on it in future years and prohibit underground testing as well.[55] A treaty that bans such testing has yet to be ratified.

After Kennedy's death, the United States never invaded Cuba, nor did war break out with the Soviet Union; however, the military-industrial complex finally got an Americanized war in Vietnam.

CIA Interests

CIA interests overlap significantly with anti-Communist, pro-war, and powerful financial interests. The CIA itself was a tool created by Wall Street. This section will focus on the CIA as an institution, not an instrument of these other interests.

Even though JFK publicly took full responsibility for the Bay of Pigs debacle, he knew he had a significant problem in his government. He confided in aide Arthur Schlesinger Jr., "It is a hell of a way to learn things, but I have learned one thing from this business—that is, that we will have to deal with the CIA."[56] Schlesinger informed Kennedy that the CIA possessed many of the characteristics of a "state within a state."[57] According to an unnamed source in a 1966 *New York Times* article, Kennedy vowed to an aide after the Bay of Pigs fiasco that he wanted to "splinter the CIA in a thousand pieces and scatter it to the winds."[58]

While Kennedy did not accomplish such drastic changes to the CIA, he did manage, to some extent, to rein them in. In 1961, he issued National Security Action Memoranda (NSAMs) 55 and 57. NSAM 55 called for the Joint Chiefs of Staff, and not the CIA, to be the primary military advisors.[59] NSAM 57 declared: "Any large paramilitary operation wholly or partly covert which requires significant numbers of militarily trained personnel, amounts of military equipment which exceed normal CIA-controlled stocks and/or military experience of a kind and level peculiar to the Armed Services is properly the primary responsibility of the Department of Defense with the CIA in a supporting role."[60] During the same year, he asked the three principal CIA planners for the Bay of Pigs, the top three men at the CIA, Director Allen Dulles, Deputy Director Richard Bissel Jr., and Deputy Director General Charles Cabell, to resign. Allen Dulles later told a *Harpers* reporter his honest thoughts about JFK: "That little Kennedy, he thought he was a god."[61]

JFK also moved quietly to cut the CIA budget in 1962 and again in 1963, aiming at a 20 percent reduction by 1966.[62] Kennedy then gave authority to ambassadors to oversee and coordinate all the activities of the United States government within their assigned countries, with the exception of military forces in the field. These instructions were aimed particularly at the CIA. The ambassadors now, for the first time, had the authority to know everything the CIA was doing in their countries.[63]

The CIA felt the impact of Kennedy's changes. CIA officer David Atlee Phillips, writing about this period in his book *The Night Watch*, described "the few officers remaining" as "moving up and down the halls as attendants at a sepulcher." *The American Heritage Dictionary* defines sepulcher as a "burial vault." According to Phillips, the perception among the CIA officers was that "the Agency is finished."[64]

Most of the changes Kennedy imposed on the CIA occurred in 1961, resulting from the Bay of Pigs disaster. However, it is possible that Kennedy would have pursued further adjustments to the agency, particularly in his second term. After Kennedy's death, the CIA remained a powerful institution and still holds immense power today.

Israeli/Zionist Interests

According to Israeli minister Mordechai Gazit, "The US/Israeli relationship was entering a state of crisis" by late 1963.[65] Four major points of contention led to this "state of crisis": 1. the Palestinian refugee issue; 2. JFK's relationship with Arab countries; 3. attempts to register the American Zionist Council, a Zionist lobby group in the U.S., as a foreign agent; and 4. Israel's nuclear weapons program.

Upon the establishment of Israel in 1948, many of the Palestinians who had been living on the land took residence in refugee camps. During his early months in office, JFK committed himself, via letters to Arab leaders, to UN Resolution 194, Article 11, which called for the right of return for the refugees. JFK's stated support for Resolution 194 prompted Israeli Prime Minister David Ben-Gurion to react in the fall of 1962 with his own letter, to the Israeli ambassador in Washington, intended to be circulated among Jewish American leaders, in which he stated, "Israel will regard this plan as a more serious danger to her existence than all the threats of the Arab dictators and kings, than all the Arab armies, than all of Nasser's missiles and his Soviet MIGs. ... Israel will fight against this implementation down to the last man."[66]

JFK preferred to pursue the refugee issue under the auspices of the United Nations. As such, he brought on Joseph E. Johnson, president of the Carnegie Endowment for International Peace, who would spend the next year and a half working on a plan known as the Johnson Plan, which was then presented to and negotiated with the Arabs and Israelis. The plan offered three options to the refugees: repatriation (return to Israel), reparations (no return, but compensation for lost property), or resettlement, with compensation for lost property, to primarily other Arab countries or potentially non-Arab nations.[67]

However, due to the difficulty of negotiations with both sides, the plan fizzled in the fall of 1962, and Johnson resigned on February 1, 1963.[68] However, JFK made clear to Israel in the fall of 1962 that "We cannot and will not accept the status quo on this matter."[69] The U.S. continued bilateral talks with Israel to try to come to some resolution regarding the refugees. On November 20, 1963, two days before JFK's assassination, the US delegation at the United Nations once again gave its support to UN Resolution 194, Article 11, which triggered fury among Israeli supporters.[70]

The second source of tension with Israel was JFK's desire to build good relations with Arab leaders, and in particular, with Egyptian leader Gamal Abdel Nasser, whom Israel viewed as an archenemy—Ben-Gurion going as far as comparing Nasser to Hitler in a letter to Kennedy.[71] In early 1962, Kennedy approved a three-year, $500 million Public Law 480 food package for Egypt and a loan designed to stabilize the Egyptian economy. This surge in American aid led Kennedy foreign policy advisor Chester Bowles to predict Nasser would take up a "key role in bringing the Middle East peacefully into our modern world."[72]

In a December 1962 meeting between President Kennedy and Israeli Foreign Minister Golda Meir in Palm Beach, Florida, Kennedy attempted to express his need for Israel to understand the United States' overall interests in the Middle East. He made it clear that US and Israeli interests were not necessarily the same. In a memorandum from the meeting, JFK expressed that while the United States has a "special relationship" with Israel, it "cannot afford the luxury of identifying Israel" or any other country "as our exclusive friends." He further elaborated, "We know that Israel faces enormous security problems, but we do too. We have to concern ourselves with the whole Middle East." He then said that the U.S. would like to "maintain our friendship with Israel without constantly cutting across our other interests in the Middle East. When Israel takes actions ... we hope it will understand our problems as well as its own."[73]

R. W. Komer, a senior staff member of the National Security Council who was responsible for Middle Eastern affairs, wrote in a memo to JFK on November 21, 1963, a summary of what he had expressed to Israeli minister Gazit:

We were expected to subsidize Israel, both privately and publicly, to support her to the hilt on every issue, to meet all of her security requirements, and to defend her if attacked. In return, we did not even know what she intended to do in such critical fields as missiles and nuclear weapons. ... What kind of a relationship was this? ... Couldn't the Israeli government acknowledge just once that the U.S. had a defensible position in attempting to maintain good relations with the Arab states?[74]

The third source of tension between JFK and Israel was the attempt by the Justice Department, run by his brother Robert Kennedy, to register the American Zionist Council (AZC), a lobbying group, under the Foreign Agents Registration Act of 1938. This registration was intended to prevent Israel from influencing US foreign policy. During the 1960 presidential campaign, Zionist financier Abraham Feinberg approached JFK. According to close JFK friend Charles Bartlett, "As an American citizen, he was outraged to have a Zionist group come to him and say, 'We know your campaign is in trouble. We're willing to pay your bills if you let us have control of your Middle East policy.'" Bartlett recalled that Kennedy was deeply upset and concluded that "if he ever did get to be president, he was going to do something about it."[75]

On November 21, 1962, the Department of Justice made its initial request to the American Zionist Council to register as a foreign agent.[76] A few weeks later, on January 2, 1963, Isaiah L. Kenen incorporated the American Israel Public Affairs Committee, known as AIPAC today.[77] Kenen originally ran the American Zionist Committee for Public Affairs as a lobbying division of the AZC; this division was renamed AIPAC in 1959.

After the completion of hearings held by the Senate Foreign Relations Committee in May and August 1963, the Department of Justice determined that it "should insist on the immediate registration of the American Zionist Council under the Foreign Agents Registration Act, and if such registration is not forthcoming, appropriate action should be taken to enforce such a request."[78] On October 11, 1963, the Department of Justice submitted a letter to the American Zionist Council requesting registration, concluding, "the Department expects a response from you within 72 hours with regard to this matter."[79] A memo from an October 17, 1963, meeting between the Department of Justice and the AZC outlined the response to the registration request:

> Judge Rifkind [representing AZC] then made a plea for no registration, stating it was the opinion of most persons affiliated with the Council that such registration would be so publicized by the American Council on Judaism [which opposed Zionism] that it would eventually destroy the Zionist movement. ... Judge Rifkind said that he would discuss the matter further with his principles and that he thought the council would probably supply all the information to the Department required of the average registrant but that he did not believe his clients would file any papers or sign any papers indicating that the organization was an agent of a foreign principal.[80]

The Department of Justice indicated it could only reach a position after examining the material filed. No material was filed until after JFK's assassination.[81]

The fourth source of tension between John F. Kennedy and Israel was Israel's nuclear weapons program. In his December 1962 meeting with Golda Meir, Kennedy expressed concerns about Israel's nuclear facility, Dimona. The U.S. had done a cursory inspection of Dimona in 1962; however, Kennedy wanted more thorough and frequent inspections.[82] Kennedy made his first formal request for semi-annual inspections in late March 1963, requesting they begin in May.[83]

On May 5, Israeli Ambassador Walworth Barbour met and discussed the matter of semi-annual US visits to Dimona with Ben-Gurion. The State Department's reaction was that it "appears here [the prime minister] may now be attempting [to] throw [the] question of Dimona inspections into [the] arena of bargaining for things Israel wants from us, such as [a] security guarantee."[84]

However, given that the U.S. failed at a desired quid pro quo the prior year, after selling Israel defensive Hawk missiles and making no progress on the refugee issue in return, they were not keen on such an approach in 1963, as Komer detailed in a memo to JFK: "Given the Hawk/refugee episode of last year, we want to avoid giving if possible before we've taped down the quid pro quos."[85]

Ben-Gurion wrote several letters to JFK in late April and early May. In his letters, he ignored the topic of inspections and instead wrote about his concerns for the security of Israel along with other topics. He even offered to fly to Washington, DC, to meet with JFK, but on May 4 Kennedy denied the request for an in-person discussion.[86] In his reply letter of May 12, Ben-Gurion discussed the possibility of an assassination on Jordanian King Hussein: "He has survived a number of attempts of assassination, but there is always a danger that one single bullet might put an end to his life and regime. ... In light of past events one cannot dismiss the possibility that what was done to his grandfather, King Abdullah, could be done to him."[87]

On May 18, JFK responded to Ben-Gurion and refused to allow him to change the subject continually. He returned the focus of the conversation to Dimona inspections and expressed to Ben-Gurion that US commitment and support to Israel could be seriously jeopardized if inspections could not be secured.[88] On May 29, 1963, Ben-Gurion finally responded to JFK regarding inspections and suggested an inspection either at the end of the year or early 1964.[89]

Kennedy responded on June 15, 1963, just a few days after his famous

American University "Peace Speech," in which he called for a nuclear test ban treaty as the first step to potential disarmament. In this letter to Ben-Gurion, JFK requested more detailed, more frequent inspections, starting immediately, during the early summer of 1963, not at the end of the year, otherwise: "This government's commitment to and support of Israel could be seriously jeopardized if it should be thought that we are unable to obtain reliable information on a subject as vital to peace as the question of the character of Israel's effort in the nuclear field."[90]

As Kennedy's letter arrived in Israel on June 16, Ben-Gurion resigned, never accepting receipt of the letter.[91] Ben-Gurion, however, was not deterred from supporting a nuclear future for Israel. In his farewell speech to the Armaments Development Authority (RAFAEL) on June 27, 1963, he expressed, "I am confident that science is able to provide us with the weapon that will ... deter our enemies."[92]

It is believed some of the highly enriched uranium used for Israel's weapons development may have been supplied from the NUMEC (Nuclear Materials and Equipment Corporation) plant in Pennsylvania and that this funneling of materials was known by James Jesus Angleton.[93] Angleton was the head of counterintelligence at the CIA as well as the head of the Israeli desk at the CIA. After Ben-Gurion resigned, according to Efraim Halevy, who served as the liaison officer of the Israeli spy agency Mossad to the CIA station in Tel Aviv in the early 1960s, Angleton went to visit Ben-Gurion:

> He [Angleton] used to meet with David Ben-Gurion, who[m] he knew for many years. Ben-Gurion ultimately left office and Angleton went down to Sde Boker [Ben-Gurion's home] to meet him. I didn't attend those meetings. Those were just the two of them. He had business to transact.[94]

On July 4, 1963, JFK sent a similar letter to the new prime minister, Levi Eshkol, repeating the same ultimatum he had given to Ben-Gurion.[95] Eshkol responded on July 17, and stated he needed time to review the issue in detail before providing a substantive response. To Ambassador Barbour, Eshkol mentioned his great "surprise," "searching for the right word," he added, over Kennedy's near-ultimatum statement that the US commitment to and support of Israel could be "seriously jeopardized."[96]

In a July 23 White House meeting, CIA director John McCone explained that they estimated that Dimona would go critical late in 1963 or early in 1964, and inspection must begin beforehand as once the reactor was critical, much of it would be radioactive and closed off. Kennedy reiterated his desire to keep up the pressure on inspections.[97]

On August 19, 1963, Eshkol replied to Kennedy. He informed him that due to technical reasons, they could not proceed with an inspection at that moment, but he agreed to a Dimona visit "toward the end of 1963" and assured Kennedy it would be *before* the reactor reached criticality.[98]

JFK did not live to see the end of 1963, and proper US inspections of Dimona never happened. By the Old Man, as Ben-Gurion was publicly known, resigning, Israel was able to get a six-month delay on JFK's demands for immediate inspections of Dimona. However, JFK did not live to see six months. Isaiah L. Kenen, the man who incorporated AIPAC, when writing about the Kennedy Administration, referred to 1963 as "the turbulent year."[99] After the assassination of JFK, these various conflicts with Israel were all resolved in Israel's favor. Kenen referred to Lyndon Johnson as "Israel's Texas friend."[100]

The refugees were neither repatriated nor compensated. Lyndon Johnson cut the economic aid to Egypt and boosted the aid to Israel. He lifted the embargo on offensive military equipment and sent US-made tanks and aircraft to Israel.[101] JFK had sold only defensive weapons, not offensive weapons, and only did so when refugee negotiations appeared to be progressing, in hopes of finalizing those negotiations. According to historian Stephen Green, in *Taking Sides: America's Secret Relations with a Militant Israel*, "The $92 million in military assistance provided in fiscal year 1966 was greater than the total of all official military aid provided to Israel cumulatively in all the years going back to the foundation of that nation in 1948."[102]

This equipment and Johnson's cover-up of Israel's attack on the USS *Liberty* helped Israel double her territory in 1967,[103] something JFK would have been firmly opposed to, as he had assured Nasser the U.S. was against Israeli expansion.[104] It is almost certain that neither the 1967 Six-Day War and the resulting occupation of the Palestinian territories nor the USS *Liberty* attack would have occurred if Kennedy had remained president.

Johnson also invited Israeli prime minister Levi Eshkol to come on an official state visit, something JFK had denied to Ben-Gurion while remaining open to a Nasser visit.[105]

Regarding the USS *Liberty* attack, Under Secretary of State George Ball wrote, "By permitting a cover-up of Israel's attack on the *Liberty*, President Johnson told the Israelis in effect that nothing they did would induce American politicians to refuse their bidding. From that time forth, the Israelis began to act as if they had an inalienable right to American aid and backing."[106]

The replacement of the American Zionist Council, AIPAC (American Israel Public Affairs Committee), has never registered as a foreign agent. There is no doubt today about the influence the lobby group AIPAC has on American policy. In 1973, Senator William Fulbright, who led the hearings against the American Zionist Council in 1963, told CBS, "Israel controls the US Senate. ... The great majority of the Senate of the U.S.—somewhere around 80 percent—are completely in support of Israel; anything Israel wants, Israel gets."[107]

As for the Dimona nuclear reactor, annual cursory inspections did occur under Johnson, but they were limited in nature, and the first inspection did not occur until early 1964 *after* the reactor had already gone critical. According to historian Stephen Green, Lyndon Johnson's White House "saw no Dimona, heard no Dimona, and spoke no Dimona when the reactor went critical in early 1964."[108] And CIA counterintelligence chief James Angleton was not the only one in close contact with Ben-Gurion in 1963. According to Lyndon Johnson himself, "I spent a lot of time with him [Ben-Gurion] back when they were in real problems, and they were getting ready to sanction [in 1963 over Dimona]. I just came down here and said, 'Hell no. That can't be.' And I stopped it."[109] It must be asked, why were Lyndon Johnson and James Angleton talking to David Ben-Gurion behind JFK's back?

It is also important to note that Ben-Gurion had a personal and multi-generational disdain for Kennedy. According to Abraham Feinberg, a ladies' hosiery manufacturer who organized the financing for Israel's nuclear weapons program via approximately twenty-five private donors, Ben-Gurion "had such a hatred for the old man" (JFK's father).[110] In 1938, US British Ambassador Joseph Kennedy had wanted to negotiate the emigration of German Jews to other lands.[111] Ben-Gurion felt Joe's plan would "endanger the existence of Zionism." Ben-Gurion wanted the emigration of Jews to Palestine and not to other lands.[112] It is worth noting that JFK's brother, Attorney General Robert Kennedy, had ordered a Federal Bureau of Investigation (FBI) background check on Abraham Feinberg in March 1961. The background check confirmed Feinberg's close ties to Israel but did not uncover anything regarding the financing of nuclear weapons.[113] JFK had felt Feinberg tried to buy him off during his presidential campaign to gain control of US Middle East policy.[114] Eighteen of the approximately twenty-five private donors to Israel's nuclear weapons project were Americans. Most of the donor names remain undisclosed to this day.[115]

Kenen, the man who incorporated AIPAC, also had a multi-generational dislike of the Kennedy family. Kenen had lobbied for American involvement in World War II and smeared those who opposed the war, stating that it was vital to "isolate the isolationists." He labeled those that opposed the war as anti-Semitic. JFK's father was one of the most vocal opponents of the war and very public about his isolationist views.[116]

As for CIA Chief of Counterintelligence James Angleton, he would have also had his own personal motives for wanting Kennedy removed. Were Kennedy to find out about the funneling of nuclear material from the NUMEC plant to Israel, which he may very well have uncovered had he gotten his desired inspections, he would have removed Angleton from the CIA even more quickly than he had CIA Director Allen Dulles. And he may even have had Angleton tried for treason. Instead, Angleton was honored with two monuments in Israel after his passing.[117] And if JFK was already threatening to cut off funding to Israel over the building of nuclear weapons how much further would he have gone if he had uncovered the funneling of nuclear materials?

It is also important to note that these various Israeli interests overlapped. Kenen worked closely with Abraham Feinberg, the man who was responsible for gathering private donations for Israel's nuclear weapons program.[118] Kenen spread stories that the nuclear reactor was for peaceful purposes.[119] And Feinberg, according to reporter Seymour Hersh, "enjoyed the greatest presidential access and influence ... with Lyndon Johnson. ... Even the most senior members of the National Security Council [under Johnson] understood that any issue raised by Feinberg had to be answered."[120]

According to the Israeli newspaper *Haaretz*, "Historians generally regard Johnson as the President most uniformly friendly to Israel" and "Israel has had no better friend" than Lyndon Johnson.[121] And according to *The Jewish News of Northern California*, "President Johnson firmly pointed American policy in a pro-Israel direction. In a historical context ... the constant diplomatic support, the economic and military assistance, and the strategic bonds between the two countries can all be credited to the seeds planted by LBJ."[122]

Powerful Financial Interests

The last major interests to benefit from JFK's removal from office were powerful financial interests. There was much hostility towards JFK in the upper echelons of economic power. Private interests felt threatened by his insistence on following policies that served the public good. More than any other president, JFK was deeply committed to serving the public. He viewed it as his duty, proclaiming, "[The president] must serve as ... the defender of the public good and the public interest against all the narrow private interests which operate in our society."[123]

JFK emphasized that it was the government's responsibility to nurture and protect a genuine free market, one where everyone had equal opportunity to participate:

> I regard the preservation and strengthening of the free market as a cardinal objective of this or any administration's policies. ... A market of course, is not a fact of nature. It is a creation of man and, as such, we have no guarantee that it will work effectively and impartially if we pay no attention to it. ... We must encourage and protect the availability of full information, safeguard competition, and extend freedom of opportunity to individuals and businesses to participate fully in the economy in accordance with their desires and their abilities. The full benefits of the market system can only be felt when all of our people and all of our resources are used as wisely and effectively as possible.[124]

JFK made multiple attempts to reform tax laws and eliminate tax privileges. He viewed such reform as vital to the public interest, declaring:

The present tax code contains special preferences and provisions, all of which narrow the tax base (thus requiring higher rates), artificially distort the use of resources, inhibit the mobility and formation of capital, add complexities and inequities which undermine the morale of the taxpayer, and make tax avoidance rather than market forces a prime consideration in too many economic decisions.[125]

He made proposals to increase government powers during a recession.[126] He wanted presidents to have the authority to quickly reduce income taxes, implement public works programs, and improve unemployment compensation programs during times of recession. JFK was trying to increase the power of the president, i.e., the elected authority, to respond quickly to economic downturns. Today, for example, the Federal Reserve may adjust interest rates, but the Federal Reserve is not a public institution, even though the president of the United States nominates its chair. But even the chair's term does not coincide with the president's. As such, JFK also proposed to modify the selection of the Federal Reserve chairman to coincide with the presidential term so that each new incoming president could immediately pick their own chairman of the Federal Reserve.[127]

Another quite interesting proposal being looked at under JFK's administration was the loosening of bank regulations—in particular, giving banks more freedom from the Federal Reserve System. James Saxon was Kennedy's Comptroller of the Currency. That position regulates national banks. In November 1963, Saxon gave an interview to *US News and World Report* shortly before Kennedy's assassination. In the introduction to the interview, the editors wrote:

A little-known federal banking agency suddenly has burst into the news, stirring controversy. James J. Saxon, Comptroller of the Currency, who has shaken up many banking regulations, now finds himself at odds with the Federal Reserve Board and some of this country's leading bankers. The Comptroller approved scores of new national banks, and branches, spurred key mergers, revised outmoded rules. Result: Keener competition for deposits and customers.

In the interview, Saxon declared that communities would benefit from greater bank competition as he felt banks were currently failing to meet the customer needs of both individuals and businesses, including not paying sufficient interest on savings accounts and not supplying enough customer installment loans or enough loans to farmers. "You can't find a vibrant and growing community where there is not a live bank … show me a live bank and I'll show you a live community," he stated. He called for less regulation of banks and more freedom from the Federal Reserve System: "My contention is that the Reserve Board shouldn't go beyond determining the adequacy of the total supply of money and credit. It shouldn't determine how money is to be used." When asked if he felt the Federal Reserve System ought to be updated or overhauled, he responded, "Yes, that's exactly what I think. Membership in the System ought to be voluntary." When asked if he had the support of the White House, Saxon replied, "I am well satisfied with the understanding and support I have received." When asked if he was surprised when the Federal Reserve Board came out vigorously in opposition to his proposals, he replied, "No, I wasn't. I'll tell you why. The Federal Reserve Board is the principal regulatory spokesman and champion of the state banks. These include some of the country's big state banks, like the Chase Manhattan, which are plainly apprehensive of the growth in competitive capacity of the national banking system."[128]

In addition to trying to create a climate of fairer competition and greater federal government power and flexibility in responding to economic downturns, Kennedy also focused heavily on creating a production-based economy and supported many programs to assist the needier sectors of society. The first tax change he proposed was an investment tax credit that allowed companies to deduct part of the value of their investments in plant and equipment from their taxes. JFK described the aimed benefits of the tax credit:

> The tax credit increases the profitability of productive investment by reducing the net cost of acquiring new equipment. It will stimulate investment in capacity expansion and modernization, contribute to the growth of our productivity and output, and increase the competitiveness of American exports in world markets.[129]

He expressed, "I would like to see this country's small businessmen improve and expand and not have the control over economic life in either the hands of the government or a few larger groups."[130]

In other efforts to serve individuals and their families, Kennedy pursued the expansion of social welfare benefits. He doubled the amount of surplus food available to those in need and doubled the number of people eligible to receive the surplus food.[131] By March 1961, Kennedy signed a bill extending unemployment benefits from twenty-six to thirty-nine weeks. In May, he signed a bill to extend aid to children of unemployed parents.[132] He also signed off on increasing the minimum wage and expanding the number of industries and professions eligible for the minimum wage.[133] In June 1961, JFK signed off on increased Social Security benefits.[134]

As part of Kennedy's goal to defend "the public good and the public interest against all the narrow private interests which operate in our society," he also stood up to industry in various ways. His most intense conflict with industry was the 1962 steel crisis. Keeping inflation low was essential to JFK's economic policy. He referred to inflation as a "cruel tax upon the weak."[135] What good would his 25 percent increase in the minimum wage accomplish if it would just be eaten up by inflation?

Steel prices were critical to price stability because steel was a major element in industrial costs. Its price was either a direct or indirect cost in every other commodity. A steel price increase would quickly reverberate throughout the economy, creating an inflationary spiral.

The United Steelworkers of America union and the company U.S. Steel were due for contract renegotiations in 1962. JFK had reached out to both the company and the union to express his concerns over the possible creation of an inflationary spiral. JFK offered his help to negotiate an agreement that would not require an increase in prices. Both parties agreed to his involvement. The president was able to negotiate an agreement with the union to forgo a wage increase, thus eliminating the need for a price increase.[136]

Nevertheless, on April 10, 1962, after the last major contract of agreement on no wage increase was signed, JFK was informed by Roger Blough, chairman of U.S. Steel, that the company would be increasing its prices. After Blough left, Kennedy bitterly commented, "My father always told me that all businessmen were sons-of-bitches, but I never believed it till now." Kennedy also understood that this was a direct attack on the prestige of the office of the president. The U.S. Steel board of directors consisted of some of the heaviest Wall Street power players. They were essentially letting Kennedy know that they were running the show. Kennedy felt his entire economic program, as well as his presidency, was at stake here.[137]

The next morning U.S. Steel was joined in its price increase by Bethlehem Steel, the second-largest steel company, and soon after by four others. Kennedy played hardball. He publicly called out the steel industry and urged his defense secretary, Robert McNamara, to give new contracts only to companies who had not raised their prices.[138] JFK then had his brother, Attorney General Robert Kennedy, convene a federal grand jury to investigate price-fixing. The attorney general also ordered the FBI to begin an investigation.[139]

On April 13, Bethlehem Steel became the first steel company to buckle and rescind its price increase. The reported reason was that "Bethlehem had gotten wind that it was to be excluded from bidding on the construction of three naval vessels the following week." By the end of the day, all six steel companies announced that they were rescinding their price increases.[140] Robert Kennedy's Justice Department, however, continued its anti-trust investigation. U.S. Steel and seven other steel companies were eventually forced to pay maximum fines in 1965 for their price-fixing activities between 1955 and 1961.[141]

In an ominous press attack, *Fortune* came out with an article titled "Steel: The Ides of April." According to Shakespeare, Julius Caesar was warned of his coming assassination by a soothsayer with the message "Beware the Ides of March."[142] At a New York dinner in May 1963, Kennedy referred to the fact that down the hall at the same hotel, President Eisenhower was receiving a reward as the man who had done the most for the steel industry that year. "Last year," quipped Kennedy, "I won the award, and they came to Washington to present it to me, but the Secret Service just wouldn't let them in."[143]

In addition to the steel industry, Kennedy also stood up to the chemical and pharmaceutical industries. Rachel Carson was a biologist who became concerned with the impact of pesticides on both the environment and human health. In early 1962 she completed her book on the subject, *Silent Spring*. Kennedy strongly supported the book, and the chemical industry was not pleased. He gave the book credibility and treated it as something that should be taken seriously. The industry responded with a propaganda campaign attacking the book. Kennedy, meanwhile, formed a committee to study the environmental and health impacts of pesticides. In May of 1963, that committee issued a report essentially vindicating Carson and called for greater study of pesticides and alternate methods of pest control in hopes of ultimately removing toxic pesticides from the market.[144]

Kennedy responded in a similar fashion to a scandal in the pharmaceutical industry. In 1961 an epidemic of severe birth defects was uncovered in Germany. Some doctors suspected that the drug thalidomide, a popular remedy for insomnia, headaches, and nausea, was the cause. The drug manufacturer rejected the claims as speculation. However, Dr. Frances Kelsey, a new FDA employee, refused to approve the drug, and Kennedy presented her with the President's Award for Distinguished Federal Civilian Service at a ceremony at the White House, the highest honor for a civilian. Kennedy then signed legislation in October 1962 requiring the FDA's approval before a drug could be marketed. The legislation transferred to the FDA control over prescription drug advertising, which would have to include accurate information about side effects. It required the FDA to approve efficacy (previously, it was only responsible for safety approval). Finally, it mandated that the FDA conduct a retrospective evaluation of the effectiveness of drugs approved for safety between 1938 and 1962.[145] This led to a retrospective review of all drugs approved during those decades. By the early 1970s, this review had categorized approximately six hundred medicines as "ineffective" and forced their removal from the market.[146]

It was not only legal drugs that Kennedy went after, but also illicit narcotics. In September of 1962, JFK convened the White House Conference on Narcotic and Drug Abuse.[147] Then, on January 15, 1963, he signed Executive Order 11076, establishing a presidential commission to study how best to prevent the abuse of narcotic and non-narcotic drugs and how to provide appropriate rehabilitation for habitual drug misusers.[148] An interim report was delivered on April 1, 1963, calling for the Justice Department to "launch a massive attack on the big-time smugglers and sellers of narcotic and dangerous drugs" and at the same time to reduce punishment for "small peddlers" and for "possession." It suggested that the Attorney General, Robert Kennedy, be authorized to organize and put into operation a new special unit of investigators and attorneys to focus on the prosecution of "large-scale illegal operators in narcotics." It also recommended tasking the Attorney General with authoring new legislative proposals regarding more lenient sentencing and punishment for addicts.[149] Robert Kennedy expressed, "The answer is not solely putting them in jail. There has to be some hospitalization of some kind to help and assist them."[150] JFK viewed the addict more as a victim than a criminal. He proclaimed that "the real heart of the matter" when it comes to crime is "the growing power of the organized underworld – the criminal syndicates which have achieved control over an increasing number of legitimate business enterprises." He elaborated:

> These illicit activities are now concealed by or associated with legitimate commercial enterprises, which in turn become the subject of murder and extortion: the building trades, the trucking business, the motion picture industry, the coin machine business, garment manufacturing, and export-import trade.

> Frequently, the nature of a legitimate business serves to assist these illicit operations. Narcotics smugglers, posing as importers, conceal drugs in barrels of olive oil or in the heart of huge cheeses. Those posing as garment manufacturers have access to acetic anhydride, which is used to treat rayon but can also be used to convert raw opium into a morphine base for heroin. Those engaged in trucking operations have access to the waterfront, to facilitate their smuggling.[151]

In its final report, issued November 1, 1963, the commission recommended "that the functions of the Bureau of Narcotics in the investigation of illicit traffic in narcotics ... be transferred ... to the Department of Justice," in other words, to Robert Kennedy.[152] Such changes would have required legislative approval, but JFK would likely have submitted the necessary legislation, which his aide Ted Sorensen considered "extremely controversial,"[153] for review in 1964.

Another area where Kennedy threatened powerful financial interests was his support of broadening campaign contributions. JFK created a Commission on Campaign Costs in October 1961 to review and recommend alternate ways of financing campaigns. In his announcement of the commission, he proclaimed:

> To have Presidential candidates dependent on large financial contributions of those with special interests is highly undesirable. … Traditionally, the funds for national campaigns have been supplied entirely by private contributions, with the candidates forced to depend in the main on large sums from a relatively small number of contributors. It is not healthy for the democratic process—or for ethical standards in our government—to keep our national candidates in this position of dependence. I have long thought that we should either provide a federal share in campaign costs, or reduce the cost of campaign services, or both.[154]

In April 1962, the commission issued its findings.[155] On May 29, 1962, JFK wrote a letter to the president of the Senate and the speaker of the House, stating, "It is essential to broaden the base of financial support for candidates and parties." JFK indicated that this could be accomplished via an incentive system. He specifically recommended a tax incentive that would give each taxpayer the choice of receiving a 50 percent tax credit on their contribution amount, up to $10 annually (valued at approximately $100 in 2024), or a reduction in taxable income, up to $750 annually. If that was not acceptable to the legislators, he suggested that the government match all contributions under $10. So, for every $10 donated by a citizen, the government would contribute another $10 to the citizen's chosen candidate. He also requested that all large donors be required to disclose their donations.[156] He resubmitted a similar letter to the Senate and the House on April 30, 1963, declaring, "The people of the United States are entitled to know their candidates for public office and to be free of doubts about tacit or explicit obligations having been necessary to secure public office."[157] He urged them again to consider his proposed legislation.

JFK opposed setting contribution limits not because he felt they were unnecessary but because he thought that practically they could never be enforced. The commission explained to him that placing limits would only increase the number of political action committees (PACs). PACs are generally formed by corporations, labor unions, trade associations, or other organizations or individuals.[158] They fund campaign activities and are subject to federal limits. Super PACs are independent expenditure-only political committees that raise money to influence elections through advertising and other efforts. They cannot directly contribute to or work with a campaign. Their donations are not subject to federal limits.[159]

The commission pointed out that "there is doubt whether individuals could be prohibited from making certain expenditures, instead of contributions, if the latter were effectively limited, in view of constitutional guarantees of freedom of expression."[160] In place of limits, JFK proposed the "establishment of an effective system of disclosure and publicity to reveal where money comes from and goes in campaigns." He declared that in the commission's view "full and effective disclosure ... provides the greatest hope for effective controls over excessive contributions and unlimited expenditures."[161]

JFK proposed these legislative changes in 1962 and again in 1963. There is no guarantee that he would have been able to pass the legislation, but he would likely have continued to try, and it is not uncommon for legislation to take several years to be enacted into law successfully. When considering that JFK's brother, Robert F. Kennedy, may have been elected as president after him had he not been assassinated while running for the presidency in 1968, it is pretty likely the legislation would have eventually passed. In its place, Congress passed the Federal Election Campaign Act of 1971, which failed to create an incentive system to encourage vast numbers of small, federally financed donations and instead set hard limits on financial contributions. The act had the end result of accomplishing what the commission predicted such policies would accomplish: a vast increase in the number of PACs and multiple Supreme Court decisions striking down parts of the law as unconstitutional.[162] It failed to broaden the base of political contributions or remove the influence of wealth on political campaigns.

It is important to note that Kennedy's foreign policy also greatly impacted powerful private financial interests. Wall Street interests created the CIA to serve their needs. For example, in the Congo, Kennedy not only put in great effort to get a constitutional government re-established, but also strongly opposed the secession of the richest region in the Congo, Katanga. Kennedy felt the Congo would remain destitute if Katanga was able to successfully secede as most of the Congo's tax revenue came from the region.[163] Many wealthy interests, in both Europe and the U.S., supported the July 11, 1960, secession, as it ensured control of the lucrative resources in the area. It was Kennedy's steadfast determination that ultimately reintegrated the Congo in 1963.[164] Similarly, in Indonesia, there was great desire to overthrow President Sukarno to secure access to the rich region there. Indeed, Allen Dulles, the CIA director ousted by JFK, had his own personal reasons for wanting Sukarno removed. There was a secret Rockefeller-controlled gold mine in the region that he wanted to ensure remained in Rockefeller hands.[165]

Kennedy's financial aid policies to poorer regions of the globe were also problematic to powerful financial interests. *The Wall Street Journal* accused JFK of interfering with private investment abroad and accused his foreign aid of fostering "statist and socialistic institutions." It criticized JFK for providing soft loans (long-term with little or no interest) and recommended that he follow more closely the policies of the World Bank. It accused him of having an overly rigid anti-colonialism policy and admonished him for not being more supportive of European allies.[166]

On November 18, just a few days before his death, JFK spoke at the Florida Chamber of Commerce and shared what he felt truly mattered:

I realize that there are some businessmen who feel only they want to be left alone—that government and politics are none of their affairs—that the balance sheet and profit rate of their own corporation are of more importance than the worldwide balance of power or the nation-wide rate of unemployment. But I hope it's not rushing the season to recall to you the passage from Dickens's Christmas Carol in which Ebenezer Scrooge is terrified by the ghost of his former partner Jacob Marley. And Scrooge, appalled by Marley's story of ceaseless wandering, cries out, "But you were always a good man of business, Jacob." And the ghost of Marley, his legs bound by a chain of ledger books and cash boxes replied, "Business? Mankind was my business. The common welfare was my business. Charity, mercy, forbearance, and benevolence were all my business. The dealings of my trade were but a drop of water in the comprehensive ocean of my business." … Mankind is our business. And if we work in harmony, if we understand the problems of each other and the responsibilities that each of us bears then surely the business of mankind will prosper.[167]

After Kennedy was assassinated, powerful private financial interests were no longer hindered by a president in the White House who insisted on serving the public good, both at home and abroad.

Conclusion

Various interests benefited from John F. Kennedy's removal from office. These interests often overlapped. For example, Allen Dulles, the CIA director let go by JFK, was connected not only to the CIA, but also to Wall Street, where he had served as an attorney. James Angleton, the chief of counterintelligence and the head of the Israeli desk at the CIA, was not only an ardent Zionist, but also staunchly anti-Communist. Dulles and Angleton themselves were linked to each other through friendship. Angleton carried Dulles's ashes at his funeral.[168] It was not only the military and the CIA who pushed for the Vietnam War but also powerful financial interests who saw value in the region. Even Zionist interests benefited from the war. French President Charles de Gaulle felt that under the climate of the Vietnam War, Israel would never be forced to withdraw from the captured Arab territories, stating, "One cannot see how such an agreement can be reached as long as one of the greatest among the four will not withdraw from the heinous war that they are waging elsewhere. ... Without the tragedy of Vietnam, the conflict between Israel and the Arabs would not have become what it has become."[169] Indeed, Soviet Foreign Minister Andrei Gromyko wrote in his memoirs that JFK had confided in him that Zionists, along with ideological anti-Communists, were the president's primary opposition to improved relations between the Soviets and the United States as they believed the Soviets would always support the Arab nations over Israel. According to Gromyko, Kennedy stated of Zionists, "This group has effective means for making improvement between our countries very difficult. That is the reality. But I think it is still possible to improve relations, and I want Moscow to know that."[170]

Among powerful financial interests, many were ardent anti-Communists and/or Zionists. They supported a strong CIA and a strong military as tools of empire.

It is also important to note that Lyndon Johnson himself was a beneficiary of Kennedy's assassination. He had a lifelong aspiration to become president, and it is doubtful his goal would have ever been achieved without Kennedy's murder. And while not substantiated, there were many rumors in the fall of 1963 that Lyndon Johnson would be dropped as vice president from the 1964 ticket.

All of these various motives and players should be kept in mind when studying the details of the assassination. It is also worth asking why the culprits chose assassination over blackmail. Was there no blackmail material on Kennedy? Undoubtedly, the intelligence agencies would have had access to any dirt on him. Given how much the press smeared Kennedy's reputation after his death, could they not have done the same for the 1964 election cycle and used such smears to remove him through more legitimate means? Or was his removal from office so urgent as to bypass the blackmail route? Or would the character assassination not have held up if he had been alive to defend himself? These questions are worth asking as typically bribery, blackmail, manipulation, and other forms of election interference are pursued before action as monumental as assassination is undertaken.

Throughout the following chapters, this book will delineate potential links between these interests and possible players in the assassination. When trying to solve a political crime, it is crucial to point out all potential connections to those interests that benefited from that crime. Thus, in this case, it is critical to point out where parties potentially involved in the murder were connected to anti-Communist, pro-war, CIA, Israeli/Zionist, and/or powerful financial interests. Connections to Lyndon Johnson and to organized crime will be pointed out as well. This does not in any way, shape, or form imply that all people tied to such interests would have supported or condoned assassination as a means of furthering those interests. Nor does it mean that even those mentioned were witting participants, and even if witting, that they acted on behalf of such interests. These connections will merely be pointed out because, ultimately, to solve a political crime and determine which parties/interests initiated the crime, every possible relationship to such interests, no matter how tenuous, must be documented and explored. The reality is that there will never be documented proof of who ordered the assassination. The best that can be done is to point out connections to the beneficiaries of the assassination wherever possible to help determine if a pattern forms. Unfortunately, such sophisticated crimes leave few paper trails. Nevertheless, much has been uncovered about the murder over the years. Now that the proper lens has been established, let us explore that evidence.

2

The Alleged Assassin

Oswald was not a Communist or a Marxist. If he was, I would have taken violent action against him and so would many of the Marines in the unit. – Marine Jim Botelho

Who was Lee Harvey Oswald? The history books have written him as the leftist/Marxist lone-nut assassin of President Kennedy. But who was he really? An understanding of Oswald will give a greater understanding of what happened that fateful day in Dallas and Oswald's role in it.

Lee Harvey Oswald was born in New Orleans in 1939.[171] His older brother, Robert Oswald, joined the Marines in July of 1952.[172] In 1955, Lee joined the Civil Air Patrol (CAP), where he met David Ferrie, who would revisit his life in later years, closer to John F. Kennedy's assassination.[173] The CAP is a federally supported non-profit corporation that serves as the official civilian auxiliary of the United States Airforce.[174] Prior to him joining the CAP, Oswald's friends did not recall Oswald reading any Communist literature or expressing any Communist sympathies. His brother Robert stated, "If Lee was deeply interested in Marxism in the summer of 1955, he said nothing about it to me. During my brief visit with him in New Orleans, I never saw any books on the subject in the apartment. ... Never in my presence did he read anything that I recognized as Communist Literature."[175] It was not until after joining the CAP and meeting Ferrie that Oswald began to express Marxist sympathies periodically in public. By October of 1956, Oswald had joined the Marine Corps. His occasional public sympathies towards Communism did not prevent the Marine Corps from enlisting him.[176]

In August of 1957, the military sent Oswald to the Naval Air Facility Atsugi in Japan, which was the main operational base in the Far East for the Central Intelligence Agency. The Lockheed U-2, a high-altitude reconnaissance plane, flew out of Atsugi. One of Oswald's duties in Japan was to guard the U-2 and use state-of-the-art radar equipment to track the plane.[177] Oswald's anti-aircraft unit required a highly classified security clearance. A high, heavily wired fence surrounded the unit. Even a mail truck could not enter without a sergeant's approval.[178]

Some of Oswald's Marine mates felt he had intelligence connections. Marine David Bucknell told JFK assassination researcher Mark Lane that in 1959 he and Oswald, among others, were pitched on becoming part of an intelligence operation against Communism. Bucknell claims that Oswald informed him that the recruiter they met with was Oswald's intelligence contact at Atsugi and that he, Oswald, would go to the Soviet Union as part of an American intelligence mission. While many of Oswald's Marine mates said he was studying Russian language and culture, only one, Kerry Thornley, who featured prominently in the Warren Report, claimed Oswald was a Marxist.[179] The Warren Report was the document resulting from the Warren Commission, the official government investigation into the assassination of John F. Kennedy. Thornley had not served with Oswald as long as the others had and never lived on the same part of the base as Oswald.[180] The rest denied that Oswald had Marxist interests. Marine Jim Botelho, who was friends with Oswald and even took him to meet his parents, told Mark Lane, "Oswald was not a Communist or a Marxist. If he was, I would have taken violent action against him, and so would many of the Marines in the unit."[181] Nelson Delgado, who lived closest to Oswald and for the most prolonged period, stated that Oswald "never said any subversive things." He elaborated, "He would discuss his ideas but not anything against our government or—nothing socialist."[182]

The Marines tested Oswald for marksmanship with a rifle. He was tested twice, once in December 1956 and again in May 1959. There are three marksmanship classifications in the Marines. From highest to lowest, they are expert, sharpshooter, and marksman. On his first test in 1956, Oswald scored 212, two points above the minimum, to qualify as a sharpshooter, just putting him into the middle range. In 1959, Oswald scored 191, one point over the minimum ranking for a marksman, barely qualifying him for the lowest category. In later years, Oswald's Marine Corps acquaintances spoke of how horrible a shooter Oswald was. One acquaintance, Sherman Cooley, stated, "I saw that man shoot. There's no way he could have ever learned to shoot well enough to do what they accused him of doing in Dallas." Oswald was called a "shitbird," someone who repeatedly failed his test and had to do it over and over. Some Marines stated Oswald never did pass the test but was given a final qualifying mark so that the unit could continue with basic training.[183] Delgado testified, "It was a pretty big joke because he got a lot of 'Maggie's drawers,' you know, a lot of misses, but he didn't give a darn. ... [He] wasn't as enthusiastic as the rest of us. ... We all loved—liked going to the range." He added, "[Oswald] was mostly a thinker, a reader, he read quite a bit."[184] Oswald's poor shooting skills should be kept in mind considering the herculean task attributed to him in the assassination of John F. Kennedy.

In March 1959, Oswald picked up an application to attend Albert Schweitzer College (ASC) and applied for the spring term of 1960. ASC was not your typical college; it was hardly a college at all. It was high in the Swiss Alps, not easily reached, and accommodated only thirty students. The college officially opened to students in the fall of 1955, yet none of the thirty students in the entering class were from Switzerland. The school was practically unknown to Swiss authorities. When the FBI tried to find the place, they had to ask for help from their agents in Paris, who in turn asked for help from the Swiss authorities, and it took two months to track down the school. The question raised is how did Oswald find out about this obscure college if even the authorities had great difficulty in finding it?[185] Worth noting is that Albert Schweitzer College was closed in early 1964, shortly after President Kennedy's assassination.[186]

Oswald's service in the Marines was scheduled to end on December 7, 1959; however, on August 17, 1959, he requested an early discharge to assist his mother with health-related issues. Colonel B. J. Kozak, a senior board member who reviewed Oswald's discharge, stated that it usually took three to six months for a hardship application to be approved. Nonetheless, the Marines approved Oswald's application in two weeks. Seven days before his release, he applied for a passport and mentioned in his application his intent to attend Albert Schweitzer College. His passport application was approved a mere six days later. Despite giving his mother's health as the reason for his discharge request, Oswald spent all of three days with her upon leaving the Marines.[187]

He then left for New Orleans, from where he traveled by ship to Europe, arriving in Southampton, England, on October 9. He told officials he planned on staying in the country for a week before departing for Albert Schweitzer College in Switzerland. Instead, Oswald left for Helsinki, Finland, the next evening, October 10. Upon arriving in Finland, he checked into the Hotel Torni for a day and then the Klaus Kurki hotel for four days. The Hotel Torni was a lavish hotel at which President Herbert Hoover had stayed. It served as an espionage headquarters for the British and Soviets during World War II. Klaus Kurki was a similarly upscale hotel.[188] The US dollar was strong at the time, but nonetheless, Oswald's trip would have been costly for someone of his means. Would he have been able to finance it on his own?

The Soviet Embassy in Helsinki had direct ties to Intourist, the Russian state-owned travel bureau. Intourist was typically able to obtain visas for travelers in five to seven days. Oswald applied for a one-week tourist visa on October 13 and received an approved visa by October 14. Oswald then left Helsinki by train on October 15 for the USSR.[189] When Oswald arrived at the Moscow train station, he was met by Intourist guide Rimma Shirkova. Oswald informed Rimma he held classified information about US airplanes and wanted to apply for Soviet citizenship. The Soviet Union denied his request for citizenship, and Rimma informed him he would have to leave before his short-term visa expired. Instead of departing, Oswald attempted suicide. The doctor who examined Oswald stated it was a "show suicide" and not a genuine attempt. As a result, Oswald was placed in the hospital's psychiatric ward for seven days and then released to a hotel. Oswald then went to the US embassy to renounce his US citizenship. While there, he stated he would turn over radar secrets to the Soviets. Oswald likely made these statements believing that the KGB, the Soviet spy agency, had bugged the US embassy and that this would entice the Soviets to allow him to stay in Russia. The US embassy did not detain or charge Oswald for intending to divulge US military secrets. Instead, they told him to return in a couple of days to sign papers to renounce his citizenship. Oswald never did.[190]

Meanwhile, the US embassy contacted US officials about Oswald's defection to the Soviet Union. As a result, the FBI issued a FLASH warning on Oswald, which essentially alerted agents to be on the lookout if Oswald re-entered the U.S.[191] At the CIA, the information about Oswald's defection went into a "black hole" and finally surfaced approximately thirty days later at Counterintelligence Chief James Angleton's CI/SIG (counterintelligence/special investigation group) unit on December 6, 1959. It should have gone to the Soviet Russia division. A 201 file (an information file on any person of interest to the CIA) was not opened on Oswald until over a year later, on December 8, 1960. Despite taking over a year to open a 201 file, the CIA placed Oswald on a watch list in November 1959, during the "black hole" period. This list, which Angleton supervised, allowed the CIA to intercept Oswald's incoming and outgoing mail. There were only approximately three hundred people on the list at the time. Oswald was simultaneously so inconsequential as not to have a standard 201 file but so consequential as to be on an exclusive watch list. Intelligence analyst John Newman indicated this may have been the case if James Angleton was running Oswald as an off-the-books agent.[192] A 1954 FBI memo outlines how the FBI became aware of Angleton running a mail intercept operation. Angleton informed the FBI that the "sole purpose" of his having access to the mail of others was to find persons who could serve as "contacts and sources" for the CIA.[193] It is presumed Angleton's interest in Oswald was a result of Angleton's suspicion that there was a Soviet mole in the Soviet Division of the CIA. Angleton had a spy in the Soviet Union, Petr Popov, who told him that the Soviets knew many details of the U-2. Since Oswald had worked with the U-2, by closely monitoring Oswald and, more importantly, the Soviet reaction to him, Angleton could try to determine if Popov's claims were legitimate. For example, if the Soviets took no interest in Oswald, it would confirm that they already had a high-level source on the U-2 project.[194]

In the late 1970s, there was a reinvestigation into the Kennedy assassination conducted by the House Select Committee on Assassinations (HSCA). During the hearings, Ann Egerter, who worked under James Angleton, was asked why she opened a 201 file on Oswald on December 9, 1960, more than a year after the CIA had found out about his defection. She responded it was because his name was on a list of defectors received from the State Department. The question raised is why was the CIA willing to open a file for this reason in 1960 but not in 1959? This point is especially important since in 1959, Oswald was not just a defector, which was not unlawful, but openly discussed giving away military secrets to the Soviets, which was illegal. When the HSCA asked CIA director Richard Helms in 1978 why it took more than a year to open a 201 file, he responded, "I can't imagine why. ... I am amazed."[195] A declassified CIA memo written by Angleton's successor, George T. Kalaris, in 1975, perhaps gives the answer; he stated the CIA opened the file due to "queries" Oswald was making in December 1960 "concerning possible reentry into the United States." Officially, no one was supposed to know where Oswald was at the time or what he was trying to do.[196] Angleton, however, would have perhaps known because of his access to Oswald's communications. Another item worthy of mention is that the CIA opened the 201 file under the name Lee Henry Oswald and not Lee Harvey Oswald. Indeed, Angleton's counterintelligence staff disseminated much inaccurate and contradictory information about Oswald. For example, in one of two cables drafted on the same day and by the same people, Oswald was described as approximately thirty-five years old and six feet tall, and in the other, twenty-three years old and five feet ten inches tall. Professor Peter Dale Scott argued that Angleton's staff disseminated such disparate information to assist in finding the mole. For example, if someone later referred to Oswald as thirty-five, Angleton would be able to narrow down the source of the leak of information on Oswald.[197] In terms of why the CIA did not open a 201 file in 1959, author Jefferson Morley argued that by opening an Office of Security file instead, Angleton would know who was looking for information on Oswald as they would need to request permission to see the file. Permission is not required to view a 201 file.[198]

In early January 1960, Oswald was given a residence document in Russia and 5,000 rubles and told to go to Minsk. Once there, he quickly found work at a radio factory. He was given a rent-free apartment by the mayor of Minsk and a generous salary of 700 rubles per month. The Red Cross supplemented this with a stipend of the same amount. In March, he was moved to a 60-rubles-per-month apartment, which he called "a Russian dream."[199]

In mid-March 1961, Oswald met his future wife, Marina. Just a few weeks later, on April 10, they filed an intent to marry notice, and the marriage took place on April 30. Marina had been living with her uncle, a high-ranking member of the Communist party and a colonel in the MVD, a Soviet secret police equivalent to the FBI.[200] Was Marina an intelligence asset planted on another intelligence asset, i.e., Oswald? To add credence to this possibility, Marina was not just the niece of a colonel in the MVD, but before spending time with Oswald, she had spent time with Robert Webster, one of two other Americans who had defected to the Soviet Union in 1959 before Oswald. Like Oswald, Webster had military ties and, after a short period, returned to the U.S.[201] What are the odds that Marina would meet up with two defectors when there were so few in total? Marina's potential intelligence background is relevant considering her future odd and contradictory statements after JFK's assassination.

By July of 1961, Oswald began making plans to move him and Marina to the United States, and by December, the couple received news of their visa approval. They had a child while still in Russia in February of 1962, applied for a US State Department loan for their return trip, and received the funds by June. On June 2, they left Russia by train to Holland, where some believe the CIA debriefed Oswald. The Oswalds then boarded a ship across the Atlantic and disembarked in Hoboken, New Jersey, on June 13, 1962. Spas T. Raikin, whom the US State Department had asked to assist the Oswalds, greeted them at the port. Raikin was a former secretary of the American Friends of Bolshevik Nations, an anti-Communist lobby with wide ties to the CIA and other US intelligence agencies. In later years, Donald Deneselya recounted receiving a debriefing report from the New York City field office about a Marine defector returning from Russia in 1962. Deneselya reported to Robert Crowley, a close friend of James Angleton. The Oswalds shortly left New Jersey and flew to Dallas.[202]

If Oswald was a genuine defector rather than a US intelligence asset, why did the State Department issue him funds to return to the U.S., and why was he greeted so warmly upon his return, particularly during the height of the Cold War? According to the State Department, they cannot issue such a repatriation loan unless the recipient's "loyalty to the United States" is "beyond question." Given that Oswald defected and supposedly handed over military secrets to the Soviet Union, it is odd, to say the least, that the State Department considered his loyalty to the U.S. to be "beyond question." Indeed, back in August 1961, the State Department's passport office found no reason they should not allow the renewal of Oswald's passport and authorized the American embassy to renew it. Typically, in the case of defectors, the passport office prepares a "lookout" card in case the party attempts to renew their passport. They never created a "lookout" card for Oswald.[203] Much later, in 1978, James A. Wilcott, a former CIA finance officer who served in Japan at the time Oswald was there, told the House Select Committee on Assassinations that Oswald had been recruited from the military by the CIA.[204] Wilcott testified under oath that "Oswald was a CIA agent who received financial disbursements under an assigned cryptonym." Other agency witnesses denied Wilcott's claims.[205]

Upon Oswald's return to Texas, he began subscribing to Communist papers. His mail also showed he reached out to the Communist Workers Party, which was considered a subversive organization. Despite knowledge of Oswald's recent subscriptions to Communist papers, as well as his defection to the Soviet Union and his Soviet wife, the FBI closed its file on him in October of 1962, claiming he was "unworthy of any further consideration."[206] FBI Agent James Hosty later re-opened Oswald's file in March 1963, purportedly for the Communist subscriptions, even though those were known when his file was closed.[207] According to Hosty, his job was to determine if either Oswald or Marina were Soviet spies.[208]

Equally questionable, upon his return to the Dallas area, Oswald began spending time with upper-class, right-wing Russians who loathed Communism. Why was a poor and allegedly left-wing Oswald hanging out with a wealthy right-wing crowd? George de Mohrenschildt, an affluent, CIA-connected man who, during World War II, had worked for French intelligence, befriended Oswald.[209] The majority of de Mohrenschildt's contact with Oswald was during the six-month period in which the FBI had closed their file on Oswald, October 1962 through March 1963. During this time, the Oswalds made many visits to the de Mohrenschildt's home.[210] According to District Attorney Jim Garrison, among de Mohrenschildt's close friends was Jean de Menil, president of Schlumberger Corporation, which had close ties to the CIA and which, like the CIA, had an interest in the OAS, a French paramilitary organization that had revolted against President Charles de Gaulle when Algeria was in the process of winning its independence.[211] John F. Kennedy had been strongly supportive of Algerian independence and had even given a highly controversial speech in its support in 1957, which was anathema not only to the CIA but to the Mossad as well. De Menil sat on the board of a company called Permindex (Permanent Industrial Exposition).[212] In the only criminal investigation into John F. Kennedy's murder, Garrison charged Clay Shaw, another board member of Permindex, with conspiracy to murder John F. Kennedy.[213] (Permindex and Shaw's trial are covered in later chapters.) It is worth noting as well that France supplied Israel with its initial weapons development in the 1950s in exchange for Israel providing intelligence to France to combat Algerian independence.[214] Furthermore, France also supplied to Israel the Dimona nuclear reactor.[215] De Mohrenschildt also had ties to former CIA director and dominant member of the Warren Commission Allen Dulles. In the early 1920s, Allen Dulles, on behalf of Rockefeller's Standard Oil, negotiated with the head of Baku oil, Sergey von Mohrenschildt, George's father. Then in 1940–41, de Mohrenschildt worked with Allen Dulles in Humble Oil. It is not clear if these connections were close, but they did exist.[216] Later, when de Mohrenschildt testified in front of the Warren Commission, he stated, "Dulles ... did not interfere in the proceedings, but there was a distant threat."[217]

De Mohrenschildt found Oswald a job at a graphic arts house in Dallas, Jaggars-Chiles-Stovall.[218] This company was a Pentagon contractor that produced maps and charts for military use, including in relation to top-secret U-2 missions. They hired Oswald in early October 1962, a month made infamous for the thirteen days of the Cuban Missile Crisis, when the world came closest to nuclear war and the U.S. was flying U-2s over Cuba to gather intelligence on the Soviet missiles. It would have been highly derelict to have given a former defector to the Soviet Union such access during such a crucial and tense moment of the Cold War.[219] In his unpublished manuscript, de Mohrenschildt claimed that he went to Dallas CIA station chief J. Walton Moore and mentioned to him that he had met Oswald. De Mohrenschildt then asked Moore if Oswald was safe to associate with, and Moore said yes.[220] Author Edward Epstein claimed that de Mohrenschildt divulged to him that Moore had actually asked him to "babysit" Oswald. Moore denied this.[221] It should be noted that Epstein used James Angleton as a consultant for his book. In the book, he wrote that Oswald killed Kennedy while working as a Russian agent, so anything claimed by Epstein should be taken with a grain of salt.[222] Nonetheless, regardless of if it was Moore or not, it appears someone had asked de Mohrenschildt to watch over Oswald. In February 1963, de Mohrenschildt introduced the Oswalds to Ruth and Michael Paine. In April 1963, de Mohrenschildt left Dallas for Haiti, where he received a lucrative oil consulting contract with the Haitian government and never saw Oswald again. The Paines became the Oswalds' new "babysitters." They remained so up to the assassination of President Kennedy.[223] There is no indication that de Mohrenschildt had any involvement in or knowledge of the assassination plot.

Furthermore, he had first connected with Oswald more than a year before the assassination, so it is doubtful the assassination was even in the works at the time de Mohrenschildt initially met Oswald. While de Mohrenschildt made incriminating statements against Oswald to the Warren Commission, he and his wife later told District Attorney Jim Garrison that Oswald had been a scapegoat. Garrison stated that he "was particularly affected by the depth of [de Mohrenschildts'] unhappiness at what had been done not only to John Kennedy but to Lee Oswald as well."[224] De Mohrenschildt was subpoenaed to testify before the House Select Committee on Assassinations, but shortly after being served the subpoena, he died of a gunshot wound to the head, in an alleged suicide. Some investigators believe he was murdered.[225] In the police report, his wife, Jeanne de Mohrenschildt, and others stated that he was constantly in fear of what he termed the "Jewish Mafia" and the FBI. However, they attributed his fear to his deteriorating mental state.[226] Did he have legitimate reasons to be fearful of the Jewish Mafia and the FBI? Were perhaps one or both entities concerned about his potential testimony in front of the House Select Committee on Assassinations?

Like de Mohrenschildt, the Paines also were interesting characters. Michael Paine was an engineering designer who did highly classified work for Bell Helicopter, a major Defense Department contractor. Ruth Paine's father and her brother-in-law had been employed by the Agency for International Development, believed by many to be a front for the CIA.[227] Furthermore, Ruth Paine's sister worked for the CIA as a psychologist.[228] The Paines also had an odd connection to the former CIA director let go by Kennedy, Allen Dulles. Dulles's mistress, Mary Bancroft, was close friends with Ruth Forbes, the mother of Michael Paine.[229] Lastly, Ruth had worked in a leadership role with various organizations supportive of Israel, including the Young Men's Hebrew Association and the Young Women's Hebrew Association in Philadelphia as well as Jewish community centers in both Indianapolis and Columbus, Ohio.[230] The Jewish Community Center Association of America sponsors trips to Israel as well as other events in support of the nation.[231] Ruth even hired a tutor to teach her Yiddish when she was working with the Golden Age Club,[232] which she said consisted of "people over the age of sixty" who spoke "Yiddish in conducting their business meetings."[233] Ruth's ties to these organizations are brought up only to raise the possibility that in her work she may have made connections to individuals with Zionist interests. Regardless of on whose behalf the Paines accepted their task, it is doubtful they had any knowledge of a brewing assassination plot, nor do we definitively know at which point the assassination plot began, whether it was before or after the Paines became involved with the Oswalds. Most intelligence operations function on a need-to-know basis, and it is doubtful the Paines knew much beyond what they were asked to do.

As can be seen, Oswald was not your typical "lone nut." He appeared to be some sort of intelligence asset, either witting or unwitting, who James Angleton closely monitored. Because he defected to Russia, Oswald had the perfect background to be manipulated and set up as the "Communist/Marxist lone nut" assassin of President Kennedy. Furthermore, what are the mathematical odds that of all the people in the United States, the alleged killer just happened to be someone already under the close monitor of James Angleton, a man on the short list of the prime beneficiaries of JFK's assassination? This is even smaller odds than Allen Dulles's mistress knowing the mother of Michael Paine. It can be a small circle in the upper echelons of American society. Indeed, George de Mohrenschildt was friends with Jackie Kennedy's mother, but no one suspects her of being involved in the crime. Connections between upper society players are not rare, but Angleton's links to a random lone-nut assassin, out of the many millions of people in the United States, should raise eyebrows.

3

The Lead Up to the Crime

A mansion has many rooms. ... I'm not privy to who struck John. – James Jesus Angleton

On April 18, 1963, Oswald wrote to the Fair Play for Cuba Committee (FPCC) New York office, a pro-Castro entity. In the letter, Oswald indicated that he had passed out FPCC literature in the street the day before and requested more copies. Oswald asked that they send the literature to his Dallas address. However, on April 24, Oswald moved to New Orleans. This timing indicates the move to New Orleans may have been a last-minute decision.[234] On the same day, April 24, on the front page of the *Dallas Times Herald* was the headline "LBJ sees Kennedy Dallas Visit."[235] District Attorney Jim Garrison believed that Oswald might have been moved from Dallas to New Orleans to separate him from the anti-Communist, upscale Russian community he was spending time with, to better "sheep dip" him into the patsy role.[236] Given that the timing of his move to New Orleans coincided with the first public announcement of a potential upcoming Kennedy visit to Dallas (JFK would confirm on June 5),[237] it is likely, but not definitive, that at least some planning for the assassination was in place by late April.

Upon Oswald leaving for New Orleans, his wife Marina moved in with Ruth Paine, whom she barely knew. After arriving in New Orleans, Oswald stayed with his aunt and got a job at Reilly Coffee Company on May 10, after which Ruth drove Marina down to live with Oswald. In mid-July, Reilly terminated Oswald's employment for his spending too much time reading gun magazines at Adrian Alba's Crescent City Garage. Oswald's superiors, Alfred Claude and Emmett Barbee, left in July to work for NASA, as did two of Oswald's co-workers. Oswald himself told Alba he expected to move on to NASA as well. A declassified document confirms that Reilly Coffee Company was of interest to the CIA dating back to 1949. Furthermore, some witnesses claim to have seen Oswald either speaking to or handing documents over to FBI agents while working at Reilly, implying Oswald may have been an FBI informant.[238]

While in New Orleans, Oswald continued to write to the Fair Play for Cuba Committee. On August 5, Oswald began to appear in public as an agent of the FPCC. During this time, the CIA ran an anti-FPCC counterintelligence operation headed by David Phillips and James McCord. Oswald handed out pamphlets titled "The Crime Against Cuba." The first printing of these pamphlets was in 1961 when Oswald was in Russia. The current printings were for the fifth edition; however, Oswald handed out the first-edition flyers. The CIA had ordered copies of the first printing back in June of 1961, so Oswald may have gotten his copies from a source linked to the CIA.[239] It is worth pointing out that the leader of the Cuban exile group Alpha 66, Antonio Veciana, told House Select Committee on Assassinations investigator Gaeton Fonzi that he had seen Oswald with David Phillips in early September 1963 in Dallas. The timing is problematic as Oswald was still in New Orleans later in September, but it is possible Veciana was mistaken about his timing.[240]

Oswald also handed out "Hands off Cuba" flyers. On those flyers, he stamped the address 544 Camp St., which was the address of Guy Banister's office.[241] Banister was a detective and former special agent in charge of the Chicago office of the FBI.[242] He had started his career working for the Office of Naval Intelligence during World War II.[243] His office was across the street from the ONI and the Secret Service. A short walk away was the headquarters of the CIA. His office was in the heart of the intelligence community in New Orleans.[244] According to Banister's secretary, Delphine Roberts, Banister had engaged in closed-door meetings with Oswald that summer and had arranged for a room for Oswald's use.[245] Other witnesses had also seen Oswald in Banister's office. Consuela Martin did part-time work for Banister and stated that Oswald had come to her office more than once to get items translated. Since Oswald's documents were pro-Castro and Banister was anti-Castro, she assumed Oswald was trying to find pro-Castro sympathizers for Banister. She indicated she saw Oswald inside Banister's office on multiple occasions. In addition to seeing Oswald there, she often saw anti-Castro Cuban exiles in the office.[246] Jack Martin, who had spent quite a bit of time in Banister's office, also admitted to often seeing Cuban exiles in the office. He told Garrison that he had frequently seen David Ferrie there too, who he said "practically lived there." Oswald had met Ferrie in 1955 when he joined the Civil Air Patrol. Lastly, Martin also admitted to seeing Oswald there, revealing, "Sometimes, he'd be meeting with Guy Banister with the door shut. Other times he'd be shooting the bull with Dave Ferrie."[247]

Ferrie was spending time in Lake Pontchartrain, Louisiana, supervising the training of Cuban exiles, in hopes they would one day return to the island and remove Castro from power.[248] In 1975, the Church Committee, a Senate select committee investigating the abuses of the CIA and FBI, among others, conducted interviews with two Immigration and Naturalization Service (INS) agents who stated that in their tracking of Cuban refugees to see if they were in the country illegally they came across Ferrie since he spent so much time with Cuban exiles. They confirmed that Ferrie spent much time in Banister's office and that Oswald had his own room there.[249] George de Mohrenschildt, Oswald's initial Dallas "babysitter," was close friends with Jean de Menil, Permindex board member and president of Schlumberger Corporation. Banister and Ferrie would pick up explosives from Schlumberger Corporation in support of their anti-

Castro activities.[250] According to the *New Orleans States-Item*, "50 to 100 crates" of ammunition, rifles, grenades, landmines, and the like were found in Banister's storeroom, labeled "Schlumberger."[251] If Oswald was a pro-Castro lone nut, why was he hanging around an anti-Castro, intelligence-linked community?

The answer is that he was likely an "agent provocateur," someone expressing sympathy with a cause to infiltrate and incite those supporting such a cause into committing illegal actions. On August 9, as Oswald was handing out pro-Castro pamphlets, he got into an altercation with two anti-Castro supporters and was arrested for disturbing the peace. The arresting officer stated that Oswald "seemed to have set them up, so to speak, to create an incident, but when the incident occurred, he seemed absolutely peaceful and gentle." Indeed, Oswald had described the incident in a letter to the national office of the FPCC five days before it happened. After being arrested, Oswald asked the police to call the FBI, specifically asking for Agent Warren Debrueys. It is believed Oswald may have been an informant for Debrueys—in fact, according to another FBI employee, Debrueys had an informant file on Oswald.[252] It is worth noting that the person Oswald got into the altercation with was Carlos Bringuier, who had headed the New Orleans branch of the Cuban Student Directorate (DRE), an anti-Castro propaganda operation which had been created and funded by the CIA.[253]

Another vital character linked to Oswald in the summer of 1963 was Clay Shaw, whom Garrison later charged with conspiracy to murder John F. Kennedy. That summer, Shaw had sent Oswald to attorney Dean Andrews to assist Oswald with his military discharge and the citizenship of his wife.[254] Another witness saw Shaw hand over money to Oswald.[255] There was also a slew of witnesses that saw Shaw, Ferrie, and Oswald together at a voter registration event in Clinton, Louisiana. Late in the summer, Oswald began asking around about how he could get hired at the East Louisiana State Hospital, a mental hospital located in a rural area approximately ninety miles northwest of New Orleans. Several residents told him he would have a much better chance of being hired if he was a registered voter in the area.

The day Oswald went to register, there was a Congress of Racial Equality (CORE) voting drive happening. The event was packed, and Oswald stood out as virtually no other white people were in line. According to witnesses, he arrived in a Cadillac with Shaw and Ferrie.[256] Because of the out-of-place appearance of the Cadillac, and the three white visitors, who waited for hours, the local sheriff, John Manchester, spoke with the driver. The driver mentioned that he worked for the International Trade Mart. Manchester later, under oath, identified the driver as Shaw.[257] Clinton Registrar of Voters Henry Palmer corroborated Manchester's testimony and testified under oath that Manchester had told him that day that the vehicle was from the International Trade Mart and also identified Shaw as the driver.[258] Palmer is the one Oswald spoke to about registering when he got to the front of the line. Palmer informed Oswald that because he did not have proof that he had lived in the parish long enough, he could not register him, but that one wasn't required to be registered to apply for a job at the hospital.[259] Oswald then applied for a job at the hospital but was never hired. Garrison was not sure why Oswald made such a great effort to get employment at the hospital; he thought perhaps it was to show him as someone wandering haplessly from one job to another, or even worse, to perhaps somehow switch his files from an employee, maybe a lowly janitor that no one saw, to a patient, completing the picture of a mentally deranged lone nut.[260] It is difficult to imagine how the person who hired him would not have remembered. Still, perhaps with some ingenuity or simply some manipulation by the press, it would not have mattered.

Clay Shaw, the man who took Oswald to the voting drive, was the director of the International Trade Mart in New Orleans.[261] He was also connected to the CIA. Even CIA Director Richard Helms admitted in 1979 that Shaw "was one of the part-time contacts of the domestic contact division, the people that talked to businessmen, professors, and so forth."[262] Shaw, just like Jean de Menil, the president of Schlumberger Corporation, was also on the board of Permindex (Permanent Industrial Exposition) and its sister company CMC (Centro Mondiale Commerciale). On the surface, the purpose of Permindex/CMC was to offer a centralized site where businessmen could display goods and make deals. Underneath, however, Permindex/CMC was tied into various covert networks. Louis Mortimer Bloomfield, who lived in Montreal, Canada, has often been described as the founder of Permindex and its majority shareholder, but this is not entirely accurate. He was Permindex's attorney and was responsible for coordinating all the different players involved. He acted as a proxy for particular interests, effectively hiding their identities. These interests held stock in his name, and he occupied their spot on the board.[263]

Bloomfield was connected to a number of Zionist organizations. He served as honorary counsel to the World Jewish Congress. He was also involved in building up the Canadian branches of the Histadrut, Israel's trade union complex, and was president of the Israel Maritime League. Both entities were involved with organizing Zim Shipping, a key supplier of weapons to Israel.[264] Indeed, Bloomfield was involved with smuggling arms to the Haganah in the 1930s.[265] The Haganah was the central Zionist paramilitary organization before the establishment of Israel, when it then became the core of the Israeli Defense Forces.

Furthermore, according to a whistleblower at the NUMEC facility in Pennsylvania—the facility that has been accused of smuggling uranium to Israel for nuclear weapons development—it was the aforementioned Zim Shipping that transferred the material.[266] Edmond de Rothschild appears all over Bloomfield's correspondences and appears to have been intimately involved with Permindex/CMC.[267] It was Lord Rothschild to whom the Balfour Declaration was addressed. The declaration was a public statement issued by the British government in 1917 which announced its support for a "national home for the Jewish people" in Palestine.[268] Lastly, and most critically, Bloomfield was one of approximately twenty-five key donors to Israel's nuclear weapons program. Also among the donors was

Bloomfield's brother, Bernard, as well as the British and French branches of the previously mentioned Rothschild family.[269] Indeed, the two Bloomfield brothers first met Israeli Prime Minister David Ben-Gurion at a celebration of Israel's first anniversary.[270] Permindex/CMC also had ties to the CIA as well as Italian intelligence, in addition to various connections to the Mossad, the Israeli intelligence agency.[271] It received funding through J. Henry Schroder Banking Corporation, for which former CIA Director Allen Dulles had served as general counsel.[272] With Bloomfield having access to the majority of the shares, he, and those he represented who are not known, essentially controlled Permindex/CMC.[273] Some view Permindex/CMC as a sort of intelligence apparatus functioning transnationally. Indeed, Permindex/CMC, the International Trade Mart, and those affiliated with these entities greatly supported globalism over nationalism. Their views, in general, were opposed to Kennedy's views of a more decentralized system of power where national sovereignty played a significant role. They preferred a system of international banking and transnational and multinational corporations controlling the global economy.

Permindex has also been suspected in the death of Enrico Mattei, whose plane exploded in October 1962. Mattei sought to sign oil agreements with the Soviet Union, as well as Egypt and Algeria, which were, at the time, opposed to Israel. There have been multiple official inquiries into the incident. Italian journalist Fulvio Bellini turned over information to one of these inquiries alleging that Permindex had funded the assassination of Mattei.[274]

According to a Garrison witness named Jules Kimble, Ferrie, a pilot, flew Shaw up to Montreal on at least one occasion. Garrison speculated that Ferrie may have flown Shaw up to Montreal to visit Bloomfield.[275] The witness went with them on one such trip and was asked by Ferrie to go on another but declined. To say the very least, Oswald had some interesting companions in the summer of 1963. One would not expect a lone-nut Communist to be spending time with the highly connected Shaw and the anti-Communist Ferrie.

Oswald's street theater of early August, which had led to his arrest, was not the only street theater he performed that summer. On August 16, Oswald went to the unemployment office and hired a couple of young men, promising to give them two dollars for fifteen to twenty minutes of passing out leaflets in front of Clay Shaw's International Trade Mart. One of Clay Shaw's men then phoned WDSU-TV, and they arrived to cover the "event." Shaw was aware of this event because a photographer captured him walking into the building and looking at Oswald, and Oswald looking back at him. After the incident, Oswald walked over to WDSU. Once there, WDSU television and radio interviewed him. A reporter then arranged for Oswald to participate in a debate on WDSU radio on August 21.[276] These video and audio events played a critical role in the setup of Oswald as they offered documented proof of Oswald as a Communist, which was then widely disseminated after the assassination.

WDSU was owned by Edgar Bloom Stern Jr.[277] Shaw was a close friend of the Stern family. Indeed, Edgar B. Stern Sr. had been on the board of the International Trade Mart (he passed away in 1959).[278] Before passing away, he had been given clearance on a CIA project for a period of three years, from 1953 to 1956.[279] The Sterns, who ultimately gave the public platform to Oswald, were strong supporters of Israel.[280] It has even been claimed that they were key financiers behind NUMEC,[281] the plant in Pennsylvania suspected of funneling uranium to Israel for nuclear weapons development purposes. However, this author has been unable to substantiate whether the Sterns were financiers or not, though Edith Stern's son, Philip M. Stern, did write a book about J. Robert Oppenheimer, often referred to as the "father of the atomic bomb," dedicating the book to his mother "with love." Hence, the family had at least some interest in the area of nuclear weapons. Within hours of the assassination, the corporate media used the footage captured by the Stern's WDSU to display to the whole world Oswald's Communist leanings. This footage gave the public immediate "proof" of Oswald being a Communist lone nut and was crucial in quickly establishing the official narrative regarding the crime. Getting ahead of a narrative before the public starts asking questions is critical, so this footage captured by the Sterns was an integral part of the assassination plot. Given that Oswald was a "nobody" during the summer of 1963, it is unlikely the Sterns gave him the public platform without being asked. Who might have asked them for the favor?

On September 16, the CIA informed the FBI that the "Agency is giving some consideration to countering the activities of the FPCC [Fair Play for Cuba Committee] in foreign countries."[282] Coincidentally, or perhaps not, the following day, on September 17, Oswald visited the New Orleans Mexican Consulate, where he obtained a tourist permit. The person in line in front of him, who received the tourist permit with an issue number one less than Oswald's, was William Gaudet. Gaudet's CIA files indicated he had been a "contact" for the New Orleans office.[283]

Ruth Paine drove Oswald's wife, Marina, back to Dallas on September 23, and Marina moved in with Ruth, who lived in Irving, about twenty minutes outside of Dallas, where she would stay until the assassination.[284]

On September 24, Ferrie made a phone call to Chicago. Garrison had gotten access to Ferrie's phone records as part of his investigation. Garrison speculated that perhaps Ferrie was calling to report to some intermediary that the "sheep dipping" job in New Orleans was complete and Oswald was leaving the city. Garrison determined this was someone by the name of Jean Aase. According to an FBI report, Jean traveled to Dallas with Lawrence V. Meyers, a friend of Jack Ruby. She served as Meyers' female companion, and they visited with Ruby the night before the assassination.[285] Ruby is the person who shot and killed Oswald two days after the assassination. Meyers supported Ruby's cover story as to why he shot Oswald, even going as far as telling the Warren Commission that Ruby had "worshiped" JFK for years.[286] Garrison felt he had stumbled upon a "message center," what he called "a customary intelligence community device to throw off a would-be pursuer of a phone-call listing." In this instance, the message center had resulted in a communication with Jack Ruby via Lawrence Meyers.[287]

Meyers was employed with Farber Bros., Inc and was integrating them into the sporting goods business. This author was unable to find a connection between Meyers and Klein's Sporting Goods (the Chicago store alleged to have sold Oswald his rifle). Meyers' daughter worked as a nuclear chemist for various nuclear reactors, including Argonne in Illinois, and his son worked in Army intelligence.[288] Argonne was one of five laboratories that arose out of the Manhattan Project, the program that led to the building of the first atomic bomb.[289] In the 1950s the Israelis asked to visit Argonne[290] and today researchers at Argonne receive various grants from the U.S.-Israel Energy Center.[291] Meyers was affiliated with B'nai B'rith, an organization staunchly committed to Israel.[292] B'nai B'rith has long been suspected of having Israeli intelligence ties and indeed on its board of overseers sat Edgar Bronfman,[293] son of Samuel Bronfman, one of the twenty-five key funders of Israel's nuclear weapons program.[294] In 1960, Abraham Feinberg, the man who was organizing the funding for Israel's nuclear weapons program, was named the B'nai B'rith man of the year.[295] Louis Mortimer Bloomfield, the aforementioned de-facto head of Permindex/CMC, was an attorney for the law firm that represented the Bronfmans, though it is not clear if Bloomfield himself represented the Bronfmans.[296] As far back as 1878 the *New York Times* referred to B'nai B'rith as "one of the most powerful secret organizations in the United States."[297] B'nai B'rith rewarded JFK with a Presidential Gold Medal on the night of January 31, 1963.[298] Had Garrison been aware of JFK's intense behind-the-scenes battle with Israel, which intensified in the spring of 1963, he may have dug into this line of inquiry more deeply to see if it led anywhere, but at the time he had no awareness of the conflicts between John F. Kennedy and Israel and as such could not figure out what made Meyers unique or why he would potentially have been tied into the assassination plot.

Oswald allegedly arrived in Mexico City on September 27 and left on

October 3.[299] There is much debate on whether Oswald actually went to Mexico City or whether an imposter went on his behalf. While in Mexico City, Oswald went to the Cuban and Soviet consulates and stated that he would like to travel to the Soviet Union via Cuba.[300] He showed them all the FPCC and pro-Castro literature that he had.[301] They informed him that he could not get a transit visa to Cuba without first obtaining a Soviet visa, which would take four months. After being told it would take four months, Oswald did not bother to fill out the application.[302] It is claimed that Oswald offered information to the Soviet consulate in exchange for money. If true, this may have been a "counterintelligence dangle." In 1966, an apparently disgruntled US Army sergeant offered the Soviet Embassy information in exchange for money and, for the next ten years, fed them disinformation while being rewarded by the CIA.[303] Oswald's claim to want to travel to the Soviet Union via Cuba made no sense since in the summer of 1963, the State Department had approved his passport for travel to the Soviet Union but stamped a warning that a person traveling to Cuba would be liable for prosecution. It would have made more sense for Oswald to travel to the Soviet Union via Europe as he had previously done.

It seems the trip's primary purpose was to create contact between Oswald and the man who issued Soviet visas in Mexico City: Valery Kostikov. Only a handful of counterintelligence officers knew who Kostikov really was. He worked for the KGB (Soviet spy agency) assassinations group. It is unlikely that Oswald would have known this. But James Angleton, as head of counterintelligence, and perhaps a few people under him would have known.[304] This contact between Oswald and what was allegedly KGB assassinations is critical to keep in mind and this book will return to this topic when discussing the events after the assassination. Indeed, back on May 23, 1963, Angleton had distributed to the Joint Chiefs of Staff and various other agencies a document titled "Cuban Control and Action Capabilities" containing the following example of problems to be solved: "An American citizen, for example, can enter Mexico with a tourist card ... and obtain a separate visa to Cuba from the Cuban Consulate in Mexico

City. He can go to Cuba and return ... without any indication that he has ever been there." This shows that Angleton had an interest in the Mexico City Cuban consulate back in May of 1963, was familiar with its operations, and had outlined a scenario that Oswald followed a few months later.[305]

On October 2, the *Washington Daily News* published an article by Richard Starnes outlining the disagreements between the various governmental agencies on what to do about Vietnam. In the article, Starnes quoted a US official as stating, "If the United States ever experiences a 'Seven Days in May,' it will come from the CIA, and not from the Pentagon."[306] *Seven Days in May* was a fictional book about a planned military coup in the U.S. as a reaction to the US president signing a disarmament treaty with the Soviet Union. It was published in 1962 and released as a film in early 1964. President Kennedy supported the making of the film and allowed the use of the White House for filming while he was away for the weekend.[307] Quotes from Starnes' article were then picked up by Arthur Krock and published in the *New York Times* the following day.[308] Some have argued that JFK was the one that offered the quote since his father had worked closely with Krock. However, Krock was not who originally published the quote; Starnes was.

Furthermore, Robert Kennedy stated in his oral history that JFK "grew to dislike Arthur Krock" and viewed him as "unfair."[309] Jackie Kennedy disclosed that Krock had "enmity" for her husband.[310] So if JFK did offer the quote, it was almost certainly not to Krock. Others have argued that the culprits planted the statement to steer skeptics of the upcoming assassination towards a domestic governmental institution as the culprit rather than a private or transnational source. Most likely, the article was just coincidental. There was much squabbling between different governmental institutions regarding Vietnam, and Starnes quoted various anonymous sources in his article, most of whom, if not all, were in Vietnam. And the book and film were popular then, so a reference to it was not wholly out of place. Nevertheless, given that the media printed this series of articles the month before JFK's assassination, this information is worth at least a mention.

In early October, Oswald returned to Dallas.[311] On October 8, Marvin Gheesling, a supervisor at FBI headquarters with considerable experience in espionage, intelligence, and counterintelligence,[312] took Oswald off the espionage watch list, a list Oswald had been on since his defection to the USSR in 1959. This removal ensured that Oswald would not be placed on the security index and, therefore, would not be removed from the motorcade route in Dallas, as he would not be seen as a security threat. It is unclear who or what prompted Gheesling to do this, but he likely was given the impression that Oswald was involved with some intelligence operation and thus did not need to be monitored. After the assassination, the FBI reprimanded Gheesling for taking Oswald off the list.[313]

On October 14, Ruth Paine told Oswald about a job at the Texas School Book Depository (TSBD). Oswald interviewed for the job on October 15 and started on October 16. It is important to note that Oswald visited the Texas Employment Commission upon returning to Dallas. As a result of that visit, the Paine residence received a phone call on October 15 about a job for Oswald at Trans Texas Airways, a position that paid significantly better, approximately 30 percent more, than the TSBD job. Robert Adams, the man who phoned the Paine residence, says he was told Oswald was not home. Adams called the following day again but was told Oswald had taken another job. This is critical, as it is from the TSBD that Oswald was accused of shooting JFK. He would not have been on the motorcade route had he been informed of and taken the higher-paying job. Ruth Paine initially denied receiving a call from Robert Adams but later admitted Oswald had told her about it. This is different from what Adams testified. He indicated he tried to reach Oswald and left a message for him but was unable to get in touch with him.[314]

On November 2, JFK had a planned visit to Chicago; however, it was canceled at the last minute after the press plane had already left for the city. It was officially canceled due to a crisis in Vietnam. It is not known whether additional factors played into the decision to cancel the trip.[315] On the morning of November 2, a Chicago man named Thomas Arthur Vallee was arrested for threatening to kill the president.[316] The Secret Service found rifles in his rented room.[317] Vallee had a similar profile to Oswald. He was an ex-Marine who was supportive of Communism[318] and had recently moved from New York City to Chicago and gotten a job at a warehouse directly over Kennedy's planned motorcade route. The building he was employed in was located shortly after a slow and sharp turn off the expressway, the turn that was scheduled to be taken during JFK's motorcade route, similar to the slow turn in front of the Texas School Book Depository building. According to Vallee, like Oswald, he had been assigned to a U-2 base in Japan, Camp Atsu.[319] There are many striking similarities between the potential Chicago plot and the Dallas plot, from the disgruntled ex-Marine recently hired along the motorcade route to the slow and sharp turn in front of the kill zone. Was this pure coincidence, or did the assassination plotters realize they had to plan for multiple cities to ensure the successful removal of John F. Kennedy?

Abraham Bolden was the first-ever African American Secret Service agent. He was hired personally by John F. Kennedy. According to Bolden, on October 30, a few days before the planned November 2 visit to Chicago, Special Agent in Charge Maurice Martineau informed the Chicago Secret Service agents that a potential plot to assassinate Kennedy had been uncovered. The FBI learned from an informant that four snipers planned to shoot Kennedy with high-powered rifles along his motorcade route. The informant stated his name was "Lee." The following day, a landlady phoned the FBI and said she had rented rooms to four men. In one of their rooms, she had seen four rifles with telescopic sights along with a newspaper sketch of JFK's motorcade route.[320] On November 1, two of the men were picked up and brought to Secret Service headquarters for questioning, but they stonewalled during the interrogation.[321] According to Bolden, a Secret Service informant had revealed that the money for the assassination had been put up by "Israeli sources."[322] Bolden did not link the ex-Marine Vallee to the four-man assassination team, but he did indicate he remembered Vallee's name coming up in 1963 concerning a possible assassination attempt. Other Secret Service agents did not corroborate Bolden's claims of a four-man rifle team; however, this may have been due to fear of punishment.[323] In 1964, Bolden was arrested and prosecuted for soliciting a bribe from a counterfeiter and served a six-year sentence. He claimed it was a set-up to silence him. The main witness later recanted, and Bolden was ultimately pardoned.[324] There is also some evidence of a potential plot in Tampa on November 18, but less is known about it.[325]

On November 1 and November 5, FBI Agent James Hosty visited the Paines' residence and spoke with Marina. Hosty was the Dallas FBI agent in charge of keeping tabs on any potential connections Lee and Marina had with Soviet intelligence. Both Marina and Lee held hostility towards Hosty. They found him "harsh," according to Lee's brother, Robert.[326] FBI employee Nannie Lee Fenner testified that somewhere between November 6 and 8, Oswald came to the FBI office. She stated,

> He was awfully fidgety, and he had a 3 x 5 envelope in his hand. It was not sealed. And in it was a piece of paper, and it was folded. The bottom portion of the letter was visible. ... He kept pulling this letter in and out of this envelope. When I informed him Hosty was not in the office, he threw it on my desk and said, "Well, give this to him." ... As the bottom portion of that letter was visible, I could not help but read the last two lines. And the last two lines stated, "I'll either blow up the Dallas Police Department or the FBI Office." ... It was something about speaking to his wife; that was what he was going to do if it didn't stop.

When Hosty testified before Congress, he denied Fenner's claim. He admitted there was a letter in which Oswald asked that his wife be left alone, but there was no threat about blowing up a building. Hosty testified that a few hours after Oswald's death, his supervisor Gordon Shanklin told him to destroy the note. Shanklin denied all of this to Congress. Obviously, someone lied under oath because the three told inconsistent stories.[327] If Oswald had indeed made a threat after recently having his security profile reduced, why was his security profile not raised again? The blatant way in which Oswald, or potentially an imposter, handed the note over to Fenner ensured she would see what he had written at the end of it. In the weeks leading up to the assassination, there were various sightings of a man who resembled Oswald attracting attention to himself in over-the-top ways. For example, in perhaps the most egregious instance, a man who appeared at a car dealership referred to himself as Oswald but didn't fit his description. He test-drove a vehicle at high speed and informed the salesman that he would have the money to purchase the car in several weeks. When a fellow salesman mentioned to him that he needed a credit rating, the man replied, "Maybe I'm going to have to go back to Russia to buy a car."[328] Garrison called these scenarios "about as subtle as roaches trying to sneak across a white rug."[329] The Warren Commission discounted the story as mistaken identity.

The months of planning that went into the assassination, the "sheep dipping" of Oswald, and the placing of Oswald inside the Texas School Book Depository building all would have been for nothing if a motorcade route going past the building, and the slow and sharp 120-degree turn, could not have been secured. As such, it is vital to try to understand how the motorcade route came to be.

Though the trip had been in the works since April, the Kennedy party had not agreed to an exact itinerary or date. Only on September 26, 1963, did the Dallas papers confirm that Kennedy would visit Texas on November 21–22.[330] In early October, Texas Governor John Connally, an ex-military man who had previously worked for Lyndon Johnson, visited JFK in the Oval Office to discuss arrangements for the trip. JFK suggested four or five consecutive fundraising dinners, but Connally opposed this, letting

JFK know that Texans would consider this "financial rape" of the state. The governor then suggested that JFK attend several "non-political" events and meet with moderate and conservative business leaders who had not supported him in 1960 and that he attempt to convert them in a non-political setting.[331] JFK won Texas in the 1960 election by a very slim margin and was often accused of being "anti-business." Hence it was essential to secure support from the more conservative elements of the Democratic Party, which Connally represented.

This then led to the sponsoring of the trip by the Dallas Citizens Council, the Dallas Chamber of Commerce, and the Assembly of Young Businessmen, who then, in combination with Governor Connally, would have a say over the location of events along with the motorcade route.[332] It was the fateful choice of the Trade Mart as the location for the luncheon that determined the fatal motorcade route. Before the selection of the Trade Mart, the culprits could have deduced that the motorcade route would likely pass through Dealey Plaza because the plaza was part of the traditional parade route through Dallas. However, knowledge of eastward versus westward direction was vital, as only the westward approach gave any opportunity to make the 120-degree turn directly underneath the Texas School Book Depository.[333] The eastward direction would have been a block away from the building and going in a straight line at higher speed down Main Street. It is essential to note that even going westward the 120-degree turn could have been avoided by continuing straight on Main Street.

JFK's advance man, Gerald Bruno, known as Jerry, was informed of the trip on October 20. An advance man is someone who scopes the selected city that is to be visited beforehand and ensures suitable arrangements. The White House asked Bruno to contact Walter Jenkins, Lyndon Johnson's right-hand man (Johnson was a former senator from Texas), and current Texas Senator Ralph Yarborough for ideas regarding the trip. Bruno recalled Yarborough as "bitter" because he felt Johnson and Governor Connally would run the show and did not trust either. He stated, "They never liked Jack Kennedy.

They never have, and they never will." On October 28, Bruno flew down to Texas. On October 29, he met with the president of the AFL/CIO, a federation of unions in the United States representing millions of workers, who informed him that "Connally would try to run the show and prevent labor from participating." Bruno then met with Connally, who made it clear that he "had planned an itinerary and that at each stop, his man would be in charge." Bruno responded that the White House would make the final decision, to which Connally replied, "Either we select the stops and run the trips, or the president can stay home. We don't want him."[334]

Bruno then met in Dallas with the chairman of the Dallas Citizens Council, J. Eric Jonnson, the co-founder of Texas Instruments, a defense contractor, and with Robert Cullum, president of the Dallas Chamber of Commerce.[335] Another key figure on the Dallas Citizens Council was Julius Schepps. He was the wholesale distributor in Dallas for the Seagram Company,[336] established by Samuel Bronfman, another of the twenty-five key funders of Israel's nuclear weapons project.[337] There is no concrete evidence that Schepps was influential regarding the planning of the trip, but there is no doubt that the Dallas Citizens Council, of which he was a leading figure, was. According to Bruno, his first choice for the luncheon site was the Statler Hilton, as it was the site JFK had spoken at during his 1962 trip to Dallas,[338] but the American Bottlers of Carbonated Beverages was holding a convention there and refused to give up the site.[339] The Bronfmans' Seagram is a member of the American Bottlers of Carbonated Beverages as is Perrier,[340] whose founder, Gustave Leven, was another of the twenty-five financiers of Israel's nuclear weapons project.[341] According to Bruno, it was this bottlers convention that "necessitated looking for another site."[342] Did perhaps the Bronfmans, Schepps, or Leven ensure that the popular Hilton site that JFK had relied on in the past would be unavailable at the time of JFK's visit?

Due to the unavailability of the Hilton, Bruno first looked at Dallas Memorial Auditorium, but Jonnson and Cullum did not like the location. Bruno then stated, "We talked of other possibilities but could arrive at no place that suited their requirements." They then suggested the Trade Mart, but Bruno objected to the location, thinking the Secret Service would not approve it due to the layout of the building. Governor Connally was unhappy with Bruno for his dislike of the Trade Mart location and wanted to see Bruno again before Bruno left Dallas. They went to see the Trade Mart again, but Bruno still did not like it and insisted on visiting more locations. The only other suggestion they gave was the Women's Building. Bruno favored the Women's Building because, in addition to his dislike of the Trade Mart building, he stated, "It didn't make any sense to me that we go downtown and then backtrack to the Trade Mart."[343] It is important to note that the Women's Building, just like the Statler Hilton, would have had the motorcade go in an eastward direction, hence avoiding the fatal intersection where Oswald was stationed.

On November 5, Bruno met at the White House with Walter Jenkins, Kennedy aid Kenny O'Donnell, and the head of the Secret Service, Gerald Behn. Behn declared that he preferred the Women's Building.[344] As a result of the meeting, Bruno and O'Donnell decided against the Trade Mart.[345]

On November 6, a letter was sent to the chairman of the Democratic Party, John Bailey, from the Dallas District 3 Democrats expressing concern that "articles in the local newspapers indicate that President Kennedy's visit to Dallas might be placed under the auspices of the arch-conservative Dallas Citizens Council." The letter further expressed that "99 percent of the members ... have consistently fought every Democratic ticket and administration." It recommended that control of the president's visit be given to the Democratic Clubs Council.[346]

As of November 7, Bruno's schedule listed the Women's Building as the location for the luncheon.[347] However, Governor Connally continued to insist that if the president would not speak at the Trade Mart, he not come to Dallas. Bruno stated that Connally was "violently opposed" to the Women's

Building. On November 15, exactly one week before the assassination, the White House announced they had approved the Trade Mart location. According to Bruno, O'Donnell stated that "Connally was unbearable and on the verge of canceling the trip" and that, as such, they decided to let the governor have his way.[348] O'Donnell confirmed in his Warren Commission testimony, "The governor felt very strongly on it. And we finally acquiesced to his views."[349]

It appears Governor Connally was the central figure pushing for the Trade Mart location, and without his insistence, the White House would have selected the Women's Building. This would have led to an alternate motorcade route that would not have made the 120-degree turn in front of the Texas School Book Depository building. It appears Connally was supported in this by the Dallas Citizens Council and the Dallas Chamber of Commerce. This decision does not in any way imply Connally had any prior knowledge of the assassination. Indeed, at least one bullet struck Connally during the shooting. He yelled out, "My God, they are going to kill us all!" as the bullets rained down.[350] However, what is clear is that his insistence is what ultimately led to the selection of the fatal motorcade route. Neither the Warren Commission nor the House Select Committee on Assassinations asked Governor Connally why he insisted so ardently on the Trade Mart location. They did not ask him if anyone had sold him on that location or encouraged him to push for it, such as one of his benefactors. Neither did they ask him if anyone had encouraged him to press for a "non-political" visit before his October trip to the White House, hence handing over the planning of the trip to the Dallas Citizens Council.

Despite not being asked, Connally did state in his HSCA testimony that the Trade Mart "was a new, exciting building ... a magnificent facility," and he personally went to Dallas in preparation for the trip and spoke with the Dallas Citizens Council, which he stated was a "group that for forty years dominated the political leadership of Dallas."[351]

According to Elizabeth Harris, who worked on planning the trip with Dallas Citizens Council member Sam Bloom, whom she called her "mentor," "Dallas was run by the Dallas Citizens Council." Membership was composed of one hundred or more CEOs. Bloom ran the Bloom Advertising Agency, and according to Harris, the agency was Bloom's "means of playing a major role in the management of the city of Dallas." Bloom's agency was responsible for the luncheon arrangements.[352] Bloom was close to both Governor Connally and Lyndon Johnson.[353] He was also a supporter of Israel. He served twice as president of Temple Emanu-El,[354] which encourages its members to visit the nation.[355] According to one of Bloom's employees, "That project [JFK's trip to Dallas], like all non-advertising projects at Bloom, was total madness. Secret Service men, aides to the President, press people—they all swarmed around the agency for days."[356] Did perhaps Bloom push Connally for the Trade Mart location? He would have had a lot of say over the site since he was responsible for the luncheon arrangements. Or was it obvious Connally would favor the Trade Mart location once the Hilton was unavailable and no urging was needed? Frank Erwin, the executive secretary of the Texas State Democratic Committee, who assisted Connally on the planning of the visit, stated there was no chance that the conservative and affluent supporters of Connally would have been willing to mix at a public occasion with elements of the liberal wing of the party, hence the governor's insistence that the Trade Mart serve as the location of the lunch. Kennedy's staff, in contrast, preferred the Women's Building because it allowed for a much larger crowd, and they felt it would give them better contact with liberal elements in the party and would have increased their ability to reach the poor and middle class.[357]

When Secret Service agent Winston Lawson visited Dallas to scope out the city beforehand on November 13, as is customary for a special agent from the White House detail to do before a trip, he was taken to both the Trade Mart location and the Women's Building. When taken to the Trade Mart, Sam Bloom was there to greet him.[358] According to Harris, it was through the "ubiquitous Bloom" that Lawson worked with the host committee, implying Bloom was the key figure on the Dallas Citizens Council who was responsible for the trip arrangements.[359] After the White House had finally agreed to the Trade Mart location on the fifteenth, Lawson met with several individuals, including Bloom, on the eighteenth, to discuss the motorcade route.[360] Others in attendance included Robert Cullum, president of the Dallas Chamber of Commerce, and Erik Jonnson, president of the Dallas Citizens Council, both of whom had previously urged Bruno to select the Trade Mart.[361]

On the morning of the twenty-first, Lawson went to Bloom's office to finalize the plans for the twenty-second, including confirming that Bloom had secured the necessary motorcade signs and vehicles.[362] Researcher Vince Palamara wrote that, according to witnesses he spoke to, the police were not informed of the final route until the evening of the twenty-first and that they had assumed the vehicles would go straight on Main Street and not make the turn in front of the Texas School Book Depository building,[363] however, Bloom would have had to know the route earlier since according to Lawson he checked in with Bloom on the motorcade signs on the morning of the twenty-first. It would make sense for Bloom, as a public relations man, to prefer the ultimate route chosen, with the 120-degree turn in front of the TSBD building over the alternate route straight on Main Street as the alternate route required going through a less desirable part of the city. Indeed, the correct route had been printed earlier in the week in some newspapers. However, the papers published various routes and were not consistent, some showing the turn onto Elm Street and some going straight on Main Street. It is not clear if this inconsistency in the papers was due to incompetence or if it was intentional, but Bloom's agency handled the coordination with the press. Was perhaps the correct route printed so that the claim could be made that Oswald brought his gun to work after seeing the motorcade route in the papers? And at the same time, was the incorrect route printed so that the location in Dealey Plaza would be less crowded than earlier parts of the route, which indeed it was? In this same vein, typically, presidential motorcades have in front of the president's car a flatbed truck for the press to take photos of the president. This did not happen in Dallas.[364] Bloom appears to have also been involved in this decision. He is the one that supplied the three convertibles for the press that were used in place of the flatbed truck.[365] The three convertibles were then placed near the rear of the motorcade. This ensured no press people were there to take photographs and videos at the time of the assassination. As a public relations man, one would think Bloom, of all people, would have been aware of the importance of having good press coverage for the motorcade. However, if the goal was the assassination of a president, then the less press coverage, the better.

Bloom was the brother-in-law of Morty Freedman, who shared a telephone number with the Dallas Uranium and Oil Company and Marilyn-Belt Manufacturing. The *Denton Record Chronicle* named Freedman as the president of Dallas Uranium and Oil.[366] There is no evidence that Dallas Uranium and Oil was involved with the smuggling of uranium; however, it is not clear at all what this entity did. It appears to have been some sort of dummy operation or front. Both Dallas Uranium and Oil Company and Marilyn-Belt Manufacturing were listed as being located inside the Dal-Tex building. Most of the firms in the building dealt with textiles, hence the name of the building, Dallas Textiles, so Dallas Uranium and Oil stands out. Marilyn-Belt Manufacturing was located on the western side of the third floor of the Dal-Tex Building, facing Dealey Plaza. Since the Dallas Uranium and Oil Company seems to have been a dummy operation, it appears not to have had a physical office inside the building but rather to have been somehow connected to Marilyn-Belt Manufacturing, as they shared the same phone number. The Dal-Tex building is immediately behind the Texas School Book Depository, and some researchers believe a shooter and/or shooters may have been firing from the western side of the building.[367] Bloom's name will come up again when it comes to the silencing of Oswald after the assassination.

It should also be mentioned that the mayor of Dallas at the time was Earle

Cabell, the brother of Charles Cabell, one of the top three men at the CIA who Kennedy had asked to resign in 1961. Earle himself had also worked for the CIA.[368] Furthermore, Cabell was a member of the Dallas Citizens Council.[369] However, there is no indication that Cabell had any involvement with the decision of the luncheon site. To be clear, this author is by no means saying definitively that Bloom was the one who pushed for the luncheon site and hence the ultimate motorcade route, just that he had at least some involvement with the selection of both the Trade Mart and the route, as well as the press coordination and vehicle arrangements and (as will be seen later) with Jack Ruby and the fateful transfer of Oswald that ultimately led to Oswald's murder. He was even involved in Ruby's trial afterward. According to FBI Agent James Hosty, Dallas City Manager Elgin Crull hired Bloom to "advise the police department on how to handle the Kennedy visit."[370] According to Police Chief Jesse Curry, when it came to choosing the parade route, the police "left it entirely up to the host committee and the Secret Service."[371] Thus Bloom is a character that should be examined and scrutinized closely, particularly since he was also connected to the Dal-Tex building. For some reason, he has, for the most part, wholly escaped scrutiny.

It is also possible that there was a plan B had the motorcade gone eastward, just as Dallas appears to have been a plan B after Chicago. And there is some evidence for this. According to Statler Hilton employee Laura Layfield, Oswald applied for a job at the Statler Hilton on October 31.[372] On this date, JFK's advance man, Gerald Bruno, was in Dallas expressing his dislike of the Trade Mart Location after making known his initial preference for the Statler Hilton.[373] Layfield also claimed that she had briefly met Jack Ruby in 1960 when he offered her a job at his nightclub, which she turned down. The Statler Hilton personnel director, Jo Fischer, stated that she could not find an application for Oswald on file. Other employees in the personnel office indicated that they had never seen Oswald. Layfield claimed Oswald had torn up his application and that is why it was not on file. Fischer did indicate that a man by the name of James Murphy, who had allegedly arrived with

Oswald to also apply for a job and was hired, resigned a few days after the assassination and informed her at such time, without being prompted, that he did not know Oswald, giving credence to Layfield's claim.[374] Regardless, any plan that relied on Oswald in the Texas School Book Depository was crucially dependent on the motorcade route. Therefore, understanding how the luncheon site and the corresponding motorcade route came to be selected is critical. There is often debate over who added the Elm Street turn to the motorcade route, but that debate would be irrelevant if the luncheon site had not been secured first. This is an often-overlooked part of the assassination, but its importance cannot be overstated.

With the luncheon site chosen and the motorcade route set, the last part needed was the assassins. A witness, Rose Cheramie, claimed to have traveled from Florida to Dallas with individuals involved in the assassination in the days leading up to the crime. A few days before the assassination, a vehicle ran into her while she was hitchhiking near New Orleans. As a result of the accident, she was taken to a hospital. Lieutenant Francis Fruge of the Louisiana State Police testified to the House Select Committee on Assassinations that Cheramie had told him that she had been traveling with two men from Florida to Dallas and that during the trip the two men had discussed killing Kennedy. After an argument with the two men, they left her, leading to her hitchhiking. It is important to note that she relayed this story not only to Fruge but to employees at the hospital a few days before the assassination.[375]

After the assassination, Fruge attempted to check out Cheramie's story by visiting the bar she had popped into with her traveling companions before they ditched her. The bar owner told him he saw her with two men he knew as pimps who hauled prostitutes in from Florida. Fruge claims he showed the bar owner a stack of photographs and that the bar owner picked out Cuban exile Sergio Arcacha Smith as one of the men he saw with Cheramie. Back in 1961, Arcacha Smith had been active as the head of the New Orleans Cuban Revolutionary Front and had befriended David Ferrie, the same David Ferrie who was spending time with Oswald in 1963.[376] Smith had been assisted in his move from Cuba to the U.S. by an Office of Naval Intelligence officer, Guy Johnson, who was a friend of Guy Banister and Clay Shaw.[377] It is difficult to definitively assess the credibility of Cheramie's story or the accuracy of the bar owner's identification. However, the story is worth a mention. Garrison attempted to investigate it further. Arcacha Smith was living in Dallas at the time of Garrison's investigation. Garrison first sent an arrest warrant to Dallas for Arcacha Smith's role in the Schlumberger raid, which transferred ammunition and weapons from Schlumberger Corporation to Banister's storeroom. Arcacha Smith was arrested and released on a $1,500 bond. Garrison then sent extradition papers to Texas, but Governor Connally refused to sign them; thus the bond was released and Garrison was unable to bring Arcacha Smith in for questioning.[378]

Another witness who claims to have potentially come in contact with the assassins was Marita Lorenz. She testified under oath that in November 1963 she and several Cuban exiles had traveled in a vehicle from Miami to Dallas with a man by the name of Frank Sturgis. She was told the purpose of the trip was "confidential." She said they were transporting weapons and that when they arrived in Dallas on November 21, they met up at a hotel with Howard Hunt, a CIA agent. Hunt handed money over to Sturgis. After Hunt left, Jack Ruby arrived, the man who would later shoot Oswald. Lorenz then left and flew back to Miami. Lorenz testified that they had transported cases of machine guns and shotguns and that one of the major tasks in her job for the CIA was to transport weapons; however, this time felt different, as though it was something bigger than a typical gunrunning. She testified that Frank Sturgis later confirmed to her that he was involved in the Kennedy assassination.[379] Sturgis had ties not only to the CIA but to Israel as well. He had been a Haganah mercenary during the 1948 Israeli-Arab war.[380] Lorenz has made contradictory statements over the years, so her claims should be taken with a grain of salt. Hunt denied under oath that he was in Dallas; however, he was caught lying under oath about where he was that weekend. It was not proven that he was in Dallas, but it was proven that he was being dishonest about his whereabouts.[381] According to Hunt's son, Hunt later confessed to him that he had been asked to participate in the Dallas plot but had declined.[382] Unfortunately, when it comes to potential assassins, there is not much to go on beyond he said/she said statements made by people with changing stories. Nonetheless, because Lorenz made her claims under oath and because Hunt was dishonest under oath about his whereabouts, the claims are worth at least a mention.

William Harvey ran Task Force W, the CIA unit responsible for attempts to subvert the Cuban government. This task force included the highly secretive ZRRIFLE, an assassination program. According to Angleton's Church Committee testimony, he used a Mossad agent as an intermediary between himself and Harvey for the "Cuban business." Some researchers believe ZRRIFLE may have been re-directed at Kennedy.[383]

There is also suspicion that the culprits used at least one French assassin. According to CIA Counterintelligence Chief James Angleton's HSCA testimony, he met with a high-ranking official of the French intelligence service (SDECE), Georges de Lannurien, on the afternoon of November 22. Since Kennedy was gunned down during the lunch hour in Dallas, Angleton's meeting would have been at the time of the Kennedy assassination. Officially, the meeting was regarding a potential mole.[384] There was at least one potential French assassin in Dallas on the day of the assassination. According to a CIA document dated April 1, 1964, the French were looking for Jean Souetre, who had been associated with attempts to assassinate French president Charles de Gaulle. The document stated he had been in Dallas on November 22, the day of Kennedy's assassination. The French believed he had been expelled to Canada or Mexico.[385] In the mid-1960s, de Gaulle issued an order terminating all joint operations between the SDECE and the CIA[386] and ordered that the French intelligence service cut ties with the Mossad.[387] There is no indication that de Gaulle did this because he felt that the two intelligence agencies had pulled the SDECE into the JFK assassination, but it does indicate that he did not trust either.

If there was a conspiracy to murder John F. Kennedy, then the assassination plot's successful execution depended on seven key pillars. The first was the upper-level control of Oswald and his movements, as well as his files within the government bureaucracy. James Angleton, who had close ties to both the CIA and the Israeli intelligence service Mossad, is the prime suspect for this role. Indeed, he received files on Oswald as late as November 15, 1963.[388] It is unclear if anyone underneath him, who may have assisted him, had prior knowledge of an assassination plot. The second pillar was the on-the-ground control of Oswald. In New Orleans, this appears to have been the responsibility of Clay Shaw, who had ties to both the CIA and Permindex, whose de-facto head was financing Israel's nuclear weapons program. In Dallas, this role appears to have been played by Ruth Paine, who likely had connections to the CIA and possibly even Zionist interests.

The third pillar was the selection of the luncheon site and the corresponding motorcade route/arrangements. While it is not fully clear here as to who was responsible, the Dallas Citizens Council, and particularly Sam Bloom, are key suspects in this role. Bloom oversaw the arrangements in Dallas as head of the host committee. At the very least, he was in charge "on paper." It is unknown if Bloom had intelligence links, but he was a supporter of Israel and a friend of Lyndon Johnson and held a massive influence in the city of Dallas. The Dallas Citizens Council, in general, was a group of wealthy men who were largely opposed to Kennedy's policies and likely had some connections to intelligence. The scheduling of the American Bottlers of Carbonated Beverages convention at the Statler Hilton (and their refusal to give up the site) also appears to have perhaps played a role, as it necessitated the search for another location for the luncheon.

The fourth pillar was control over the Texas School Book Depository as well as potentially other buildings in Dealey Plaza. Who might have had control of these sites also is not fully clear. Bloom was connected to the

Dal-Tex building, but it is unknown if shooters were stationed there. As for the TSBD building, it was owned by David H. Byrd, a defense contractor who owed a portion of his wealth to both oil and uranium. But the building could have easily been controlled without the owner's permission as it was leased out to various entities. Furthermore, the top three floors were typically empty as they were used to store books, and staff only sporadically accessed them. During the week of the assassination, the sixth floor, the floor Oswald allegedly shot from, was occupied by outside contractors doing floor work.[389]

The fifth pillar was the publicity given to Oswald prior to the assassination via radio and TV. This publicity was used after the assassination to display to the whole world Oswald's Communist sympathies. It allowed the culprits to immediately provide "proof" to the public of the official narrative regarding the assassination. The Sterns supplied this spotlight. Edgar Stern Sr., though deceased at the time of the assassination, did have some ties to the CIA while he was alive. The Stern family were supporters of Israel and appeared to have had some interest in nuclear weapons.

The sixth pillar was lax security along the motorcade route and the assurance that the Secret Service would fail to protect the president. This will be discussed later. The seventh pillar was the guarantee of a cover-up. This also will be discussed later.

At the lowest level of the plot, it appears the culprits may have used the Cuban exiles. The exiles would have had their own motive for assassinating Kennedy. They were angry over his refusal to give military support during the Bay of Pigs invasion and his attempts to pursue normalized diplomatic relations with Castro. Were the exiles used to provide a cover for those who ordered the assassination? Layering an assassination plot gives added protection to those at the top. If the culprits were forced to admit to a conspiracy, they could have then blamed the murder on disgruntled exiles.

Although there were seven key pillars, that does not mean all involved knew an assassination plot was in the works. Some of them likely did not know. As James Angleton cryptically told the *New York Times*, "A mansion has many rooms. … I'm not privy to who struck John."[390] It is not clear if Angleton was referring to the Kennedy assassination when he made his cryptic comment; however, what is clear is that if any of the seven pillars had fallen apart, the assassination plot could not have been successful.

4

The Crime

I'm just a patsy. – Lee Harvey Oswald

What happened on the day of the crime? Getting lost in the myriad details is easy and distracting. What matters is who ordered the assassination and why and what changed as a result. Overanalyzing the granular details of that grisly day will not supply that answer. In many ways, the conversation often is intentionally steered to the technicalities, forcing the attention of skeptics towards the nitty-gritty minutia of the crime when the focus should be on the big picture, on policy, and on what changed, not on how many shooters there were and from where they were firing. Nevertheless, a basic understanding of such details is essential, as it establishes the fact that there were myriad issues with the official story. And it shows that innumerable investigative avenues were never followed. It also sheds some light on who the culprits may have been.

Dealey Plaza was chosen as the location for John F. Kennedy's murder. It is an upside-down triangular plaza with Houston Street at the top of the triangle, Elm Street going down on the left side, and Main Street going down the right side. A grassy area sits in between Elm and Main. There is also a second grassy area to the left of Elm, known today as the infamous Grassy Knoll.

On the afternoon before the assassination, Thursday, November 21, Oswald was driven by a co-worker, Buell Frazier, to Irving, Texas, where Marina was staying with Ruth. Oswald had rented a small room in Dallas, where he lived during the week, and spent the weekends in Irving with Marina. He typically rode to Irving on Fridays, so leaving on a Thursday was an exception, though not entirely out of character. He had cashed a check a few weeks prior in Irving on a Thursday.[391] Furthermore, he had not visited the previous weekend and had quarreled with Marina during the week, so he may have wanted to go to mend fences.[392] According to Frazier, Oswald told him that he was visiting on a Thursday because he needed to pick up curtain rods for his room. Frazier testified that Oswald brought a bag into the Texas School Book Depository the following morning. The Warren Commission used this to allege that Oswald brought a rifle into the building; however, the only two people to see Oswald with the bag, Frazier and his sister, were both clear in their testimony that the bag was too small to hold even a disassembled rifle. The only person other than Frazier to see Oswald walk into the building that morning was a man by the name of Jack Dougherty, who testified that Oswald was not carrying anything.[393] Based on Dougherty's testimony and Oswald's denial that he brought anything into work other than his lunch, some have questioned Frazier's story.[394] Dougherty's testimony however is not wholly inconsistent with Frazier's, as Frazier testified, "From what I seen walking behind he had it under his arm, and you couldn't tell that he had a package from the back."[395] Regardless, the package, according to Frazier, was too small for a rifle and Oswald had been manipulated into the patsy role for months up to this point, so if he did bring something into work, he may have been encouraged to do so for what he understood to be a completely unrelated reason.

That morning, as witness Julia Ann Mercer, a twenty-three-year-old Dallas resident, was driving down Elm Street, she saw a truck parked illegally, partly on the curb, at the base of the grassy knoll. At the top of the knoll were a fence, bushes, and a half dozen trees. The truck protruded onto the street, blocking traffic, forcing Mercer to stop and wait behind it until the lane to the left of her opened. Mercer saw one man "slouched over the wheel" and another remove "what appeared to be a gun case" from the truck. She then saw the second man walk up the grassy knoll. She described the man in the vehicle as a heavy-set middle-aged man and the other as being in his late twenties or early thirties and wearing a plaid shirt and brown pants.[396] She would later identify the heavy-set man as Jack Ruby, the man who later shot and killed Oswald.[397]

Later in the morning, employee James Jarmon Jr. encountered Oswald on the first floor. Oswald asked him why people were gathering outside, and Jarmon informed him that the president was supposed to pass by the building.[398] Witnesses Bonnie Ray Williams and Bill Lovelady saw Oswald on the fifth floor waiting for an elevator to go down at around 11:45 a.m.[399] According to witnesses Eddie Piper and William Shelley, they saw Oswald on the first floor at noon and ten minutes of noon, respectively, corroborating the witness accounts that at 11:45 a.m. Oswald had been waiting for an elevator to go downstairs. This would also match Oswald's claim that he ate lunch on the first floor and then went to the second floor to get a Coke from the vending machine. Oswald claimed he saw two African American employees eating lunch in the downstairs room at the same time as he was. Indeed, two African American employees did testify that someone else was in the room while they ate lunch, but they could not recall who. But the fact that Oswald could remember who they were implies that he may have been there. Another employee in the building, Carolyn Arnold, told the FBI that she believed she had seen Oswald downstairs around 12:15 p.m., though her story became inconsistent over the years as to where exactly she saw him.[400] One witness, Charles Givens, claimed he (Givens) went up to the sixth floor at 11:55 a.m. to retrieve his cigarettes and saw Oswald walking from the southeast corner to the elevator; however, there are issues with Givens' testimony as he could not have seen Oswald unless he also walked all the way to the eastern part of the building. Furthermore, Givens had a criminal record and did not mention this encounter in his initial statements to the police. He is someone who could have easily been encouraged to make inaccurate claims at a later time.[401]

As JFK's motorcade started to make its way out of the airport and towards downtown Dallas, a Secret Service agent began jogging along the rear of JFK's limousine on JFK's side, but another agent, Emory Roberts, assistant to the special agent in charge, called him off. Though not always, agents were often on or near the presidential vehicle. During this trip, however, they were not. The called-off agent looked back in disbelief.[402] It is also common for police motorcycles to ride next to the presidential car, making it more difficult for a shooter to hit his target. However, they were behind the vehicle in the Dallas formation, leaving the President completely exposed.[403] It is unclear from whom these orders for lax security along the motorcade route originated. The police claimed that the Secret Service told them JFK wanted a better connection with the crowd and that the motorcycles were obtruding that.[404] Agent Winston Lawson testified that JFK gave them no direct orders regarding the vehicle arrangements; however, his general impression was that the President preferred not to have too many motorcycles next to the vehicle unless necessary because they made it difficult for him to hear others in his car.[405] Dallas Police Department motorcycle officer B. J. Martin stated, "I'd never heard of a formation like that, much less ridden in one, but they said they wanted to let the crowds have an unrestricted view of the President. Well, I guess somebody got an 'unrestricted view' of him, all right."[406]

Who gave the Secret Service and the police the impression that JFK wanted better crowd connection? Is this an idea that could have perhaps originated from an advertising and publicity man, since crowd connection is a public relations concept? There is no indication it came from Bloom; however, as previously mentioned, Bloom worked closely with the Secret Service on the motorcade details, and according to FBI Agent James Hosty, Bloom had been hired to "advise the police department on how to handle the Kennedy visit." Or was the Secret Service given direct orders, and if so, by whom? The Secret Service was technically the responsibility of the Department of Treasury, run by Douglas Dillon, who was connected to many powerful Wall

Street interests, but there is no evidence that Dillon was involved with the planning for Dallas. Furthermore, if the Secret Service as an institution was involved in the assassination, then why did the head of the Secret Service, Gerald Behn, choose the Women's Building as the lunch location? This implies that someone outside the typical command line encouraged the on-the-ground agents. Similarly, who urged the police to essentially end their motorcade duties after the turn off Main Street, i.e., right before entering Dealey Plaza?[407] Police Chief Curry stated about the parade route that the police "left it entirely up to the host committee and the Secret Service."[408] As for agent Emory Roberts, Lyndon Johnson ultimately made him his personal receptionist at the White House and decorated him in 1968 with a Special Service Award from the Treasury Department.[409] Johnson stated of Roberts in 1968, "He greets me every morning and tells me goodbye every night."[410]

In addition to the lax formation surrounding the president during his motorcade route, the agents' alertness to respond to an unexpected event was also in question. Agent Emory Roberts had taken his team out drinking and partying until five in the morning the evening before the assassination.[411]

Witness Lee Bowers, a railroad tower man, had a view of the area behind the fence at the top of the grassy knoll from his fourteen-foot tower. He saw two men standing behind the fence shortly before the shots rang out. The description he gave was similar to the one Mercer gave of the two men she had seen earlier that morning carrying what appeared to be a gun case up the grassy knoll. He said one was in his mid-twenties and wearing a plaid shirt and the other heavy-set and middle-aged.[412] Mercer had identified the heavy-set man as Jack Ruby; however, it is not clear that the man Bowers saw could have been Ruby, as other witnesses had claimed to have seen Ruby at around 12:20 p.m. and again at 12:40 p.m. at *The Dallas Morning News* building, located a short distance from Dealey Plaza.[413]

At approximately 12:15 pm, witness Arnold Rowland saw a man with a rifle standing a few feet back from the southwest window of the sixth floor of the Texas School Book Depository. Oswald allegedly fired from the opposite side, the southeast window. The witness assumed the gunman was part of the presidential security team. Rowland testified that at the same time, at 12:15 p.m., he saw a dark-skinned man hanging out on the southeast side of the sixth floor. He testified that the dark-skinned man was bald or practically bald and that the man stayed there until approximately five minutes before the motorcade passed. As the motorcade approached, Rowland did not take any further looks at the building.[414] The testimony of Bonnie Ray Williams corroborated Rowland's testimony to some extent, as Williams, an African American worker inside the TSBD building, stated he was on the sixth floor, a few windows from the southeast window, eating lunch until approximately ten to twenty minutes before the motorcade arrived. Williams was not bald, but he did have white dust in his hair, which may have made him look bald from a distance. He did not see Oswald while he was on the sixth floor, though with the many stacks of books on that floor, it is very possible Williams would not have seen anyone.[415] Williams then went down to the fifth floor and met up with two other workers, Harold Norman and James Jarvis Jr., and they watched the motorcade from there.[416]

John F. Kennedy's limousine moved slowly in a westward direction down Main Street as it approached a slow 90-degree right turn onto Houston Street. It then moved slowly down Houston Street, preparing for a slow 120-degree left turn onto Elm Street. The most obvious question to ask, if Oswald was indeed a "lone nut," is why did he not shoot Kennedy as his car was slowly driving down Houston Street and approaching the Texas School Book Depository building on the corner of Houston and Elm? He had a perfect shot, not obstructed by any trees. Anyone who has stood on the corner of Houston and Elm can see what a perfect shot it was. Yet, if one believes the official thesis of the crime, for some reason, Oswald chose not to take the optimal shot and instead waited until after Kennedy's limousine had turned onto Elm Street and until a tree obstructed his view. However, if one believes there were multiple shooters, waiting until after the turn on Elm makes perfect sense, as Elm Street offered the ideal kill zone for multi-directional shots.

As Kennedy's limousine turned onto Elm Street and began slowly driving down the hill, a man stepped forward and opened an umbrella. It was a perfectly sunny day, and for years researchers were confused as to why this man opened an umbrella and wondered if it was in any way related to the shots that were about to ring out. The man, Steven Witt, testified in front of the House Select Committee on Assassinations that he opened the umbrella to heckle Kennedy over his father's appeasement policies during World War II. JFK's father, Joseph Kennedy, supported and was friendly with British Prime Minister Neville Chamberlin, who always walked with an umbrella and wanted to negotiate with Hitler and avoid war.[417] Most researchers have laughed off Witt's explanation. However, Lyndon Johnson, while battling Kennedy for the Democratic Party nomination, had referred to JFK's father as a "Chamberlain-umbrella policy man" who thought "Hitler was right."[418] In addition to Johnson, who else would have understood the symbolism? And, more importantly, who would have wanted that symbolism captured at the moment of Kennedy's murder? It is important to note that Kennedy's father was not a Hitler supporter; he merely wanted to avoid a war that resulted in over seventy million deaths when taking into account war-related famine and diseases.[419]

In the seconds that followed, Kennedy was shot from the back and seemingly from the front as well until the fatal headshot sent him violently backward and to his left. In what was, at best, gross incompetence and/or negligence, the Secret Service failed to protect the president. None of the Secret Service agents in the trailing vehicle ran to his protection. Some did start to move toward JFK's car, but agent Emory Roberts called them off as he felt JFK's vehicle was moving too quickly for the agents to catch up with it.[420] Roberts was the agent who had earlier called off the Secret Service agent running alongside JFK's vehicle as the cars were departing Love Field Airport toward downtown Dallas and who had taken his team out drinking the night prior.

The driver of JFK's car, also a Secret Service agent, slowed down as the shots rang out, according to many eyewitness accounts, instead of speeding up and out of the location, as agents are trained to do. The only agent to run towards the car was assigned to JFK's wife, Jackie, and he did catch up with it, an indication of how slowly the vehicle was moving.[421]

Governor John Connally was also struck by at least one bullet, as was a bystander, James Tague. Tague was approximately 260 feet from the president when he was struck in the face by an apparent bullet fragment. A fresh bullet mark was found on the curb next to where Tague was standing.[422] It is not clear why a bullet would stray so far from the presidential vehicle or if perhaps there is another explanation for Tague's injury and the apparent bullet mark on the ground near him.

Complete chaos ensued. Many witnesses thought the shots came from the grassy knoll area and ran towards there.[423] Bowers, the railroad worker who had earlier seen two men behind the picket fence, stated, "At the time of the shooting, in the vicinity of where the two men I have described were, there was a flash of light ... something I could not identify ... but ... something which caught my eye ... a flash of light or smoke or something."[424]

Mary Woodward, an employee of *The Dallas Morning News*, stood to the front and left of the wooden fence when the shots rang out. She stated, "Suddenly there was a horrible ear-shattering noise coming from behind us and a little to the right."[425] The two motorcycle policemen behind Kennedy's limousine and to the left were both splattered with blood and brain matter, implying the bullet entered Kennedy from the right front. One of the officers, Bobby Hargis, testified that the flesh particles hit him with such impact that he thought he had taken a bullet.[426] Jackie, JFK's wife, who was sitting to the left of him, jumped onto the back trunk of the car to pick up a piece of her husband's skull, again implying a shot came from the right front.

Witness J. C. Price, standing on top of a nearby building, stated in an affidavit that he saw a man run from behind the fence, carrying something in his hand, he thought perhaps a headpiece. His description of the man matched the description given by Mercer and Bowers. He stated the man was in his mid-twenties and wearing brown pants. He later told researcher Mark Lane, "He was running very fast, which gave me the suspicion he was doing the shooting."[427] Another witness, S. M. Holland, stood on the bridge directly over Elm Street as the shots rang out. He immediately looked towards the wooden fence area on the grassy knoll and saw "a puff of smoke." Another witness who ran behind the fence after the shots were fired stated that he saw "footprints in the mud around the fence." Multiple witnesses said they saw muddy footprints on a car bumper as if someone had been standing there, looking over the fence.[428]

At the time of the motorcade, thirteen railroad employees and two police officers were on the railroad bridge overlooking Elm Street, the grassy knoll just to their left. Of those who were questioned, five said the shots came from the knoll, and six others said their attention immediately went to the knoll when the shots were fired. These witnesses were among those closest to the knoll area. Eleven indicated, either explicitly or implicitly, that they felt the sniper was behind the fence on the knoll. Seven of them stated that they saw smoke above the bushes and under the trees.[429] While only those with a side view of the knoll witnessed smoke, many witnesses standing in front of the knoll, with their backs to the picket fence area, felt the shots came from the knoll area behind them.[430]

Seymour Weitzman was one of the first police officers to reach the fence area on the grassy knoll.[431] When he got there, he stated the Secret Service was present. Police officer J. M. Smith also ran towards the knoll area and said when he arrived, he could smell gunpowder,[432] but a Secret Service agent flashed his credentials to him, essentially halting him.[433] The significant problem these accounts raise is that all the Secret Service agents were accounted for and none were in Dealey Plaza.[434] This implies that men with fake Secret Service credentials were in the area where many witnesses felt shots had come from. Where did these men get their Secret Service credentials? Researchers have speculated that perhaps they came from Sidney Gottlieb, head of the CIA Technical Services Division, whose responsibilities included "issuance of forged personal identity documentation," including Secret Service documentation.[435] After he had learned no Secret Service agents were in Dealey Plaza, Officer Smith gave his testimony about the appearance of the "agent" who'd stopped him: "He looked like an auto mechanic. He had on a sports shirt and sports pants. But he had dirty fingernails, it looked like, and hands that looked like an auto mechanic's hands. And afterwards, it didn't ring true for the Secret Service."[436]

Other witnesses thought shots came from the rear of the motorcade, where in fact some shots did originate. Sixteen-year-old Amos Euins testified that he saw a man with a bald spot on the top of his head shooting from the southeast window of the sixth floor, where Oswald was allegedly located, but Oswald was not bald.[437] Euins initially told a reporter that the man was dark-skinned, but later in his Warren Commission testimony he said he could not be sure if the man were dark-skinned or white. Other witnesses said they saw a rifle protruding from the window but not a man.[438] Witness James Worrell also testified to seeing a gun shooting from the fifth or sixth floor of the east side of the building, after which he ran around to the back of the building and after a few minutes saw a white man running out of the back door of the building.[439] Euins in his testimony stated that while he was talking to a police officer, another man—a construction worker, so not Worrell—had come up to the police officer to let him know he saw a man run out of the back of the building with "a bald spot on his head."[440] So this makes two witnesses who claimed a man was running out of the back of the Texas School Book Depository building. Two other witnesses, Robert Edwards and Ronald Fischer, claimed they saw a man at the sixth-floor southeast window that fit the description of Oswald shortly before the motorcade arrived. However, they did not see a rifle. They gave their statements later after the press had set the official narrative, so their descriptions of the man may have been clouded.[441] But even if they were accurate, there is no doubt if there were a conspiracy to blame Oswald, then the conspicuous man placed in that window would likely have resembled Oswald from a distance.

Of the three men watching the motorcade on the TSBD fifth floor directly below the sixth-floor southeast window, two testified they thought the initial shot was a vehicle backfire, implying they thought the shots came from below and not above. However, one of those two stated he felt two shots came from above. One of the three, on December 4, told a Secret Service agent that he had heard the bolt action of a rifle and shells falling on the floor, but this was after the official narrative had been made public.[442] Many witnesses who had much less important things to say went to the police station and gave affidavits. However, only one of these three men provided a statement that day. It was not Norman, the one who later claimed to have heard the rifle.[443] Furthermore, the three men ran to the west side of the building to look towards the grassy knoll area immediately after they heard the shots. If they had indeed heard shots above them, why did they not yell out to the police from the window or run downstairs to let the police know? Instead, all three men rushed to look towards the grassy knoll area. They testified they did not hear footsteps above them.[444]

Witness Victoria Adams stood, with her co-worker, Sandra Styles, looking out a window on the fourth floor of the Texas School Book Depository as the president's motorcade went by.[445] A few seconds after they saw the president get shot, she and Styles ran down the stairs. Supervisor Dorothy Garner confirmed that Adams and Styles had run from the window almost immediately and then down the stairs. Shortly after, Garner followed them to the stairs to pick something up and heard them running down. A little later, she saw building superintendent Roy Truly and a policeman come up the stairs.[446] As Adams and Styles ran down the stairs, they saw and heard no one. The stairs were old and very noisy whenever anyone walked down them. This piece of testimony is crucial as the official story alleges that Oswald squeezed out of an area enclosed by boxes, hid his rifle near the stairs, then ran from the sixth floor down to the second floor in less than eighty seconds, was never seen or heard on the stairs by Adams or Styles, and calmly came across Truly and the policeman on the second floor, after which Truly and the policeman went upstairs and were seen by Garner.[447]

After being approached by the policeman, Oswald, instead of quietly leaving the building, was seen a few moments later by a clerical supervisor, Mrs. Robert Reid, with a Coke in his hand. She stated Oswald was calm and not in a rush.[448] She would be the last person to see Oswald in the building. It is unclear when Oswald got the Coke, but he told the police he already had it when the policeman approached him. Indeed, the policeman himself, officer M. L. Baker, stated in an affidavit that he saw Oswald with a Coke when he accosted him, though he later struck it from his testimony. Some initial media reports also indicated officer Baker encountered Oswald with a Coke in his hand.[449] If Oswald had a Coke in his hand, how did he manage the time to get it, since he was already allegedly moving at lightning speed to make it in time to reach the second floor after the shooting? It should be noted that researchers have questioned Baker's testimony as in his initial police affidavit he made no mention of accosting anyone on the second floor, even though at the time he gave his statement to the police, Oswald was seated in the same room.[450]

If Oswald had indeed been framed, how did the plotters ensure that Oswald would be inside the building at the time of the shooting instead of outside watching the motorcade with his co-workers? There was a public telephone downstairs, and it is believed that perhaps Oswald was told to stay indoors and await a phone call.

Assuming there was at least one gunman in the building—and based on witness statements, it appears there was—it is unclear how he got out or if he was the man that two witnesses had seen running out of the back of the building. It is worth remembering that the top three floors were typically empty, and there was a floor-laying crew working that week on the sixth floor, so people who usually did not have access to the building did have access that week, particularly to that floor. This then begs the question: If Oswald was the shooter, why did he not pick the seventh floor rather than risk being seen on the sixth floor?

According to the Warren Commission, Oswald left the TSBD building via the front door at 12:33 p.m. The front door was crowded at the time with his co-workers, and yet no one saw him.[451]

At approximately six minutes after the shooting, Sergeant D. V. Harkness arrived at the back of the Texas School Book Depository to ensure the building was sealed off and no one could escape. However, this was after a man had already been seen running away from the building. When Harkness got there, he saw men standing there who told him they were Secret Service agents.[452] Hence there were men stationed at the grassy knoll and behind the TSBD building claiming to be Secret Service agents when all Secret Service agents were accounted for. None were in Dealey Plaza at that time.

Across the street from the TSBD building, in the Dal-Tex building, two suspicious men were picked up, both of whom claimed they went to the third floor to use a telephone.[453] The third floor was where Marilyn-Belt Manufacturing, the firm which shared a phone number with the Sam-Bloom-connected Dallas Uranium and Oil, was located, directly behind the fire escape, facing Dealey Plaza.[454] After the men gave their statements, they were released. One of the men, Jim Braden, had recently changed his name from Eugene Hale Brading. If the police had known this, they would have seen a lengthy criminal history for Brading.[455] Braden had been staying at the Cabana Hotel,[456] the same hotel at which Jack Ruby met up with Lawrence Meyers the night before the assassination.[457] If the reader recalls, Meyers was the Chicago man who District Attorney Garrison thought was serving as an intermediary between David Ferrie in New Orleans and Jack Ruby in Dallas. There is no evidence that Ruby and Meyers met up with

Braden, but the possibility of such a meet-up should be investigated.

At 12:44 p.m., a dispatcher ordered police cars to Dealey Plaza. However, at 12:45 p.m., a police officer named J. D. Tippit and another officer were given special orders to go to the Central Oak Cliff area. This was an area outside of Tippit's district. Oswald's rooming house was in this area.[458] Tippit would have less than thirty minutes to live. There is debate about whether this order to Tippit was issued, as the other officer did not go to the area, and the request only appeared in the radio log months later. The original transcript did not include it. The original transcript was incomplete but was claimed to have all Tippit-related radio transmissions.[459] Regardless, Tippit left his assigned district and headed to the Oak Cliff area, where he would shortly be killed.

Also, at 12:45 p.m., a description of a suspect armed with a rifle went out over police radio. It is unclear who gave this description or where the witness saw the suspect as the policeman told the dispatcher, "It is unknown whether he is still in the building or not known if he was there in the first place."[460] The description given was of a white, slender, five-foot-ten man in his early thirties, somewhat matching Oswald's description.[461] It was never credibly confirmed who the witness was who offered this description. The Warren Commission claimed it was a man named Howard Brennan, but many researchers have thoroughly discredited that witness. Furthermore, Brennan claimed he saw Oswald only inside the building, so the dispatcher saying it was unknown if the suspect was ever in the building implies his source was not Brennan.

At around the same time, 12:45 p.m., Deputy Sheriff Roger Craig heard someone whistle, after which he saw a man, whom he believed to be Oswald, running down the hill and into a waiting station wagon on Elm Street. A dark-skinned man was driving the station wagon.[462] According to the Warren Commission, however, Oswald had left at 12:33 p.m. and thus Craig was mistaken.

96

John F. Kennedy was pronounced deceased at 1:00 p.m., shortly after arriving at Parkland Memorial Hospital.[463] The doctors who examined the president observed two wounds: a small wound in his throat and a massive wound at the back of his skull. Entrance wounds are typically small, and exit wounds large.[464] Dr. McClelland testified, "The right exterior portion of the skull had been extremely blasted. … probably a third or so, at least, of the brain tissue … had been blasted out." Some doctors also noticed a wound on the left temple. Dr. McClelland wrote, "The cause of death was due to massive head and brain injury from a gunshot wound of the left temple." The priest who administered last rites noted a "terrible wound" over the left eye.[465] However, White House Press Secretary Malcolm Kilduff announced that the fatal wound was a shot to the right temple.[466]

Approximately an hour after the announcement of the president's death, two doctors held a press conference. Dr. Malcolm Perry, the physician in charge, stated, "There was an entrance wound below his Adam's apple." Dr. Charles Carrico, the first to attend to the president, also signed a hospital report describing the throat wound as one of entrance. When the first shot was fired, JFK was facing his right, towards the grassy knoll, so an entrance wound in the neck would have had to come from that area. All doctors who expressed an opinion in the days following the assassination described the neck wound as an entrance wound. There seems to be some inconsistency regarding whether shots came from the right or left. However, it is clear the Dallas doctors thought shots came from the front.[467] Indeed, in a 2015 interview, Dr. McClelland pointed to the right temple when discussing where the emergency room doctors had thought the shot had entered, contradicting his initial statement of the left temple.[468] They had not turned JFK over to see the gunshot wound in his back. As for the neck wound, the doctors felt it was a bullet wound. However, some researchers have questioned whether the neck entrance wound was from a bullet or from perhaps exploding head matter instead. In the immediate days following the assassination, the press tried to explain the glaring issue of Oswald being in the back of Kennedy when doctors indicated shots came from the front.

The press initially stated that perhaps President Kennedy was hit while still on Houston Street, which is clearly false and untenable, and then that he had probably turned around while on Elm Street, also clearly erroneous.[469] In a 2015 interview, Dr. McClelland stated he was "as close to certain as I can be" that the fatal bullet came from the front.[470] Some of the other doctors later changed their mind and abided by the official narrative, claiming their initial assessment must have been incorrect.

A floor-by-floor search of the TSBD building by police led them to uncover a sniper's nest by the sixth-floor southeast window.[471] At around 1:00 p.m., Deputy Sheriff Luke Mooney discovered a pile of boxes in front of the window in the southeast corner. The Warren Commission alleged that Oswald set up the boxes to shield himself from view as he shot at the president. Searching the area, Mooney found three empty cartridge cases on the floor near the window. Why did the assassin not pick up the empty cartridge cases as he was making his escape? Why leave behind ballistic evidence?[472]

Since witnesses had alerted the police to the southeast window, why did the police not rush up there immediately? Instead, they only uncovered the "sniper's nest" after a standard floor-by-floor search more than thirty minutes after the crime, giving any assassin ample time to escape. Moreover, according to his testimony, Williams was eating lunch at the southeast window until 12:20 p.m. Even giving Williams wiggle room and assuming he left around 12:10 p.m., would that have given Oswald time to create the sniper's nest? The boxes were approximately fifty pounds each, and there were around twenty-four of them. Even without the boxes, anyone at the southeast window could not be easily seen by others on the floor unless those others walked to the northeast corner first, as stacks of books were everywhere, obstructing the view. Any sniper would hear someone coming and be able to assume the pose of an innocent spectator quickly. The assassin would much more likely be seen by outside spectators than by anyone inside the building. Yet he did not attempt to hide from outside spectators, as several witnesses saw either a man or a gun at the window. Lastly, given the tight way in which the boxes were arranged, the assassin would need to squeeze through to get out, delaying the time it would take him to hide the rifle and run downstairs and appear calm on the second floor eighty seconds later as Oswald was. It appears the boxes served the purpose of attracting attention after the fact more than anything else.[473]

What did Oswald do after he left the TSBD building, allegedly at 12:33 p.m.? According to Oswald and the Warren Commission, he got on a bus going back towards his rooming house; however, after the bus got stuck in traffic, he walked a few blocks and then took a cab the rest of the way. According to his alleged cab driver, Oswald offered his taxi to an elderly lady. Hence, he was not in a rush.[474] What about the police officer who had seen Oswald leaving Dealey Plaza in a station wagon? More on that in a little bit.

The housekeeper at Oswald's rooming house, Mrs. Earlene Roberts, testified that Oswald arrived in a hurry at 1:00 p.m. and went to his room. A police car then pulled up in front of the house and parked, with two uniformed police officers inside the vehicle. They lightly honked the horn twice.[475] Also at 1:00 p.m., Officer J. D. Tippit received a call from the dispatcher but did not answer.[476] After three or four minutes, at approximately 1:03 p.m. or 1:04 p.m., Oswald emerged from his room, zipping up a dark jacket. After Oswald left, Mrs. Roberts looked outside and saw the police car was gone and Oswald was waiting at the bus stop for a northbound bus.

According to witness testimony, at approximately 1:10 p.m., if not earlier, police officer J. D. Tippit was shot to death close to one mile south of where Mrs. Roberts had last seen Oswald, i.e., at a location in the opposite direction from the direction of the bus Oswald was waiting for.[477] According to Google Maps, the walk would have taken Oswald eighteen minutes. One witness claimed his watch showed 1:10 p.m. when he arrived at the scene of the Tippit shooting, and that was after the officer had already been shot. A witness radioed for help between 1:15 p.m. and 1:16 p.m. However, witness testimony makes it evident that a few minutes passed before a call for help was made due to witness fear that the shooter was still in the area.[478] A cab driver who witnessed the assailant approaching Tippet indicated that the gunman was walking west when he shot Tippit, but Oswald would have had to have been walking east.[479] The cab driver did not see the actual shooting due to shrubbery that was in the way. One witness who did see the shooting claimed that she saw two men standing near the police car. One of them then shot Tippit, and the two ran away in different directions.[480] The witness closest to the shooting, Domingo Benavides, testified that after the shooting he saw the gunman take a few steps, remove one shell from his revolver and drop it on the ground, take five or six more steps and drop another shell on the ground, before leaving the scene.[481] Why would a gunman intentionally leave ballistic evidence at the scene that could then potentially be tied back to him?

Though Oswald would have had to have been walking southeast to shoot Tippit, he allegedly then turned around and walked southwest towards the Texas Theater, a thirteen-minute walk according to Google Maps. So, according to the official narrative, Oswald was waiting for a bus going north, but instead of getting on the northbound bus, he allegedly walked rapidly southeast to shoot Tippit and then walked southwest to catch a film. Researchers have speculated that Oswald, instead, was waiting for the cop car in front of his rooming house to turn around and pick him up, which then likely drove him to the theater. According to witness and concession stand worker Warren H. Burroughs, Oswald entered the theater between 1:00 p.m. and 1:07 p.m., before the Tippit shooting, but fitting the timeline of a quick drive southwest from his rooming house to the theater (a three-minute drive). There were fewer than twenty people in the nine-hundred-seat theater. Once in the theater, Oswald sat next to a man named Jack Davis. Davis wondered why Oswald sat next to him in a largely empty theater. Oswald stayed very briefly and then went to sit next to someone else. He then got up a moment later and walked out to the lobby. Davis indicated that it seemed that Oswald was looking for someone. Warren H.

Burroughs estimated that it was 1:15 p.m. when he sold Oswald popcorn at the concession stand. Burroughs then said Oswald walked back into the theater and sat next to a pregnant woman, apparently still attempting to find whoever he was looking for.[482]

At 1:22 p.m., Deputy Constable Seymour Weitzman and Deputy Sheriff Eugene Boone discovered a rifle on the sixth floor of the Texas School Book Depository building. Deputy Sheriff Luke Mooney joined the two men shortly. Then two police officers arrived, who also examined the rifle. The Dallas authorities later informed the press that the rifle found was a 7.65 German Mauser, and Weitzman signed an affidavit declaring the same.[483] In his affidavit, Weitzman gave a very detailed description of the rifle. Other officers also confirmed it was a 7.65 German Mauser.[484]

Just after 1:25 p.m., a police officer, identified by number only and not name, stated over the police radio that he found a jacket allegedly belonging to "that suspect on shooting this officer [Tippit] out here. Got his white jacket. Believe he dumped it on this parking lot … and he had a white jacket on. We believe this is it."[485] Recall that, according to Mrs. Roberts, Oswald was wearing a dark jacket.

Theater guest Jack Davis stated that approximately twenty minutes after Oswald had sat next to the pregnant woman, at approximately 1:40 p.m., the woman got up to go to the ladies' room. The man at the concession stand, Burroughs, said the restroom door closed shortly before the Dallas police rushed into the theater. The police came in from the front and back, blocking all exits. When the police approached Oswald, he pulled out a pistol but was wrestled into submission and arrested. He did not have a jacket with him. The ticket seller, Julia Postal, had called the police because Oswald had not bought a ticket.[486] Why multiple policemen, entering from the front and rear, arrived to apprehend someone who failed to purchase a theater ticket when the president had just been murdered a few miles away is unclear. One would think they had more pressing priorities. The lady at the ticket counter, however, testified that during the arrest, a police officer came into the box office to use the telephone and stated over the phone, "I think we got our man on both accounts."[487] Several police officers testified that as they walked Oswald out of the theater, he yelled twice, "I am not resisting arrest!" This implies he may have already begun to realize that he had been set up and was worried about being killed in police custody.[488]

There is much speculation about an Oswald "double," i.e., a man who looked like Oswald playing a role in the events of that assassination day. According to another witness, Oswald walked into the theater around 1:45 p.m. The witness then informed the ticket lady, who called the police. Some witnesses saw a man in the rear of the building, who they recognized as Oswald, but the police took Oswald out of the front of the building. It may seem crazy, but it is not uncommon for intelligence operations to use look-alikes to confuse witnesses; recall the police officer seeing who he believed was Oswald leaving the TSBD building in a station wagon versus the claim that Oswald took a bus and a cab. The author felt it was worth mentioning since there were contradictory witness statements regarding the events in the theater and what time Oswald arrived there. Nevertheless, even if one discards the witness statements inside the theater and goes only with the witness who claimed he saw Oswald walk into the theater at 1:45 p.m., that would mean that after walking at a super-human pace to the scene of the Tippit slaying, Oswald then spent a leisurely half hour making a thirteen-minute walk to the Texas Theater. Typically, it is after a crime that one is in a rush to leave the scene. Lastly, it is a bit odd for someone who had just shot a president and then shot a policeman, with apparently no motive and no desire to receive attention or credit for it, to attract attention to himself by sneaking into a theater without paying.

Oswald's employer realized he was missing from work at the book depository around the same time that police brought him into custody for the theater violation. He was not the only one missing; another worker, Charles Givens, was also missing. Because Oswald had left work, he immediately became a suspect in the murder of John F. Kennedy.[489]

At 5:30 p.m., Officer Craig went to the office of Captain Fritz, where Oswald was being interrogated. Craig testified that Captain Fritz asked him if Oswald was the man he saw running into the station wagon in front of the TSBD building at approximately 12:45 p.m. Craig responded in the affirmative. According to Craig, Fritz then asked Oswald, "What about this station wagon?" to which Oswald replied, "That station wagon belongs to Mrs. Paine. Don't try to tie her into this. She had nothing to do with it." Then Oswald said, dejectedly, "Everybody will know who I am now."[490] Recall that Oswald, according to the police, had previously told them that he had taken a bus and a taxi back to his rooming house, as the Warren Commission alleged. How then did he know that someone who had looked like him had entered a station wagon that, according to Oswald, was owned by Mrs. Paine? Or was it Oswald who entered the station wagon? Mrs. Paine indeed owned a station wagon with the appearance of the one described. Was it Oswald who got into the station wagon, or was there indeed a look-alike?

At approximately 6 p.m., Oswald was administered a paraffin test.[491] When a weapon is discharged, burning powder and gasses escape, and particles containing nitrates are implanted on the skin. Warm paraffin wax is applied to the suspect's hands and face to recover nitrates. Cigarette ash, food, toothpaste, paints, and many other everyday substances may yield a positive response. Paraffin tests are typically done on both hands because a positive test on the hand that fired the rifle is of value only if a negative response is returned on the other hand. To assume that one fired a rifle that day, one would have to receive a positive test on the hand that pulled the trigger, a negative test on the opposite hand, and a positive test on the cheek. Nitrates were found on both of Oswald's hands but not on his face. The paraffin test results were thus consistent with Oswald not having fired a rifle that day.[492]

By 7:10 p.m. that evening, Oswald was arraigned for the murder of J. D. Tippit.[493] At 7:55 p.m., while being moved in front of reporters, Oswald yelled out in response to questions, "I'm just a patsy!" He told his brother that same day, "Do not form any opinion on the so-called evidence."[494] At midnight, Oswald was taken to the basement for a press conference. When a reporter asked, "Did you kill the President?" Oswald replied, "No, I have not been charged with that. In fact, nobody has said that to me yet. The first thing I heard about it is when the newspaper reporters in the hall asked me that question." Shortly after 1:30 a.m., Oswald was taken out of his cell and arraigned for the murder of John F. Kennedy.[495]

On November 23, FBI firearms expert Cortland Cunningham examined a bullet removed by doctors from Officer Tippit. Cunningham stated in his report, "The bullet ... is so badly mutilated that there is not sufficient individual microscopic characteristics present for identification purposes." The Dallas police informed the FBI that the bullet examined was "the only bullet that was recovered."[496]

Witness Howard Brennan, who had claimed to have seen a man firing from the sixth-floor window, was brought into the police station to view a line-up. He failed to pick Oswald out of the line-up. There were numerous issues with Brennan's constantly changing testimony, such as his claim that the man at the southeast window of the TSBD building was standing when he could not have been as then he would have been firing through glass.[497]

On both November 22 and 23, Oswald participated in several police line-ups. Some witnesses did pick Oswald out of the line-up for the shooting of Tippit, but the police administered the line-ups in a very unfair way. One such witness, William Whaley, stated, "You could have picked him out without identifying him just by listening to him because he was bawling out the policeman. He told them it wasn't right to put him in line with these teenagers. ... He told them ... they were trying to railroad him, and he wanted his lawyer. Anybody who wasn't sure could have picked out the right one just for that." Furthermore, the police asked each person in the line-up to state his name and place of employment. Everyone knew because of the media coverage the suspect's name and where he worked, so asking people to pick such a person out of a line-up was almost inconceivable.[498] Another witness, William Scoggins, who stated he did not get a good look at Tippit's shooter, nevertheless identified Oswald in the line-up, even though he had failed to pick Oswald out of a stack of photos.[499]

The one witness who the cops should have brought in for a line-up but did not was Domingo Benavides. He was the closest witness to the Tippit shooting. He later told the Warren Commission counsel he could not identify Oswald as the shooter.[500]

During the line-ups, Oswald complained that he had not been granted a request to put on a jacket when all the other men in the line-up were wearing a coat. If the police had in their hands the light jacket allegedly found near the Tippit shooting, as they claimed, why did they refuse to give that jacket, or any other coat, to Oswald? If the witnesses had seen the shooter in a jacket, would not giving Oswald a jacket have made it easier for witnesses to identify him? Conversely, had Oswald indeed been the shooter of Tippit, he did not realize putting a jacket on would make him easier to identify, even though he complained bitterly about other factors that made him easy to identify. This implies that Oswald was perhaps not the shooter as he appeared to be unaware that the shooter had been wearing a jacket.[501]

On November 23, the FBI alleged that Oswald owned a Mannlicher-Carcano 6.5 Italian carbine rifle. Note that the rifle that Oswald was alleged to have owned does not match the type of rifle that was claimed to have been found inside the TSBD building. The Dallas authorities then changed their statements and claimed that the rifle discovered the day before was indeed a Mannlicher-Carcano 6.5 Italian carbine. Stamped clearly on Oswald's alleged rifle were the words "MADE ITALY" and "CAL 6.5." How the initial policemen on the scene could have mistaken a Mannlicher-Carcano 6.5 Italian carbine with the words "MADE ITALY" stamped on it for a 7.65 German Mauser was never made clear.[502] The Italian rifle was considered a very feeble weapon compared to the German one. Walter H. B. Smith, the author of several National Rifle Association books, stated, "[The Italian Mannlicher-Carcano rifles] are poor quality weapons in comparison with United States, British, German or Russian equipment." An issue of *Mechanix Illustrated* stated that the Mannlicher-Carcano "is crudely made, poorly designed, dangerous and inaccurate" as well as "unhandy, crude, [and] unreliable on repeat shots."[503] During World War II, the Mannlicher-Carcano was known among Italian soldiers as the "humanitarian rifle"—on the grounds that it could not hurt anyone, at least not intentionally. Edward Voebel, a former schoolmate of Oswald's, told the Secret Service that he owned a similar rifle and that "he [Voebel] shot this rifle several times, but it is so poorly constructed he decided that it was best not to shoot it anymore for the reason he was afraid it would explode."[504]

Sebastian Frances Latona, supervisor of the Latent Fingerprint Section of the Identification Division of the FBI, examined the alleged assassination weapon for latent prints on November 23. He referred to the rifle as "a cheap old weapon." After using extensive identification methods to analyze it, he stated, "the latent prints which were there were of no value" and "that there was no indication on this rifle as to the existence of other prints." Latona also testified that he found no palm prints on the weapon. He, however, had no issue recovering prints from Oswald's personal effects, such as his wallet, pictures, papers, etc.[505]

At 6 p.m. on November 23, Oswald was confronted by police with a photograph of him holding the Mannlicher-Carcano 6.5 Italian carbine rifle along with a shotgun and Communist newspapers. The photo was one of three similar photos in a set.[506] If one wanted to be accused of a crime, one could not have taken a more obviously incriminating photograph with both weapons and motive in hand for all to see. Oswald's alleged motive itself was nonsensical. Kennedy was pursuing détente with the Soviet Union. Someone who was pro-Communist would have no reason to remove Kennedy from power and replace him with Johnson. Indeed, people who knew Oswald testified that he liked President Kennedy.[507] Oswald replied that the face in the photo was his, but that it had been superimposed onto another body and that he knew a lot about photography, and that he would be able to show that it was not his picture. Indeed, the photo had many issues beyond its over-the-top, obviously incriminating nature. One, the proportions of the body to the rifle did not match Oswald's height and the length of the rifle claimed to be the murder weapon. Two, there was inconsistency in the direction of the shadows between the man's body and his head. Three, the day the photograph was allegedly taken was cloudy, but the photo was taken on a bright and sunny day.[508] Even if the photo was authentic, that hardly conveys guilt as it is known Oswald was parading around as a pro-Communist sympathizer; but given that Oswald alleged it was fake, it is worth mentioning some arguments supporting his claim. However, it should be disclosed that there is no definitive record of what Oswald said because the police did not record their interrogations of him. His alleged statements are sourced from police notes and memory. Given they were interrogating him for the murder of a US president, this is shocking and, at best, utterly inept. Nor did they give Oswald a legal representative despite his asking for one.[509]

There is also the question: How did Oswald allegedly come into possession of this rifle? According to the Warren Commission, he ordered the rifle through the mail, leaving an incriminating paper trail instead of purchasing it at a store where he could have done so anonymously.[510] He allegedly purchased a money order on March 12, 1963, and Klein's Sporting Goods in Chicago received his order on March 13, 1963.[511] However, the rifle he allegedly ordered was thirty-six inches in length. The one reportedly used in the murder was forty inches long.[512] The location of the straps also differed on the two rifles.[513] There are other issues with the rifle allegations. Oswald allegedly had the rifle sent to his mailbox but addressed to an alias. Postal regulations do not allow mailbox suppliers to accept mail addressed to individuals who are not listed on the mailbox application.[514] Lastly, according to the Warren Commission, the entire transaction—from Oswald mailing out the order to the sporting goods store in Chicago depositing the check—was one day. This also is hard to believe since regular mail and processing is never that expeditious.[515] There is also no evidence of Oswald ever purchasing ammunition, and no ammunition was found at his house.[516]

As Oswald was being detained and questioned, Clay Shaw, the director of the International Trade Mart in New Orleans, using his often-used alias of Clay Bertrand, called Dean Andrews, the attorney he had previously asked to help Oswald with his wife's citizenship, and asked him if he could represent Oswald with the murder charges levied against him.[517] As it turned out Oswald would not need a lawyer.

On the morning of November 24, Oswald was set to be transferred from the Dallas City Hall to the Dallas County Jail in a very public fashion. According to FBI Agent James Hosty, Sam Bloom advised the police to show Oswald to the press "as openly and as often as possible."[518] How is it that Sam Bloom understood the importance of making Oswald available to the press, but when it came to Kennedy, it appears he had no issues placing the media in three convertible vehicles at the back of the motorcade, assuring no press access to the president? Would a public relations man not be consistent and insist on press access to both? During this Sunday morning transfer, Oswald was shot and killed by Jack Ruby. Inside Ruby's apartment the FBI found a card, on the back of which was written Sam Bloom's name, along with an address, phone number, and the words Times Herald.[519] Bloom had spent fifty years with the *Dallas Times Herald*.[520] Why did Ruby have Bloom's contact information? Did it have anything to do with Bloom's role in assuring Oswald was publicly available to the press?

After Oswald had been shot, the police tried to coax a dying confession from him, but he maintained his innocence to his last breath.[521]

5

The Assassin of the Alleged Assassin

Ruby arrived at the police station apparently by late afternoon or early evening Friday [November 22], and he spent a lot of time there from Friday, after the assassination, until Sunday, when he finally shot Oswald. - Police Chief Jesse Curry

Who was the man who shot and killed Lee Harvey Oswald? His name was Jacob Leon Rubenstein, better known as Jack Ruby. The study of Oswald, his background, and his comings and goings in the months preceding the assassination is essential to help determine who was in a position to set up Oswald. However, with Oswald, there was the luxury of months of advance planning, and it is not clear which characters around him were witting or unwitting in establishing him as a patsy. With Ruby, however, there was not much time available to react or plan, and clearly, Ruby was a witting participant. He may have been reluctant to assume his role, but there is no doubt he was aware of what he was doing. As such, Ruby's background is as important, if not more important, than Oswald's. He is the one person that is known to have been intentionally involved. For example, it can be argued that Clay Shaw, the director of the International Trade Mart in New Orleans, did not know; it can be argued that the Stern family, who gave Oswald the public TV and radio platform in August 1963, did not know; but it cannot be argued that Jack Ruby did not know what he was doing.

So, who was Jack Ruby? In the mid-1940s, Ruby was investigated for his role in an international drug-trafficking syndicate involving the corruption of government officials in Mexico City. The top American syndicate representative in Mexico City then was Harold Meltzer, an associate of Meyer Lansky and Mickey Cohen. According to government sources, Lansky and Meltzer organized this drug smuggling channel.[522] Ruby was not the only one connected to this network. Eugene Hale Brading, aka Jim Braden, the man police picked up from the third floor of the Dal-Tex building at the time of the JFK assassination, was also connected to this network.[523] Ruby had other potential connections to Lansky. According to an FBI informant, in the early 1950s, Ruby held an interest in the Colonial Inn, a nightclub and gambling house in Hallandale, Florida,[524] owned by Meyer Lansky.[525]

Lansky was one of the heads, if not the head, of the loosely organized National Crime Syndicate, a web of associations that at times collaborated on various organized crime initiatives.[526] According to Lansky biographer Hank Messick, Lansky was the "chairman of the board" of the syndicate. According to Ruby biographer Seth Kantor, Ruby was a "branch office errand boy" for this syndicate.[527] At the start of World War II, it was Lansky who worked with the Office of Naval Intelligence and the Office of Strategic Services, a precursor to the CIA, to help create Operation Underworld, an intelligence and organized crime project which utilized mob resources to assist the American intelligence community with the war. Operation Underworld initially assisted US ships against sabotage on US docks but then expanded beyond that.[528] Lansky also had an enormous investment in gambling operations in Cuba before the Castro regime came to power and seized those operations.[529] Lastly, Lansky financed and shipped arms to the Haganah, the leading Zionist paramilitary organization before the establishment of Israel.[530] He told the Haganah, "I'm at your service." He was also involved in the sabotage of Arab arms. He ensured Arab arms shipments fell overboard or were redirected and loaded onto ships bound for Israel.[531] Cohen, an organized crime figure who Lansky sent to work out of Los

Angeles, was also heavily involved with the smuggling of arms to Israel. Cohen explained, "Through my connections I made everybody throughout the country ... set up whatever positions there were to be helpful to the Israel cause. ... I got so engrossed with Israel that I actually pushed aside a lot of my activities and done nothing but what was involved with this Irgun war."[532] Robert Kennedy sent Cohen to prison in 1961 for tax evasion.[533] Another figure deeply involved with the equipping of the Haganah was Abraham Feinberg, the man who organized the financing of Israel's nuclear weapons program. Feinberg was the founder and first president of Americans for Haganah.[534] Whenever Israeli Prime Minister David Ben-Gurion needed to raise support for a Zionist cause, whether it be the Haganah or Israel's nuclear weapons program, he would say, "Call Abe."[535]

In 1947, Ruby moved from Chicago to Dallas. He became the owner of a nightclub and an informant for the Dallas police (narcotics division), the FBI, and for the first major federal inquiry into organized crime, the Kefauver Committee. In exchange, the Kefauver Committee agreed to ignore organized crime and police corruption in Dallas.[536] According to the House Select Committee on Assassinations, Ruby had a "friendly and somewhat unusual" relationship with the Dallas Police Department, "both collectively and with individual officers."[537] Ruby was not a stranger in town. Mayor Earle Cabell admitted in an interview that he had known Ruby "by sight" for "several years."[538]

It appears Ruby also had ties to Cuba. According to an FBI informant, during the 1950s, Ruby arranged illegal flights of weapons to Castro supporters in Cuba. The informant gave names of three others who could corroborate his story.[539] Witness Mary Thompson testified to the same.[540] After Ruby was jailed for killing Oswald, he told his lawyer, Tom Howard, that he had planned to go into the gun-running business with a man who had been involved in training anti-Castro exiles.[541]

In the days leading up to the assassination, Ruby's activities indicate that he was involved in something out of the ordinary. According to the House Select Committee on Assassinations, "The average number [of phone calls made by Ruby] leapt from around 25 to 35 in the months of May through September to approximately 75 in October and approximately 96 during the first 3 ½ weeks of November."[542]

Eleven days before the assassination, Ruby met with Alexander Philip Gruber in Dallas. Gruber had boarded with Ruby back when the two lived in Chicago, but he now lived in Los Angeles. Gruber had connections to Jimmy Hoffa, head of the Teamsters Union. Both RFK and JFK had questioned Hoffa during the 1950s for his organized crime connections when they served on the McClellan Committee, and RFK continued to pursue Hoffa as US attorney general. Gruber also had ties to the previously mentioned Los Angeles gangster Mickey Cohen, as well as to the previously mentioned Harold Meltzer, Lansky's Mexico City man.[543] Gruber later told the FBI he was unsure why Ruby called him.[544] Ruby had a number of long-distance phone conversations with Gruber both shortly before and after the assassination. Indeed, one of Ruby's earliest calls after the Kennedy assassination was to Gruber.[545]

On November 12, Ruby phoned a Cohen girlfriend, Candy Barr, whom he'd been acquainted with for some time, and spoke with her for fourteen minutes. That same day, another organized crime figure, Paul Rowland Jones, came down from Missouri and visited with Ruby in Dallas, and the two met up with Gruber the following day. The three had not seen each other since Ruby left Chicago in 1947.[546]

On or around November 15, Ruby bought and installed a safe, the first time he had done so since moving to Dallas.[547] On November 17, he made a trip up to Las Vegas. In 1963, Ruby made a series of phone calls to Lewis McWillie, a Las Vegas organized crime figure associated with Meyer Lansky's empire. He had even mailed a gun to McWillie on May 10. McWillie worked at Lansky's Thunderbird casino.[548] According to former

McWillie girlfriend Elaine Mynier, Ruby was "a small-time character who would do anything for McWillie."[549] On November 19, upon returning to Dallas, Ruby met with his attorney, Graham Koch, and signed a power of attorney, giving up certain rights to control his own money and entitling his lawyer to handle his financial dealings.[550] Ruby was heavily in debt and on November 19, three days before the Kennedy assassination, he told his attorney that he would soon be coming into the necessary funds to settle his debts.[551]

Other mob-related figures that Ruby spoke with in the days leading up to the assassination included Barney Baker and Dusty Miller, among others. Baker and Miller were both assistants of Jimmy Hoffa. Robert Kennedy wrote in 1960 that "sometimes the mere threat of his [Baker's] presence in a room was enough to silence the men who would have otherwise opposed Hoffa's reign." The summer before the assassination, Ruby had spoken with Lenny Patrick, one of the Chicago Mafia's leading assassins and, according to federal and state law enforcement files, a man responsible for the murders of over a dozen victims of the mob.[552]

A few hours after the Kennedy assassination, John Rutledge of *The Dallas Morning News* saw Jack Ruby on the third floor of the Dallas police station, outside of Captain John Fritz's office, where Oswald was being interrogated. Rutledge stated that Ruby was able to get past guards by pretending to be a reporter accompanying two out-of-town reporters. Detective Augustus M. Eberhardt, who also saw Ruby, stated that Ruby carried a notepad and professed to be a translator for the Yiddish-speaking Israeli press.[553] It was never determined who the two Yiddish-speaking men with Ruby were. Given that Ruth Paine had taken lessons to learn Yiddish, the authorities should have tried to determine if a connection could be made between her and Jack Ruby.

Later that evening, at a midnight news conference in the basement of the police station, where Oswald made a brief appearance, Ruby was in the crowd of reporters.[554] Ruby admitted to the FBI that he had on him a loaded revolver at the time of the news conference.[555] According to Police Chief Curry, Ruby told him he first thought of killing Oswald on this night.[556] Ruby, however, was not within shooting range of Oswald. When District Attorney Henry M. Wade stated that Oswald belonged to the Free Cuba Committee, Ruby, along with several other reporters, corrected him and said it was the Fair Play for Cuba Committee.[557] How did Ruby know the correct name of the organization Oswald was affiliated with?

The following day, Saturday, November 23, police considered moving Oswald to the county jail without public notice. Only sources close to the police knew about it. At approximately 3 p.m., Sergeant D. V. Harkness asked a small group of people to move from the vehicular entrance of the county jail. Among the loiterers, he saw Jack Ruby.[558] The police ultimately canceled the transfer, but it does show that Ruby was lurking around and trying to gain access to Oswald on Friday, Saturday, and Sunday, when he would ultimately shoot Oswald. According to Police Chief Curry, "Ruby arrived at the police station apparently by late afternoon or early evening Friday [November 22], and he spent a lot of time there from Friday, after the assassination, until Sunday, when he finally shot Oswald."[559]

On the morning of Sunday, November 24, Elnora Pitts, the woman who cleaned Ruby's apartment each Sunday, phoned him and asked if she could come by at 2 p.m., but Ruby asked her not to set out for his place without first making phone contact with him. She told him that was what she was trying to do, so she was confused by his instructions. She said he sounded strange and didn't seem to recognize her.[560]

George Senator, who shared Ruby's apartment with him, stated that Ruby seemed to be obsessed and mumbling to himself that morning, pacing nervously from room to room.[561] Leaving the apartment, Ruby told Senator that he was taking his dog down to his club, which was closed on a Sunday morning. Ruby wore a white shirt, black silk tie, and charcoal brown suit, dressed to fit in with the crowd at the police station he was heading to.[562] Ruby then went to the Western Union office near the police station and sent off some money at 11:17 a.m.[563] He then walked to the police station and arrived there shortly before Oswald was brought downstairs. Some have used this timing to argue that Ruby did not pre-plan the shooting of Oswald as Oswald was brought down more than an hour after the initially scheduled time, 10:00 a.m., and only minutes after Ruby arrived, 11:20 a.m.[564] Others have used this timing to argue that the police waited to bring Oswald down until Ruby arrived, because as soon as Ruby appeared, they brought Oswald down.[565] Some have argued that Ruby did not premeditate the crime because he left his beloved dog in his car. However, one can also contend that Ruby brought the dog with him to calm his nerves and to spend some last-minute time with him before his impending arrest. If Ruby was capable of murder, he was more than capable of bringing the dog with him for selfish reasons. As Oswald walked into the basement area, Ruby stepped forward and shot him in the stomach. The surrounding crowd then tackled Ruby to the ground.[566] The single shot killed Oswald, but according to detective Don Ray Archer, Ruby told him that he had intended to shoot Oswald three times, implying at least some degree of forethought.[567] At the time Ruby shot Oswald, there were forty to fifty reporters in the basement area.[568] It was Sam Bloom who had encouraged the police to make Oswald available to the press, the same Sam Bloom whose contact information Ruby had scribbled down on a card in his apartment.

Not long after his arrest, Ruby faced trial and ultimately was convicted; he died in prison a few years later of cancer. Melvin Belli represented him. Belli also served as an attorney for Mickey Cohen.[569] Indeed, Belli referred to Cohen as a "gentleman of greatly courtliness and charm" and even stated that Cohen had served as his son's babysitter, indicating a closeness between the two.[570] Sam Bloom served as a public relations counselor to the judge presiding over Ruby's trial. Belli referred to Bloom as a "volunteer" publicity man[571] and wrote that "Bloom was making legal history—the first public-relations counselor to a judge in the history of jurisprudence."[572]

Why did Jack Ruby shoot Oswald? Was it because of his debts? Was it because of other dues he owed to the world of organized crime? There are some indications that Ruby may have tried to get out of it. According to police officer Billy Grammer, he [Grammer] received a phone call the night before from a familiar voice he could not place, telling him if the plans to transfer Oswald were not changed, "We are going to kill him in the basement." Grammer informed his police chief, but the chief discarded it as the police were receiving many phone calls placing threats on Oswald. After Oswald was shot, Grammer recognized the voice as Ruby's, and though he could not definitively identify it, he stated this caller knew information about the transfer that only an insider could have known.[573] Captain Fritz, the homicide chief, later told federal authorities that he believed it had been Ruby who called in the threats.[574]

Jack Ruby's rabbi Hillel Silverman asked him on the day after the shooting why he did it. Silverman later recounted, "I don't like to mention it. I think he said, 'I did it for the Jewish people.' But I've tried to wipe that statement from my mind."[575] Ruby's defense lawyer William Kunstler corroborated the rabbi's claim. He stated that Ruby had told him, on several occasions, "I did this that they wouldn't implicate Jews." During Kunstler's last visit, Ruby handed him a note in which he stated that his motive was to "protect American Jews from a pogrom that could occur because of anger over the assassination." Kunstler stated Ruby made these statements not because he was part of a conspiracy but because the Fair Play for Cuba Committee that Oswald was promoting consisted of a number of Jewish members.[576] The question then must be asked, how did Ruby have time from when Kennedy was shot to when he shot Oswald to research the membership of the Fair Play for Cuba Committee, in the days before the internet?

Publicly, Ruby claimed, "I wanted to save Mrs. Kennedy from being put through the ordeal of a trial, and that's why I did this thing."[577]

6

The Initial Cover-Up

Whoever those who were ultimately responsible for the decision to kill Kennedy were, their reach extended into the national intelligence apparatus to such a degree that they could call upon a person who knew its inner secrets and workings so well that he could design a failsafe mechanism into the fabric of the plot. – Professor John Newman

It is doubtful the culprits would have ever attempted an assassination without prior assurance of a cover-up. The cover-up consisted of controlling the autopsy, silencing Oswald, establishing an official narrative in the media, and preventing a proper investigation from occurring.

Under Texas law, the president's autopsy should have been performed in Dallas. And indeed, the pathologist at Parkland Memorial Hospital had every intention of doing an autopsy. However, JFK aide Kenny O'Donnell, along with aides Dave Powers and Lawrence O'Brien, felt Jackie would never leave the hospital without her husband, and they worried an autopsy would take days. O'Donnell asked the Secret Service to take the body so everyone could head back to DC. O'Donnell suggested a Dallas doctor accompany them to Washington to perform the autopsy, but the hospital did not want to consider this. The hospital was reluctant to let the body go, but the Secret Service snatched it, shoving the pathologist against the wall when he tried to stop them from taking it.[578] The intentions of Kennedy's aides were almost certainly innocent; however, as a result, the slain president never received a proper autopsy.

Upon arriving in Washington, the body was taken to Bethesda Medical Center, a naval institution. The autopsy was assigned to two Navy pathologists, Commander James Humes and his associate, J. Thornton Boswell. The two had minimal experience in gunshot wound autopsies, unlike the pathologist back in Dallas, who had done many. Numerous qualified pathologists worked in the DC area, but none were called. According to Dr. Cyril Wecht, former president of the American Academy of Forensic Sciences, "You've got multiple gunshot wounds to determine angles, trajectory, range, sequence. And then you've got to correlate with the multiple gunshot wounds in Connally. This is a formidable task that would have required two or three major forensic pathologists to undertake."

As Humes and Boswell were inexperienced, they requested assistance. They were supplied with the aid of Dr. Pierre Finck from the Armed Forces Institute of Pathology. They then asked for a medical examiner, as Dr. Finck had not done an autopsy in over two years. However, they were denied any additional assistance. According to Dr. Gary Aguilar, an ophthalmologist and professor at Stanford University and the University of California,

> These three autopsy pathologists were given a body, told here's the body, he was shot from behind. He fell forward ... figure out how the wounds fit the known circumstances of the shooting. But what this really speaks to was the fact that the autopsy was not in the control of the surgeons that were charged with doing it. It was in the control of people who were there, who were telling them what they could and couldn't do.

After the autopsy was completed, Dr. Humes destroyed the notes he had taken. At this time, Oswald was still alive, and Humes should have expected to be called in to testify during his trial. Humes testified that he destroyed his notes because JFK's blood was splattered all over them, and he did not want them to become an object of morbid curiosity. Dr. Finck also took notes and complained bitterly later that his notes had disappeared.[579]

Who had access to control and ensure a cursory Navy autopsy? For starters, the Navy and the broader military itself. Reportedly present at the autopsy was bitter JFK enemy General Curtis LeMay with a big cigar in his hand.[580] LeMay allegedly flew in from Toronto that afternoon to be there.[581] JFK had once lamented, "I don't want that man near me again."[582] LBJ also had close ties to the Navy and was technically the new commander in chief. And as mentioned earlier, Meyer Lansky and the National Crime Syndicate were closely connected with the Office of Naval Intelligence. Undoubtedly, various parties in the CIA would have also had connections to the Navy. In the documentary film *Sacrificing Liberty*, which interviewed many survivors of the USS *Liberty* attack staged by Israel against a US Navy ship, the survivors alleged that Israel, Lyndon Johnson, and CIA counterintelligence chief James Angleton coordinated the attack with elements of the Navy, indicating a connection between these entities.[583]

The second aspect of the cover-up was the silencing of Oswald. The murder of Oswald gave two vital assurances. One, Oswald would never be able to speak and defend himself. Neither would he be able to implicate others. And two, the case would never be tried in a court of law, where witnesses could be cross-examined and a proper defense offered.

Arguably, the most crucial aspect of the cover-up was control over the media narrative. From the moment the crime was first reported, the mainstream and corporate press ran with the "lone-nut" thesis. They instantly concluded not only that one assassin committed the murder, but also that the assassin was essentially mentally disturbed. One must question how they could so expeditiously solve the murder of the president of the United States, who had countless enemies. An independent media would have, without delay, raised the question of cui bono. They would have looked at motives, means, and opportunity. They would have looked at each of the myriad enemies John F. Kennedy had and would have dutifully and cautiously analyzed the evidence. They would not have arrived at any conclusions until a thorough investigation had been completed.

It is unclear if this setting of the official corporate media narrative resulted from foreknowledge, intentional complicity after the fact, an implicit understanding not to rock the boat, or a combination of all three. The footage captured by the Sterns of a "pro-Communist" Oswald on the streets of New Orleans in the summer of 1963 no doubt played a heavy role as well, as it was intended to. Irrespective of the reason, what is clear is that there was never a serious conversation in the mainstream and corporate press about the crime or its political beneficiaries. This is understandable. The press is a vital part of the establishment. To question and properly investigate Kennedy's murder may have led to the tearing of the very fabric of the establishment. Within the media, there was likely an implicit understanding that it was better to protect the establishment than to reveal its corrupt core, regardless of whether those in the press knew which parties in that corrupt core were responsible for the crime.

The initial *New York Times* coverage not only implied a single assassin but also stated he committed the crime due to a "strain of madness and violence." It referred to the evidence against Oswald as "conclusive." It claimed that coups do not happen in America, only abroad, with the headline, "Lone Assassin the Rule in U.S.; Plotting More Prevalent Abroad." On the day after Ruby shot Oswald when most of the country was speculating about the potential involvement of multiple actors, the *Times* stuck to its "lone-nut" hypothesis, writing that in other countries, "assassinations were generally the culmination of detailed plans made by well-organized groups" but that in the U.S. assassinations were "by a single person, often with little advanced planning and often without any real grievance against the personage attacked."[584] And how did the *Times* report Oswald's death?

They declared in a headline, "President's Assassin Shot to Death."[585] Oswald was not afforded the word "alleged," despite the fact that he had not been convicted of any crime and had not yet been given any opportunity to offer a defense. The *Times* also took at face value Ruby's alleged motives for shooting Oswald with the headline, "Kennedy Admirer Fired One Bullet."[586] Ruby was labeled as a Kennedy admirer, not a potential cleanup man for Kennedy's murderers. No credible investigative journalist could have come to such a conclusion about Ruby in mere hours.

Other media outlets pushed similar stories. According to *Newsweek*, Oswald had "cancer of the psyche," despite indications from the Dallas police that Oswald was perfectly sane.[587] *The Wall Street Journal* wrote, "Idiots we have always amongst us, and if they have coloration at all it is more likely to be the black of night of the individual soul than the political shades of red or white."[588] In other words, it was the lone psychotic soul, not a sophisticated and politically motivated plot that removed Kennedy. The popular columnist Walter Lippman wrote on November 27, "Oswald was an extremist, outsider ... addicted to the fascination of violence in his futile and lonely and brooding existence. ... There is no limit to his hatred." *Life* magazine referred to Oswald as "strange" and "fanatic." In one of the most egregious attempts to frame the official narrative, *Life* magazine published frames of the Zapruder film, an amateur film taken of the assassination. However, they selectively published the frames so that the American people did not see Kennedy's body thrown violently backward and to the left, which would have implied a shot from the front and the right. They also explained Jackie's climb onto the back of the car as her "pathetic search for help" rather than what it actually was, an attempt to retrieve a portion of her husband's head which she then handed to doctors at the hospital.[589] Her behavior also implied a fatal shot from the front. The American public did not see the film until over a decade later.

The press were not the only ones who had managed to "solve" the crime in mere hours. The mayor of Dallas, Earle Cabell, was quoted in *The Dallas*

Morning News on November 23 as stating that the crime was "the irrational act of a single man" and "that it could only be the act of a deranged mind."[590] In Washington, the reactions were the same. But there are signs that perhaps not all fell in line with the official narrative. Former President Harry Truman published an article in *The Washington Post* on December 22, 1963, entitled "Limit CIA Role to Intelligence." Truman originally set up the agency, and while he did not refer directly to the Kennedy assassination, he did state the following:

> For some time I have been disturbed by the way CIA has been di-
> verted from its original assignment. It has become an operational
> and at times a policy-making arm of the Government. This has led
> to trouble and may have compounded our difficulties in several
> explosive areas. ... There is something about the way the CIA
> has been functioning that is casting a shadow over our historic
> position and I feel that we need to correct it.[591]

The last pillar of the cover-up was ensuring that a proper investigation did not occur. It is important to note that it is only natural that the American establishment would want to protect itself and have as smooth a transition from Kennedy to Johnson as possible. As such, it is tough to know if those pushing for a cover-up were doing so because they had knowledge of the culprits and wanted to protect them or, instead, if they were just doing so because they wanted to protect the American establishment. No matter who the culprit was, some influential establishment figures may have felt it was important to sweep the assassination under the rug and move on rather than rock the boat, not knowing what might be lying underneath. Nevertheless, it is still worth exploring how this cover-up was accomplished as it may hold clues as to who was involved in the crime and, at the very least, displays that Kennedy never had a chance for a genuine investigation.

The new president, Lyndon Johnson, and FBI Director J. Edgar Hoover wanted an FBI report and a Texas court of inquiry. The FBI report was to "settle the dust" and show that Oswald was "the man who assassinated the President."[592] Despite LBJ and Hoover's desire to quickly do away with the case, there were private individuals, outside of the government, who urged LBJ to establish a distinguished commission to essentially do what LBJ and Hoover wanted to do: "settle the dust." While the goals of those pushing for the commission were the same as those of LBJ and Hoover (i.e., to do away with the case), they felt such a commission would be more reassuring to the American public than the approach LBJ and Hoover lobbied for.

Based on telephone transcripts, it appears the first person to suggest the Warren Commission was Eugene Rostow, dean of Yale Law School, in a call to Lyndon Johnson's aide, Bill Moyers. Rostow made the call on the afternoon of November 24, shortly after the murder of Oswald. The exact timing is unknown, but he called less than two hours after Oswald's death. Rostow told Moyers that "in this situation, with the bastard killed," it was imperative to establish a commission of "very distinguished citizens" because "world opinion and American opinion is just now so shaken ... that they're not believing anything." It must be asked, when it comes to the murder of their president, why should the public "believe" anything? This was moments after the murder of Oswald. Anyone seeking truth and justice should have been asking many questions at this point. Rostow's goal appears to have been not truth but rather the establishment of a desired narrative for the public to "believe." Rostow also indicated that he had already spoken "about three times" with Nicholas Katzenbach, who was essentially taking on the role of the attorney general in the absence of a grieving Robert Kennedy. Rostow further indicated that at least one other person was present with him.[593] How did Rostow so quickly conclude, apparently with at least one other person, what the best approach was to go forward so soon after the shooting of Oswald? It must be noted that the idea of a commission could not be raised until Oswald was dead, as with a living Oswald, the investigation would have been handled via Oswald's trial.

Why was Rostow, a private individual, informing Lyndon Johnson's assistant of the approach? Who was Eugene Rostow? And why was he inserting himself into the Kennedy assassination in an interest to have the public "believe" the official narrative of the crime? A quick study of Rostow reveals that his views, in many ways, were diametrically opposed to Kennedy's. Not long after Kennedy's assassination, in 1966, Rostow left Yale to serve in the State Department as Under Secretary for Political Affairs, the third highest ranking official in the State Department. During the 1967 Six-Day War, which almost certainly would not have occurred had Kennedy lived, Rostow served on a committee in charge of negotiating a settlement to the conflict. He identified closely with the Israeli position in the dispute with the Arab states. Later, in 1972, he expressed, "The reasons for the stalemate [in the peace process] are obvious. The basic obstacle to peace has been the continuation and intensification of terrorist activities, supported or condoned by Arab governments." He did not see any responsibility on Israel's side for the ongoing conflict.[594] He summed up the Arabs as "candidates for the psycho ward."[595] Not long after the Six-Day War, at the end of 1968, Rostow left the State Department and returned to Yale. What was his purpose in moving to the State Department? Was it in preparation for the Six-Day War? According to researcher Joan Mellen, Rostow was appointed to his State Department position "precisely to support the coming Israeli war."[596]

Upon returning to Yale, he spent much of the 1970s warning Americans that détente was a dangerous illusion that "enabled a Soviet drive for dominance" and that Americans needed to let go of the "myth of détente."[597] He also worried that détente between the Americans and Soviets would drive pressure on Israel to make concessions to the Arabs.[598] He blamed the Soviets for dangling "before the eyes of Arabs the irresistible temptation ... to drive out the Israelis."[599] In the early 1980s he was confirmed as the director of the Arms Control and Disarmament Agency, an agency JFK had set up. Despite this appointment, he was a proponent of nuclear war. He stated, "We are living in a pre-war and not a post-war world." He supported fighting "limited" nuclear wars that "must" be fought, stating,

"Japan, after all, not only survived but flourished after the nuclear attack."[600] He elaborated, "The human race is very resilient. Some estimates predict that there would be ten million casualties on one side and 100 million on another. But that is not the whole of the population."[601] Eugene's brother, Walt, had worked in the Kennedy administration as deputy to National Security Advisor McGeorge Bundy. JFK referred to Walt as "the biggest Cold Warrior I've got" and further stated, "Walt had ten ideas, nine of which would lead to disaster."[602]

Nicholas Katzenbach did take Rostow's advice. He reached out to FBI director J. Edgar Hoover, who then contacted LBJ aide Walter Jenkins. Hoover told Jenkins that Katzenbach had proposed a commission and that the two of them felt that it was vital to "have something issued so we can convince the public that Oswald is the real assassin."[603] Hoover reached out to Jenkins with this message before 4 p.m. on the afternoon of November 24. So, less than two hours after Oswald died, both Hoover and Katzenbach, just like Rostow before them, were preoccupied with closing the case and declaring Oswald guilty. For anyone interested in the truth, this would have been a time to raise questions about President Kennedy's assassination and the potential for involvement of multiple parties, not a time to close the case. Katzenbach followed up on this the next day, November 25, by sending a memo to LBJ aide Bill Moyers, in which he wrote, "The public must be satisfied that Oswald was the assassin; that he did not have confederates who are still at large, and that the evidence was such that he would have been convicted at trial. ... Speculation about Oswald's motivation must be cut off."[604] This memo shows no desire for truth or justice, only to close the case and control public opinion. Why would Hoover and Katzenbach do this? A large part of it was probably an implicit understanding on their part of the need for a cover-up. To add to this, both CIA counterintelligence chief James Angleton and National Crime Syndicate boss Meyer Lansky had blackmail material on Hoover. According to a former Lansky associate, Lansky often bragged about Hoover, "I fixed that son-of-a-bitch." According to Lansky's wife, her husband had acquired "hard proof of Hoover's homosexuality and used it to neutralize the FBI as a threat to his own operations."[605]

At some point, Angleton also came into possession of these Hoover photos. It is believed he likely got them from Lansky. Angleton had pushed for the CIA to forge ties with Lansky. Angleton was not only the head of counterintelligence and the Israeli desk at the CIA, but also in charge of the CIA's relationship with the FBI, so he had much influence on Hoover and likely others in the bureau who were also pushing for a cover-up.[606] Hoover was also a neighbor of LBJ,[607] and they had been friends for thirty years. LBJ referred to Hoover as "my brother and personal friend."[608]

Katzenbach replaced Robert Kennedy as attorney general, and it was under Katzenbach that the Justice Department settled the case against the American Zionist Council without requiring them to register as a foreign agent.[609] Katzenbach had been a student and then a colleague of Rostow's at Yale.[610] Like Rostow, Katzenbach was also moved to the State Department between 1966 and 1969, as Under Secretary of State, the second highest position in the department.

LBJ was not initially receptive to the idea of a commission. He preferred an FBI report and a Texas court of inquiry. LBJ expressed his opposition in a telephone conversation with Hoover on the morning of November 25. Immediately after LBJ's call with Hoover, the new president received a telephone call from Joseph Alsop, one of the nation's best-known columnists at the time. Alsop had close ties to the CIA and was a strong proponent of escalation in Vietnam.[611] He also supported Israel and LBJ. It is Alsop and *Washington Post* publisher Philip Graham, also a strong supporter of Israel and of LBJ, who had urged JFK to offer the vice presidency to LBJ.[612] JFK offered the vice presidency to LBJ as a courtesy, assuming he would not accept. Johnson, at the time, was the senate majority leader and had been JFK's primary opponent for the Democratic Party nomination for the presidency.

According to Robert Kennedy, JFK felt if he did not smooth things over with Johnson and at least appear to offer him the vice presidency, then Johnson would make it very difficult for JFK to get legislation through as president.[613] To JFK's shock, LBJ accepted. According to presidential aide Arthur Schlesinger Jr., JFK told a friend, "I didn't offer the vice-presidency to him. I just held it out (at this point Kennedy simulated taking an object out of his pocket and holding it close to his body) and he grabbed at it."[614] According to Robert Kennedy, JFK "never dreamt that there was a chance in the world that he would accept it." After JFK met with Johnson, he returned upstairs and asked Bobby, "Now what do we do?" Bobby then went downstairs to try to talk Johnson out of it but to no avail.[615]

Alsop, like Rostow before him, also pushed LBJ to set up a presidential commission, but again LBJ was reluctant. Alsop suggested that LBJ speak with Katherine Meyer Graham, Philip Graham's widow (Philip passed away earlier in 1963).[616] Alsop told LBJ that *The Washington Post* was going to push the idea for a commission.[617] Alsop also encouraged LBJ to speak with Dean Acheson.[618] Acheson was a pillar of the American Establishment. He had been secretary of state under Democratic President Truman and reportedly thought little of JFK. He had not supported JFK's 1960 Democratic nomination for the presidency and had given his support to a competing Democrat. Acheson had been involved during the World War II period in planning post-war international policy, including the creation of the International Monetary Fund (IMF). The Bretton Woods Conference set this policy, and Acheson was a key attendant. The president of the conference was Henry Morgenthau Jr., another of the twenty-five financiers of Israel's nuclear weapons project. Indeed, Morgenthau not only donated, but also assisted Abraham Feinberg with gathering other donors.[619] Eugene Rostow, the first person to push for a presidential commission, had worked as an assistant to Dean Acheson at the State Department in the early 1940s.[620]

By the afternoon of November 28, LBJ was on board with establishing a presidential commission. By this point, there were calls for a senate inquiry. LBJ phoned Senator James Eastland to ask that he prevent any senate investigations that may occur as he had decided instead to establish a presidential commission. The following day LBJ reached out to Congressman Hale Boggs, Congressman Charles Halleck, and Speaker of the House John McCormack, urging that Congress not establish any official probe into the assassination either. LBJ stressed the importance of control over the investigation, raising the dangerous prospect of what could occur if someone publicly accused the Soviets or Cubans of killing Kennedy. He stressed the risks of potential war to get everyone in line. On the evening of November 29, LBJ signed Executive Order 11130, establishing the Warren Commission. He listed the members of the commission as Chief Justice Earl Warren, Senator Richard B. Russell, Senator John Sherman Cooper, Congressman Hale Boggs, Congressman Gerald R. Ford, former CIA Director Allen Dulles, and businessman John J. McCloy.[621]

A congressional investigation, though not a replacement for a proper murder trial, would likely have been more independently managed than the Warren Commission was. Warren had no desire to take the job, but LBJ invoked the specter of a potential nuclear war if multiple investigations occurred simultaneously and uncovered connections to the Soviet Union. That would have led to the loss of forty million American lives. Warren reluctantly obliged.[622] LBJ then applied similar pressures to Senator Richard Russell, who had been named to the commission without his agreement. LBJ told Russell of Oswald being in Mexico City and potential ties to the Soviets and Cubans and how if control was not established over the investigation, then World War III may break out.[623] Indeed, LBJ spoke of a potential worldwide conspiracy to those around him before he even left Dallas.[624] If the reader recalls, it was James Angleton who appeared to have set up Oswald in Mexico City and tied him to Valery Kostikov, a member of the KGB assassinations group. LBJ then used this information to pressure everyone into compliance with the cover-up. It should be noted that a later 1971 CIA memo indicated that the CIA could find no evidence linking Kostikov to KGB assassinations, raising the possibility that Angleton fabricated this connection to help ensure a cover-up.[625] In his book *Oswald and the CIA*, Professor John Newman described this as the "World War III virus" planted into Oswald's files. He wrote of Angleton's planting of this "virus":

> No one else in the Agency had the access, the authority, and the diabolically ingenious mind to manage this sophisticated plot. No one else had the means necessary to plant the WWIII virus in Oswald's files and keep it dormant for six weeks until the President's assassination. Whoever those who were ultimately responsible for the decision to kill Kennedy were, their reach extended into the national intelligence apparatus to such a degree that they could call upon a person who knew its inner secrets and workings so well that he could design a failsafe mechanism into the fabric of the plot. The only person who could ensure a national security cover-up of an apparent counterintelligence nightmare was the head of counterintelligence.[626]

While LBJ had to strongarm some reluctant members onto the commission, he had no trouble getting the former CIA director let go by Kennedy, Allen Dulles, to agree. According to future CIA Director Richard Helms, he "personally persuaded" Johnson to appoint Dulles. According to historian Michael Kurtz, Dulles and Helms "wanted to make sure no agency secrets came out during the investigation. ... And, of course, if Dulles was on the Commission, that would ensure the agency would be safe." Dulles allegedly spent the weekend immediately following the assassination at a secret CIA facility in northern Virginia known as "the Farm." Another commission member, McCloy, had strong ties to Rockefeller interests.[627] No commission members were Kennedy supporters. The two Democrats on the commission had opposed Kennedy's civil rights legislation.[628]

The Warren Commission had its first meeting on December 5.[629] McCloy stated at this meeting that the purpose of the commission would be to "lay the dust," both in the United States and across the globe. Meanwhile, Dulles brought up a list of books he had been reading that focused on the "psychiatric angle."[630] JFK never had a chance at a proper investigation. From day one, the commission established what its purpose would be and what sort of conclusion it would reach. On December 16, Dulles handed out a book titled *The Assassins* to all commission members and the lawyers serving them. The book's theme was that presidential assassinations were typically done by lone individuals with mental disorders. When McCloy pointed out that there had been a plot in the Lincoln assassination, Dulles corrected him, stating, "But one man was so dominant that it almost wasn't a plot."[631]

So, how did the Warren Commission "lay the dust?" There are endless examples. This book will only cover a few, enough to give the reader a sense of the process involved. First is the issue of Oswald's location at the time of the shooting. One would think that three of the most important witnesses to call in this regard would have been Victoria Adams, Sandra Styles, and Dorothy Garner. If the reader recalls, Adams and Styles were running down the stairs at the same time Oswald allegedly was, but they neither saw nor heard him. Garner was a supervisor who corroborated their story. The Warren Commission, however, only interviewed Adams, not Styles or Garner. Furthermore, they excluded Adams and Styles from the reenactment they did to verify if Oswald could have reached the second floor in the allotted time. Instead, they tried as hard as they could to discredit Adams. This is why they did not interview Styles or Garner. Discrediting one woman is always feasible. Debunking three with corroborating stories is much more difficult.

How did they discredit Adams? In her testimony, she stated that she had seen two men, William Shelley and Billy Lovelady, when she reached the first floor, but those men testified that they did not enter the building until a couple of minutes after the shooting, so the commission simply surmised that her memory was faulty. She must not have remembered waiting a little while before going downstairs.[632] While that is certainly possible, they still should have interviewed Styles and Garner and included the three women in the reenactment, as it is always possible that Shelley and Lovelady were incorrect in their estimated timing. Indeed, Lovelady testified that once he was inside the building, he asked someone what time it was. The commission did not follow up on Lovelady's statement and ask him if he had received a response to his question. The possibility that Lovelady and Shelley were on the first floor earlier than they estimated is supported by the testimony of Officer Baker, who claimed he saw two men on the first floor when he entered the building. The commission should have shown him photographs of Shelley and Lovelady and asked Officer Baker if those were the two men he saw.[633] Furthermore, it is not even fully clear if Shelley and Lovelady saw Adams at all. In their summary, the commission concluded that Shelley and Lovelady had seen Adams, stating, "Lovelady saw a girl on the first floor who he believes was Victoria Adams." But a reading of their Warren Commission testimony indicates that was not the case. The Warren Commission specifically asked each if they saw Adams. Shelley responded, "I sure don't remember." Lovelady answered, "I saw a girl, but I wouldn't swear to it it's Vickie."[634]

Adams did claim that she saw Shelley and Lovelady downstairs.[635] Nevertheless, this episode is still indicative of how the Warren Commission functioned as a whole, constantly misrepresenting witness testimony, excluding vital witnesses, and propping up other witnesses. They apparently had no time to question Styles or Garner, but they had the time to include an exhibit on the study of the teeth of Jack Ruby's mother. Styles and Garner were essential because they could have established whether the Warren Commission thesis that Oswald ran down the stairs immediately after the shooting was feasible. Meanwhile, regarding Jack Ruby's mother's teeth, Jim Garrison opined, "Even if Jack Ruby had intended to bite Oswald to death, that still would not have been relevant."[636] The priorities of the Warren Commission were, as McCloy stated, to "lay the dust."

Another vital issue is the wounds to the body. According to the doctors at Parkland, there was a massive exit wound at the back of JFK's head, and a small entrance wound in his throat. But they were not the only ones who saw the exit wound at the back of the skull. Indeed, there were over thirty people in the autopsy room, and many testified to seeing a large hole at the back of JFK's head. When combining the doctors at Parkland Hospital in Dallas with those in the autopsy room in Washington, DC, over forty witnesses have attested to a large hole in the back of Kennedy's head, implying a shot from the front.[637] So, how did the Warren Commission address this? The commission faced two major obstacles: 1) they needed to show the shots only came from behind and none from in front, and 2) they only had three bullets to work with, as three shells were found on the sixth floor. Furthermore, even getting three shots off in the allotted time was nearly impossible. To add to the commission's difficulty, it appeared one shot hit a curb and then deflected onto a bystander, limiting the commission to essentially two shots to work with. So, they had to use two bullets to explain all the injuries in Kennedy and Connally.

Concerning the first obstacle, the commission pressured doctors to concede that it was possible, if certain conditions were met, that shots did not come from the front.[638] One must also take into account the pressure, both explicit and implicit, that was placed on the doctors. The Secret Service did multiple interviews with the doctors in Dallas.[639] According to nurse Audrey Bell, when she saw Dr. Malcolm Perry the day after the assassination, he looked tired and worn. He then told her that he had been getting late-night calls from Washington.[640] Perry was the doctor who had announced to the press that the wound at the front of the neck was an entrance wound.

Concerning the second obstacle, the commission came up with the single bullet theory, infamously known today as the magic bullet theory. According to the theory, one bullet created seven combined wounds in Kennedy and Connally. It passed through JFK's neck, from back to front, without striking bone, and entered Connally's back, demolishing four inches of his fifth rib, exited his chest, and then smashed the radius bone (one of the densest bones in the body) in Connally's right wrist before landing in his left thigh. The bullet was then found in pristine condition on a stretcher at Parkland Hospital.[641] According to Dr. Cyril Wecht, "Whatever you want, whatever you need, this bullet happily and readily obliges you."[642] Most doctors testified that a single bullet could not do all of that damage and remain pristine.[643] Not to mention that Kennedy did not have a wound at the back of his neck. Admiral George G. Burkley, JFK's personal White House physician, who was both in Dallas and at the Bethesda autopsy, signed JFK's death certificate indicating a back wound at the third thoracic vertebra, far too low to exit through the neck. Furthermore, the bullet entered the back at a downward angle, not upward. The Warren Commission simply moved the back wound up to the neck area. Burkley was never called as a commission witness or deposed by a staff lawyer. One would think, given that he was the only doctor who saw the body both in Dallas and in Bethesda and had signed the death certificate, he would be worth interviewing.[644] Connally himself always swore that he had been hit by a different bullet than Kennedy. Indeed, the Zapruder film shows Connally reacted much later than Kennedy, implying a separate shot.[645]

Another obstacle the Warren Commission faced was the timing of the shots and the difficulty of accomplishing the task attributed to Oswald. According to the commission, approximately five seconds elapsed between when the first and the last bullets were fired.[646] The commission arranged a series of tests to prove that a shooter could achieve the feat attributed to Oswald. But just as with their reenactment of Oswald running down the stairs, their reenactment of the shooting was equally uninterested in getting to the truth. For starters, they hired three marksmen rated as master by the National Rifle Association, men far more skilled than Oswald. Oswald was accused of firing sixty feet from the ground. These men did their tests thirty feet from the ground. Oswald was accused of shooting at a moving target. The three men fired at a stationary target. The commission concluded that Kennedy was shot in the head and the neck, but they gave the three men a much larger target to aim at. The commission found that because an oak tree hid Kennedy's car, Oswald had less than eight-tenths of one second to take aim and fire his first shot. The three men were given unlimited time to take their first shot. Lastly, the rifle sight was improved before the rifle was given to the shooters. The three men each fired two series of three shots. Only one expert was able to fire three shots in the required time. Not one of the eighteen shots fired was able to hit the head or the neck. The commission then blamed this on the fact that they had corrected the sight on the rifle and concluded, "The defect was one which would have assisted the assassin aiming at a target which was moving away."[647] Any investigative body genuinely seeking the truth would have made sure to reconstruct the exact conditions of the crime; and when their shooters failed to duplicate it, they would have admitted their thesis was incorrect rather than concluding that the improvement they made to the rifle actually made the target more difficult to fire at, even under much easier conditions.

As with any murder case, physical evidence and chain of custody are vital. Initial tests were unable to find Oswald's prints on the rifle, which itself was not even the initial rifle reportedly found. Then on November 29, a lifted palm print arrived at the FBI laboratory. Lieutenant J. C. Day of the Dallas police claimed that he had lifted the print from the rifle before handing the rifle over to the FBI, and that is why Sebastian Latona, supervisor of the Latent Fingerprint Section of the Identification Division of the FBI, was unable to find Oswald's prints on the rifle. Day did not follow standard procedure and photograph the rifle before lifting the print, so there is no real evidence of where he acquired the palm print. Nor does it appear that Day made any mention of this print in the first couple of days. One would think this would have been explosive information.[648] It is doubtful the palm print could have been submitted in a courtroom. And what of the boxes surrounding the "sniper's nest?" There is no record of Oswald's fingerprints or palm prints ever being found on the boxes.[649]

As for the rifle itself, the commission did not allow Deputy Constable

Seymour Weitzman, the man who wrote the detailed affidavit declaring the rifle to be a German Mauser, to examine the Italian Mannlicher-Carcano and ask him if it was the rifle he had found.[650] Deputy Sheriff Eugene Boone, who was with Weitzman when the gun was found, was shown the Mannlicher-Carcano. He stated it looked like the rifle, but he was not positive.[651] Why then not show it to Weitzman, who had a much better look at it, to confirm?

And what of the initial inability to match the bullet taken from Officer Tippit, "the only bullet recovered" according to police at the time, to Oswald's gun? A quarter of a year later, the police claimed they had the other three bullets in their possession. Since they also had the gun in their possession, they could have easily fired test bullets. Nevertheless, FBI firearms expert Cortland Cunningham testified that it was not possible to determine if the bullets had been fired from Oswald's revolver. Contradicting the FBI expert, Illinois police expert Joseph D. Nicol testified that the bullets matched Oswald's revolver. As with the bullets, there were issues with the chain of possession and inconsistent police identification markings on the shells found at the scene. Furthermore, three of the four bullets allegedly removed from Tippit's body were manufactured by Winchester-Western and one by Remington-Peters. However, only two of the shells were manufactured by Winchester-Western and two by Remington-Peters, giving a mismatch between the bullets and the shells.[652] So either this evidence was not the original evidence, or five shots were fired, one missing, possibly from two shooters, as one witness testified to.

And what of the pristine magic bullet that allegedly caused seven injuries in two men with virtually no damage to the bullet? That also has massive chain-of-custody issues. For starters, it is not clear that the bullet found at Parkland Hospital had any connection to Kennedy or Connally. After Parkland, the bullet then went through several hands, and there are inconsistencies as to who took possession of it and when. For example, it is documented that Robert Frazier received the bullet at the FBI lab at 7:30 p.m. from Elmer

Todd; however, it is also documented that Todd did not receive the bullet until 8:50 p.m., which is later than the time listed for when he handed it over to Frazier. That is not possible. Furthermore, Todd reportedly initialed the bullet, but his initials are not on the bullet in the archives. According to internal FBI records, those who found the bullet at Parkland testified that it did not look like the bullet at the archives.[653]

It is doubtful how much of the physical evidence would have been admissible in court. The inconsistency in the evidence and the lack of chain of custody do not necessarily imply a grand conspiracy. It could simply be a desire by those involved to close the case or even some low-level employee wanting to look like a hero. Oswald was dead anyhow.

And what about the Zapruder film? Did the Warren Commission use it to determine what happened? The Secret Service sent a copy of the film to the CIA, and the agency's National Photographic Intelligence Center (NPIC) came to two conclusions: 1) The first shot had not come from the sixth floor of the TSBD building and 2) there were at least two gunmen. The results of NPIC's analysis were suppressed.[654] Instead, the Warren Commission, just as *Life* magazine had done before them, published the frames in the film out of order, hiding the fact that the fatal shot threw Kennedy violently backward and to the left. Hoover labeled this a "printing error."[655] After the film was made available to the public in the 1970s, the official reason given for why Kennedy was thrown back and to the left was the "jet effect," i.e., it was the exploding brain matter that caused the violent motion backward, and not a shot from the front and right.

Much of the commission's case rested on the testimony of Marina Oswald. Warren Commission records listed Reuben Efron as being present in the room when they interviewed Marina Oswald. Efron worked for Angleton and was assigned to read Lee Oswald's mail for the 20-month period prior to the assassination. Researcher Jefferson Morley believes Efron was present to keep Angleton informed of Marina's statements. In addition to working for Angleton, Efron appears to have also been a loyal supporter of Israel, living in the nation later in life.[656] Marina's statements were so inconsistent and contradictory that no truth-seeker could take anything she said seriously. As an example, when the police first showed Marina the rifle, she could not identify it as belonging to her husband. By February 1964, she confirmed it was Oswald's rifle.[657] According to Marina, "[The FBI Agents] told me that if I wanted to live in this country, I would have to help in this matter."[658] Marina was a Russian citizen who had denounced her ties to the Soviet Union and was fearful of deportation. She was poor with two young children.[659] Her husband was dead. This helps explain the endless inconsistencies in her statements. The House Select Committee on Assassinations published a report on Marina titled "Marina Oswald Porter's Statements of a Contradictory Nature." It ran for twenty-nine pages.[660]

There are many, many more examples of, at best, incompetence on the Warren Commission's part. Those details have been covered extensively in other books. The critical takeaway is that the commission's goal, as McCloy stated, was to "lay the dust." This was not a proper investigation. Oswald had no real representation and no defense. All leads pointing elsewhere were ignored or obscured. One can even argue that Oswald's government ties, apparent FBI informant status, and intelligence-linked activities helped ensure a cover-up. Institutions such as the FBI would naturally act to protect themselves and avoid being implicated in the crime through prior association with Oswald. The commission propped up bad witnesses and discredited or ignored good witnesses. Off-the-record discussion took place well over two hundred times during the examination of witnesses, as often as seven or eight times per witness, and sometimes during crucial testimony. One witness who had been deposed by counsel and subsequently appeared before the commission at his own request informed them that counsel had accused him of perjury and threatened him with the loss of his job.[661]

It is worth briefly mentioning how the Warren Commission established a pattern of behavior for Oswald. The commission alleged that on April 10, 1963, Oswald attempted to shoot General Edwin A. Walker but fired and missed.[662] It was not until after the Kennedy assassination that Oswald was linked to this attempted crime. This book will not go into the details of this shooting as it has been covered extensively elsewhere, but a few points are worth bringing up. One, given the super-human task Oswald was attributed with in the shooting of Kennedy, it would be surprising that he had failed a much simpler shot at Walker. Two, the shooting occurred on April 10, 1963, just a few weeks before Oswald moved to New Orleans. Was this shooting staged as part of the assassination planning to establish a pattern of behavior, or was it a random crime that was taken advantage of after the fact? Lastly, it is worth pointing out the amount of distracting research that is required for one who chooses to study the Kennedy assassination. Researchers are pushed to investigate not one shooting, but four: Kennedy's, Oswald's, Tippit's, and Walker's. This needlessly takes focus away from studying the who and the why of Kennedy's murder, which is what is most important.

It is often believed that the Warren Commission unanimously came to its conclusions. That is not the case. Three of the commission members expressed disagreements with the report. Those three members were Senator Cooper, Senator Russell, and Representative Boggs.[663] Indeed, Russell was skeptical from the beginning. His personal papers at the University of Georgia Library contain the following memo dated December 5, 1963: "Something strange is happening. Warren and Katzenbach know all about the FBI and are apparently planning to show Oswald as the only one considered. This to me is an untenable position."[664] The three that did agree with the conclusions were McCloy, Dulles, and Ford. The latter three were much more "establishment" figures than the former three. Ford eventually became president of the United States.

The Warren Commission was supposed to be the final word on the crime. It concluded that Lee Harvey Oswald was a lone and deranged nut who killed the president of the United States with no apparent motive but a penchant for crime. The dust may have settled, but it would not go away.

7

The Little Brother

Do you know what I think will happen to Bobby? The same thing that happened to Jack. – Jackie Kennedy

After John F. Kennedy's murder, his younger brother, Robert F. Kennedy, attempted to carry on his vision. John F. Kennedy's assassination cannot be fully understood without including his brother's assassination in the analysis. Researchers often analyze the two murders as separate events; however, if one subscribes to the hypothesis that powerful forces removed John F. Kennedy, then those same forces would be prime suspects in the removal of his brother, Robert. As such, it is imperative to analyze Robert Kennedy's murder as a potential continuation of John's.

RFK stayed on as attorney general for a short period after his brother's death, but he was in a massive state of grief and only going through the motions. He resigned in mid-1964, and the public elected him as senator of New York in November 1964.

He initially did not intend to run for the presidency in 1968 as there was an incumbent Democratic president, Lyndon Johnson, and running against a current president in the same party is a massive challenge. However, due to both the tensions at home and the seemingly hopeless war in Vietnam, RFK threw his hat into the ring and announced he was running for president on March 16, 1968.[665] A few weeks later, on March 31, to the shock of many, RFK included, Lyndon Johnson announced that he was not seeking another term in office. Did Johnson's decision have anything to do with RFK's entry into the race?

While supportive, some were nervous about RFK's presidential run, given what had happened to his brother. His brother's widow, Jackie, worryingly told a mutual friend the concerns she had shared with Bobby, revealing, "Do you know what I think will happen to Bobby? The same thing that happened to Jack."[666]

Robert Kennedy won his first few primaries, exceeding the expectations of many. He had a fervent following not seen before for a presidential candidate. After his initial winning streak, he lost the May 28 primary in Oregon, a state with a small minority population. Thus much of his presidential hopes rested on the June 4 California primary. Kennedy campaigned vigorously in the large state, working himself to exhaustion. Then on the morning of voting day, he finally had a few hours to relax. He woke up at his friend John Frankenheimer's beachside house and took it easy for a bit before heading for the Ambassador Hotel in Los Angeles, where he would await the election results in his hotel suite. Frankenheimer had directed the film *The Manchurian Candidate*, in which Communists hypnotized a US soldier and used him as a mind-controlled assassin.[667]

Approaching midnight on June 4, as it became clear RFK had won, he made his way down to the Embassy Room at the Ambassador Hotel, where approximately 1,800 campaign workers and supporters chanted, "We want Bobby! We want Bobby!" At 12:01 a.m., Kennedy entered the large room and the crowd erupted in wild cheering. Everyone was ecstatic and felt this was it—he was going to be the next president. RFK walked up to the podium to give his victory speech. He stated, "What I think is quite clear is that we can work together ... and that what has been going on within the United

States over the period of the last three years, the divisions, the violence, the disenchantment with our society … that we can start to work together." To close out his speech, he referenced the upcoming Democratic convention in Chicago, declaring, "Now it's on to Chicago, and let's win there."[668]

Upon leaving the stage, he began walking towards the Colonial Room, where the press awaited him. There was a small kitchen pantry area that he needed to pass through to reach the press area. It was dark and crowded as he slowly walked into the pantry; over seventy people filled the tiny space. As RFK made his way through, he turned to his left to shake hands with a couple of busboys and then rotated forward to keep walking. Karl Uecker, the maître d', was guiding him. Suddenly, a young man, Sirhan Bishara Sirhan, stepped in front of Uecker and Kennedy, reached around Uecker, and started firing a gun aimed at RFK. After approximately two shots, the young man was tackled onto a steam table but kept firing his weapon. RFK fell to the ground with fatal wounds. Bullets struck five other victims, all of whom suffered non-fatal injuries. After falling, RFK asked, "Is everybody alright?" in a barely audible voice.[669] Soon after, he lost consciousness. Doctors would do their best to help him survive, but the damage was too great. After surgeons made a desperate effort at brain surgery to save the presidential hopeful, Robert Francis Kennedy officially passed away in the early morning hours of June 6, 1968.

Sirhan was immediately apprehended and later convicted at trial. On the surface, this could not be a more open and shut case. Witnesses saw Sirhan fire a gun at Robert Kennedy. He allegedly had a motive. He was a Palestinian angry at Robert Kennedy for making supportive statements of Israel while campaigning. Sirhan was convicted at trial by a jury. Upon a cursory look, one would have to assume that he had killed Robert Kennedy. Perhaps he was urged, manipulated, or assisted, but he fired the fatal bullets. Or did he? Things are not always what they appear to be. The evidence raises serious doubts about his guilt. Indeed, whether Sirhan injured anyone on that fateful night is in question. Author Lisa Pease has described the RFK assassination as a magic trick. It happened in only a few seconds. The room was dark and packed like a tight subway car. It was over before anyone had time to process what had happened. When the magic trick was done and the curtain closed, Sirhan was left as the fall guy.

Before delving into the details of what happened that night, the first question to ask, as with the JFK assassination, is cui bono? The same interests that benefited from John F. Kennedy's murder also benefited from his brother's: organized crime, anti-Communist interests, pro-war interests, CIA interests, powerful financial interests, and even Israeli/Zionist interests, despite Sirhan's alleged motive. Just like his brother before him, Robert Kennedy made statements supportive of Israel while campaigning. However, it was Robert Kennedy's Justice Department that tried to register the American Zionist Council as a foreign agent. And it was Robert Kennedy who urged in a 1965 senate speech that America intensify its nuclear non-proliferation efforts, explicitly calling out Israel:

> The need to halt the spread of nuclear weapons must be a central priority of American policy. Of all our major interests, this now deserves and demands the greatest additional effort. ... We should immediately explore the creation of formal nuclear-free zones of the world. Right now, one of our greatest assets is that there is not one nuclear weapon in all of Latin America or Africa. ... We shall call on Israel and the neighboring states ... to make the same commitment. ... We should insist, at a minimum, that all reactors built with the help of other powers be subject to IAEA [International Atomic Energy Agency] inspection. Indeed, I think the time has come to insist that all peaceful reactors be subject to inspection. But we ourselves must also stop assisting nations which refuse inspection.[670]

Ultimately, his policies towards Israel would likely not have differed considerably from his brother's, particularly in the area that created the most tension between JFK and Israel, nuclear weapons. Israel itself considered JFK's policies as leading to a "state of crisis" in US/Israeli relations.[671] So, while RFK would have been generally supportive of the nation, he probably would have followed a far more balanced policy than Lyndon Johnson or Richard Nixon did. And he would not have turned a blind eye to nuclear weapons development, publicly admitting that he supported cutting off assistance to countries that did not comply with inspections.

It is also important to bring into question the motive of Sirhan himself. Many American politicians over the decades have pledged support for Israel, yet no one has tried to assassinate any of them for such support. What are the mathematical odds that only Robert Kennedy would be singled out for what so many others have done? One can also argue that in addition to the policy benefits Israel received from Robert Kennedy not being elected, Israel also benefited from increased public support and sentiment, with the public believing that a Palestinian had murdered Robert Kennedy.

The last beneficiary of Robert Kennedy's murder was, of course, the entities who murdered his brother. As president, RFK likely would have re-opened the investigation into his brother's death, and he would have ensured that this time, it was thorough and genuinely seeking the truth. What would an inquiry run by Robert Kennedy have revealed? Those responsible for the assassination of his brother would have had a great motive to ensure such an exposé never occurred.

Congressman Allard Lowenstein commented on the murders of the two Kennedy brothers:

> Robert Kennedy's death, like the president's, was mourned as an extension of the evils of senseless violence; events moved on, and the profound alterations that these deaths … brought in the equation of power in America was perceived as random … a whimsical fate interfering in the workings of democracy. What

is odd is not that some people thought it was all random, but that so many intelligent people refused to believe that it might be anything else.[672]

However, if witnesses saw Sirhan shoot at Robert Kennedy, how could the crime be anything other than what it appears to be on the surface: a lone, disgruntled individual shooting at the target of his anger? Careful scrutiny quickly peels away the facade.

Sirhan Bishira Sirhan was born on March 19, 1944, in Jerusalem, Palestine, to a Christian Arab family. He was born just four years before the establishment of Israel and witnessed much atrocity from a young age. His house was destroyed in a bombing raid, and he saw an Israeli soldier kill an Arab in front of his home. In 1956, his family, now living under Jordanian rule in East Jerusalem, applied to emigrate to the United States. Sirhan was twelve when he arrived in America.[673] The family settled in Pasadena, California, and Sirhan enrolled in the Pasadena City school system. Teachers described him as quiet, well-mannered, reserved, and sensitive, often responding to questions with a "Yes, sir" or "No, sir." He graduated from high school in June of 1963. In September 1963, he enrolled in Pasadena City College while working part-time. He often talked about horses and his desire to become a jockey. In February 1965, his sister Ayda was diagnosed with leukemia, and Sirhan stayed home to care for her until her death on March 20. At the end of that school year, he was dismissed from Pasadena City College for poor grades and poor attendance, and not given any leniency for his sister's illness.[674]

Sirhan then turned to his love for horses. He went down to Santa Anita Park racetrack in August 1965 and asked for a job. He initially volunteered for a few months and then finally landed a job there in October 1965 as a stable hand. Another worker there, Thomas Rathke, introduced Sirhan to the occult. He handed Sirhan documentation on meditation by a group called the Rosicrucians. Sirhan quit his job at the end of March 1966 and then, in early June, went to work as an exercise boy at the Granja Vista del Rio Ranch in Corona. A few weeks later, he applied for membership in the Ancient Mystical Order of Rosy Cross (AMORC), the largest Rosicrucian organization in the world. Rosicrucian teachings combine mysticism and occultism—a belief in the use of supernatural forces—and other religious teachings. After only a few months at Granja Vista del Rio Ranch, Sirhan suffered a terrible accident. On September 25, 1966, he fell off a horse and was knocked unconscious. He was hospitalized overnight but discharged the next day. The following week he fell again, returning to the hospital for more treatment. On November 13, Sirhan quit. He then got a short stint at Del Mar racetrack but again fell off a horse after a few weeks. His supervisors told him he'd never make it as a jockey and dismissed him.[675]

Sirhan was unemployed for the next nine months, and not much is known about his life during this period. According to friends and family, Sirhan changed after his falls. Sirhan's older brother Sharif explained: "He was so nice before the fall ... everybody liked him. But he changed suddenly—snap—and became reclusive and irritable. ... He'd disappear for four or five hours at a time. ... He no longer listened when family members tried to talk to him. The way he acted was abnormal."[676] Another friend commented that Sirhan "became interested in mysticism and expressed a desire to be able to control a person's mind through extrasensory perception."[677] He may have also been depressed because the falls finished his dream of becoming a jockey.

There was an important entry made in his notebook, allegedly during this period. Sirhan had kept two spiral notebooks since his days at Pasadena City College, filled with random scribbling. Dated June 2, 1967, was an entry in one of these notebooks titled *A Declaration of War Against America*. In the entry, he wrote, "The manifestation of this Declaration will be executed by its purporter(s) as soon as he is able to command a sum of money ($2000) and to acquire some firearms. ... The victims of the party in favor of this Declaration will be or are now—the President, vice, etc." Although dated, it has been questioned when this entry was actually made in the notebook. The $2,000 corresponds to Sirhan's insurance payout for his falls; however, Sirhan did not receive that payout until April 1968, and he had not known the amount back in June 1967. Additionally, the date in the notebook was written in slightly different writing and a different pen than the text, suggesting someone may have added it later.[678]

Despite this entry in Sirhan's notebook, Sirhan's closest friend, Ivan Garcia, stated that "Sirhan did not appear to be aware of any political party, was not interested in groups or being a leader, and was not openly fanatical about politics." He further stated that "Sirhan never discussed Senator Kennedy, the Arab-Israeli dispute, or racial recriminations which might have arisen out of such a dispute."[679]

On September 25, 1967, Sirhan took a job at a health food store in Pasadena.[680] In late January 1968, Sirhan asked his brother if he knew anyone with a gun to sell. By February, Sirhan was in possession of a weapon. The prior June 1967 notebook entry gave motive and forethought to the gun purchase. In February and March, Sirhan sent off two money orders to reactivate his Rosicrucian membership. In March, Sirhan lost his job at the health food store. With free time available to him, he began spending more time on his Rosicrucian studies. He also began spending time at local gun ranges, practicing shooting his new gun. He visited these gun ranges about six times before the assassination.[681]

Dated May 18, 1968, a disturbing entry was found in Sirhan's notebook. In it, he wrote, "My determination to eliminate RFK is becoming more the more an unshakable obsession ... RFK must die RFK must die RFK must die ... RFK must be killed Robert F. Kennedy must be assassinated RFK must be assassinated ... Robert F. Kennedy must be assassinated ... Robert F. Kennedy must be assassinated before 5 June 68."[682] The official narrative holds that on that day, May 18, Sirhan watched a documentary on Robert Kennedy and became enraged when he learned RFK was in support of the

U.S. sending fifty jet planes to Israel. However, there are issues with this narrative. The first is that the documentary did not air in Los Angeles until May 20, and the second is that it made no mention of the jet planes. It was a biographical piece on RFK and showed brief footage of him in Israel in 1948 when he worked as a reporter for a Boston paper.[683] It was later in Oregon that RFK indicated he would support sending fifty jet planes to Israel.[684] Ironically, on May 18, the same day the writings were dated in Sirhan's notebook, tourists in Israel heard that a radio report claimed RFK had been shot. Was there an attempt to assassinate RFK on that date that was expected to succeed but failed?[685]

On May 20, Kennedy spoke at the Temple Isaiah in Los Angeles, but his remarks were not inflammatory. He spoke mostly about the need for a negotiated settlement between the Israelis and Arabs. When he did mention weapons, he stated, "We must assist with arms, if necessary, to meet the threat of massive Soviet military buildups. ... But in the long run, an arms race helps no one. What we need is an agreement ... to defuse the Middle East and to stop on all side further shipments ... a small but important step towards peace in the world." When asked where he stood on Jerusalem, he deflected and responded, "I stand here, in Los Angeles."[686]

RFK's response regarding weapons was not markedly different from the response given by his brother in an April 1963 press conference when asked if he would comply with Israel's requests for armaments. JFK responded:

> We will just have to wait and see what the balance of military power may be in the Middle East, as time goes on. We are anxious to see it diminished rather than participate in encouraging it. On the other hand, we would be reluctant to see a military balance of power in the Middle East which was such as to encourage aggression rather than discouraging it. So, this is a matter which we will have to continue to observe. ... At the present time, there is a balance which I think would discourage military action on

either side. I would hope it will continue.[687]

Sirhan's notebook, in general, included much repetitive writing. Other examples include, "[Egyptian President] Nasser is the greatest man who ever lived in this world. Nasser is the greatest man who ever lived in this world. Nasser is the greatest man who ever lived in this world. Lived. Lived. Lived."[688]

Witness Ernest Vallero told the LAPD and FBI that approximately two weeks before the assassination, someone who looked very similar to Sirhan, of Arabic or Jewish descent, provided him with an Israeli passport and applied for a job as a waiter at the Ambassador Hotel. Vallero said the person became "rather nasty in his speech" when Vallero told him there were no openings.[689]

In the weeks leading up to the assassination, Sirhan was spotted with a mysterious young woman at various Kennedy campaign events. On May 20, a luncheon was held for RFK in Pomona. Police officer William Schneid spotted an attractive young woman standing by the restaurant kitchen door, looking like she was trying to get inside. He described her as Caucasian, five feet six, twenty-five to thirty years old, with medium blond, shoulder-length hair, and a nice figure.

He approached her and informed her she was not allowed in. She then asked, "Which way will Kennedy go in to lunch?" He told her that RFK would likely use the stairs to go up to the second floor. As Kennedy arrived and climbed the stairs, Schneid watched the girl quickly approach. She climbed over a brick flower holder and jumped onto the stairs. Then a man jumped over the rail and then onto the stairs behind her. The man resembled Sirhan and was carrying a heavy jacket draped over his right arm, despite it being a sweltering day. Undeterred by their pleas, the bartender, Albert LaBeau, denied them entry. However, after the bartender went upstairs, he later saw the girl and the man resembling Sirhan standing against the dining room's back wall as Kennedy spoke. The man still had the heavy coat draped over his arm.

LaBeau later picked Sirhan out of a set of twenty-five photos of similar-looking men. He told the FBI that the way Sirhan had his coat over his arm, his right hand was obscured and so he could have "hid a gun under there very nicely." However, when asked if he could swear with certainty under oath that the man was Sirhan, he said no.[690]

On May 26, according to Reverend Douglas Harrell, "a mumbling, apparently tranquilized Sirhan" appeared at his church in Las Vegas, and "during the service proper, he made loud, unintelligible sounds." Harrell said Sirhan was not a threat and was allowed to stay. He stated that Sirhan was "very tranquil as if he might have been under the influence of a depressant." Harrell picked out Sirhan when shown six photographs but said he could not be 100 percent certain of the identification. Researchers have speculated that perhaps this was a "dry run" to assess how a hypnotized Sirhan would behave in a public setting and how well he would follow his cues.[691]

On May 30, Kennedy campaign volunteer Laverne Botting saw two men and a woman walk into the Kennedy campaign headquarters in Azusa, California. She said one of the men resembled Sirhan, and she described the woman as twenty-two to twenty-five years old, five feet seven with an excellent figure and dishwater blond hair. The man resembling Sirhan approached her desk while the other two stood in the background. The man stated that he was from the Pasadena campaign office and asked her if Kennedy would be coming into her office that day. Botting told him no, and the three left. She later picked out Sirhan's photo from a set of pictures but said to the LAPD she could only be sure of her identification if she saw Sirhan in person. The LAPD never gave her an opportunity to see Sirhan in person and identify him. A co-worker of Botting's, Ethel Crehan, witnessed the exchange and told the FBI she was "fairly certain" it was Sirhan. She also said to them that the girl with Sirhan had a "prominent nose."[692]

Insurance executive Dean Pack stated that while on an early morning hike with his son in the Santa Ana mountains on June 1, he came upon two men and a young woman shooting at cans. One of the men strongly resembled Sirhan. The other man, he said, was six feet tall with sandy hair. The girl was in her early twenties with long brown hair.[693]

On June 2, Sirhan saw a big advertisement in the *Los Angeles Times* inviting the public to see and hear Robert Kennedy speak at the Ambassador Hotel that day. When Robert Kennedy spoke at a fountain outside, Sirhan watched and listened. He said his attitude towards Kennedy was positive that night. Two prosecution witnesses, however, testified that they saw Sirhan walking around the hotel corridors and the pantry area. Sirhan denied this.[694]

Busboy Juan Romero told the FBI that on the same day, June 2, two men claiming to be police officers and wearing Kennedy signs on chains around their necks asked him how they could obtain white kitchen staff jackets. Romero did not know if they were actually police officers as they showed no identification, but he took them to the supply room storing the uniforms. The room was locked, but perhaps they got into it later.[695] Witness Rose Gallegos told the FBI that she saw three "kitchen helpers" standing around that evening, June 2, one of whom she thought was Sirhan. Gallegos's daughter also identified one of the three as Sirhan and stated that the three wore "white jackets as kitchen help would wear." Gallegos said she approached the three men and asked them, "Are you supposed to be in the hallway? This is the way that the Senator is gonna pass by. Why are you obstructing the way?" She said they did not answer, and they left.[696]

That same evening, June 2, witness Karen Ross saw a woman in the first row of the Robert Kennedy rally wearing a white dress with black polka dots. She described the woman as five foot six, twenty-four to twenty-six years old, and she thought her nose might have been "fixed."[697]

On the afternoon of June 4, Sirhan went to a gun range to practice. Several witnesses reported seeing him there. He reportedly left around 5 p.m., though some claimed he left earlier. Despite Sirhan admitting he was there, his name being on the signature logs for the day, and witnesses identifying him, the police were unable to match any of the nearly forty thousand shell casings recovered at the range to Sirhan's gun.[698] Several witnesses described the gun the man at the range was firing as different from Sirhan's gun. If true, that would explain why the shell casings did not match Sirhan's weapon, but then from where did Sirhan get this other gun?[699] Everett Buckner, the club's line officer, told the FBI that a white couple, a slender man in his thirties and an attractive, "husky build" blonde woman in her twenties, between five foot six and five foot eight, arrived at the range shortly after Sirhan. A short while later, he overheard a heated exchange between Sirhan and the woman. Sirhan offered to help her get her shots on target, and she replied, "Get away from me, you son of a bitch; they'll recognize you." The couple left the range shortly afterward.[700]

Sirhan said he then planned to go to a Rosicrucian meeting, but when looking through a newspaper, he saw an advertisement for the Miracle March for Israel, a parade to celebrate the Israeli victory over the Arabs in the Six-Day War, which began on June 5, 1967, exactly one year prior to the shooting of Robert Kennedy. Once Sirhan arrived at the parade area, he realized the parade was the following evening, so he instead went to the nearby Ambassador Hotel, where several events were occurring. Upon arriving at the Ambassador, he consumed several alcoholic drinks. Realizing he had had too much to drink, he searched for coffee to sober up before driving home. He found a coffee urn and ran into a young woman close to his age, whom he referred to as "beautiful."[701] He stated, "So, I gave her a cup; then I made some for me, and we sat there. Then she moved, and I followed her. She led me into a dark place." The next thing he remembered was being choked on one of the steam tables in the kitchen pantry after Robert Kennedy had been shot.[702]

Numerous witnesses saw a man resembling Sirhan with a mysterious young woman that evening. While their descriptions of the woman varied to some degree, particularly regarding her hair color, all described her as young, attractive, with a good figure, and wearing a white dress with black or dark blue polka dots. There was also witness consistency as to where they saw the girl: initially in the Embassy Room, then near the pantry, and then finally inside the pantry.[703]

Some witnesses even briefly chatted with the girl in the polka-dot dress. Around 9 p.m., a girl in a "white dress with dark blue polka dots" tried to talk photographer Conrad Steim into giving her a press pass. He stated she had a funny nose. Between 10:00 p.m. and 10:30 p.m., witness Eve Hanson and her sister Nina Ballantyne, while sitting at a bar at the hotel, were approached by a young woman with a "turned-up nose" wearing a white dress with black or navy-blue polka dots about the size of a quarter. The girl offered a toast "to our next president" without specifying who she was referring to.[704]

At around 11:30 p.m., a Kennedy campaign volunteer, Sandra Serrano, sat outside about halfway down the southwestern fire escape.[705] It was too hot and crowded inside, and she needed some fresh air. As she rested there, two young men and a young woman came up the stairs, the woman saying to Serrano, "Excuse me," as the three walked past her and into the building. The taller man had straight dark hair and was wearing a gold sweater. The shorter man had curly dark hair; she would later identify him as Sirhan. Serrano stated that the girl was about five foot six, had a nice figure, and a funny, turned-up nose. She was wearing a white dress with dark polka dots. In the same southwest corner of the ballroom where the trio entered, two other witnesses, Mary Whalen and Felicia Messuri, noticed a tall, heavy-set man who held something to his face that looked like a small transistor or radio. Messuri thought the man had a "sense of urgency" to him.[706]

Witness George Green reported to the FBI that somewhere between 11:15 and 11:30 p.m., he was observing Kennedy press secretary Frank

Mankiewicz chatting with reporters in a corridor leading to the pantry area. He saw Sirhan standing at the edge of the crowd with a tall thin man and a female in her early twenties. He stated the woman had a "good figure" and wore a white dress with black polka dots.[707] While he estimated the time as between 11:15 and 11:30 p.m., and Serrano estimated the time she saw Sirhan and the girl in the polka dot dress and one other man walk upstairs as 11:30 p.m., most likely Green saw Sirhan and the girl after Serrano did.

At around 11:45 p.m., Sirhan wandered into the narrow pantry area behind the ballroom. He asked several kitchen workers, "Is Kennedy coming back through here later?" They replied they did not know. Sirhan then wandered over to the tray stacker by the ice machines.[708] One of the workers, Jesus Perez, testified that Sirhan returned to ask them if they were talking about him, and Perez responded and told him no, they were talking about the beautiful girl and not about him. The girl was presumably the girl in the polka-dot dress.[709]

There were around twenty people in the pantry as RFK gave his victory speech. They were mostly hotel staff and press people. Why was Sirhan allowed into the pantry? At around 11:15 p.m., security guard Thane Eugene Cesar began guarding the western entrance to the pantry. This would be the entrance through which Kennedy would enter. Cesar's job was to ensure no one without appropriate credentials could get into the pantry.[710] So how did Sirhan and others he was with manage to get into the pantry? Why did Cesar allow them in? No one was guarding the eastern entrance of the pantry (Cesar had previously guarded the eastern entrance before moving to the western doors), so it is possible Sirhan entered from the eastern side without Cesar realizing. But the room was small, and it was Cesar's job to watch over the area. One witness, Eara Marchman, told the LAPD she had seen Sirhan chatting with and possibly arguing with a uniformed guard standing by the pantry doors, almost certainly Cesar.[711]

Cesar was a twenty-six-year-old plumber who worked at the Lockheed facility in Burbank, where the CIA's "Top Secret" U-2 spy planes were made. He had a security clearance from the Department of Defense so that he could make repairs anywhere in the plant. He signed up for a second job as a security guard working for Ace Guard Service shortly before the assassination.[712] According to the owner of Ace Guard Service, Frank Hendrix, Cesar's first assignment was the week before the shooting. Hendrix stated that Ace had assisted with security at the hotel for approximately a year before and after the assassination. However, Ace was not incorporated until early January 1968 and did not receive its license until March 1968, so it could not have assisted with security at the hotel for a full year prior to the assassination.[713]

Witness Darnell Johnson described a group of five people he thought were together, whom he saw in the pantry shortly before the end of Kennedy's speech. One was a "well-built" girl in a white dress with polka dots. Another was Sirhan. Another was in a blue sport coat, white shirt, and tie. The fourth was in a dark jacket, dark trousers, a white shirt, and a tie. The last was in a shiny brown sport coat.[714]

Shortly after Kennedy exited the stage, at around 12:15 a.m., hotel maître d' Karl Uecker led the senator towards the pantry area. As Kennedy walked up to the entry doors, security guard Cesar took hold of Kennedy's right elbow with his left hand, and Uecker and Cesar led RFK into the pantry and began to make their way through the crowd. As Kennedy started walking through, he shook hands with waiters Martin Patrusky to his left and Vincent DiPierro to his right. He took another step or so and turned left to shake hands with kitchen porter Jesus Perez and busboy Juan Romero.[715] At this point, DiPierro noticed Sirhan hanging onto a tray stand. He said his attention was drawn to him because he was with an attractive woman. "It looked like she was almost holding him," DiPierro stated. He said that Sirhan had said something to the girl, and she smiled back in response. DiPierro explained, "I glanced over once in a while. She was good-looking, so I looked at her." He described her as having a "pudgy nose" and wearing a "white dress with black or purple polka dots."[716] When asked, "How about her build, could you see that?" he responded, "Oh, yeah." When asked what "Oh, yeah" meant, he replied, "Very shapely."[717]

Uecker then started to pull Kennedy forward with his right hand. Sirhan then stepped out from the tray stacker, reached around Uecker's left shoulder, and smiled as if he was about to offer his hand to RFK.[718] Instead, he fired a gun. Complete chaos ensued, but the shooting itself was over in a few seconds. So, what happened during those few fateful seconds in the pantry?

Only through careful scrutiny can the reality of those decisive seconds be gleaned. The first place to start is the autopsy report. The coroner, Thomas Noguchi, declared the cause of death as a "gunshot wound of the right mastoid, penetrating the brain." The fatal gunshot entered just in the back of the right ear. Noguchi estimated the gun was fired approximately "one inch from the edge of [RFK's] right ear." He identified two other gunshot wounds in Kennedy. The two other wounds entered under the armpit, also at almost near contact distance, traveling in a "right to left direction" and an "upward and back to front direction." A fourth shot passed through RFK's coat without hitting him.[719] All four shots were fired at an upward angle, three of them at a sharp upward angle: fifteen, fifty-nine, sixty-seven, and eighty degrees.[720]

So, the first question to ask is, was Sirhan in a position to inflict these wounds? The simple answer is no. According to witness testimony, Sirhan had his gun muzzle several feet in front of Kennedy, he fired at a parallel angle, and those nearby tackled him after two shots. So, there is an inconsistency between the autopsy report and witness statements when it comes to the distance, direction, and angle of the shots and the number of shots. Even if all the witnesses were mistaken on one of these characteristics, that they were mistaken on all is hard to imagine.

Karl Uecker, probably the witness closest to Sirhan, stated years later:

> I have told the police and testified [to the grand jury] that there
> was a distance of at least one and one-half feet between the muzzle
> of Sirhan's gun and Senator Kennedy's head. The revolver was
> directly in front of my nose. After Sirhan's second shot, I pushed
> his hand that held the revolver down, and pushed him onto the
> steam table. There is no way that the shots described in the autopsy
> could have come from Sirhan's gun. ... Sirhan never got close
> enough for a point-blank shot, never.[721]

During police questioning on June 5, Uecker had repeatedly told police that
Sirhan was "right in front of me ... right in front." Uecker was between
Sirhan and Kennedy, and Sirhan had to reach around Uecker to shoot,
further implying he could not have gotten close enough for a point-blank
shot.[722] Later, after he became aware of the autopsy, Uecker stated:

> I was the closest to Senator Kennedy ... Sirhan at no time was
> firing from behind Senator Robert Kennedy. No! No! Not an
> inch from Kennedy's head—I don't believe that it was Sirhan's gun
> firing from back to front in an upward direction. I think I would
> have seen it. I was the closest one. In order for Sirhan to get that
> close to Senator Kennedy from behind he would have had to pass
> me, and he didn't.[723]

Busboy Juan Romero, who had shaken hands with Kennedy immediately
before the shooting, told the FBI that the gun was "approximately one yard
from Senator Kennedy's head." Vincent DiPierro, who was just behind RFK
during the shooting, told the FBI that "the revolver was about three to five
feet from Senator Kennedy's head." Attorney Frank Burns told the LAPD
that he saw "an extended arm holding a gun" in front of him and that the
gun "was never closer than a foot and a half to two feet" to RFK. When
asked if he could be mistaken and the gun could have been closer, he replied,

"No way."[724] Writer Pete Hamill told the police that "Sirhan was four to six feet away and the gun was about two feet" from Kennedy. Valarie Schulte testified that Sirhan was "three yards" away. Robert Lubic was at Kennedy's right side when Sirhan approached. He stated, "The muzzle of the gun was two to three feet away from Senator Kennedy's head. It is nonsense to say that he fired bullets into Kennedy from a distance of one to two inches since his gun was never anywhere that near to Senator Kennedy." There is only one witness, high school student Lisa Urso, who stated that Sirhan fired at "point-blank range." However, when the police took her for a reenactment, she noted that Sirhan was three to five feet from Senator Kennedy and that the gun was closer to her head than Kennedy's head. Her original statement had merely been her misunderstanding of what the term "point-blank" meant.[725]

Virtually all the witnesses described Sirhan's gun as parallel to the floor. Some said his gun was pointing downwards. Not a single witness said he was firing upwards.[726] The distance and trajectory outlined in the autopsy report are irreconcilable with witness statements. Direction is also inconsistent, though less so. Shortly before Sirhan stepped forward and in front of Kennedy, RFK had been facing left and shaking hands. This would have exposed his right ear and shoulder to Sirhan, though only to be shot from the side, not from behind. According to busboy Juan Romero, whose hand Kennedy had turned to shake, "He was shaking my hand and had just turned away [from me and forward] when this guy came out and started shooting." Romero did state that Kennedy had not turned completely around to face Sirhan, "He turned around—no, he hadn't finished turning around, he just kept on walking, you know, sort of looking this way. He took two steps, and all of a sudden, I just seen somebody … reaching over." Uecker, who was in front of Kennedy, stated that Kennedy had turned to face him before the shots rang out, "He was still talking towards the busboy, and he starts looking at me, and we start going."[727] One witness, Frank Burns, had Kennedy still facing completely to his left as the shots rang out, but he also stated Sirhan was firing down at Kennedy, wholly inconsistent with the sharp upward angles described in the autopsy.[728] As Sirhan appeared, Romero noted that Kennedy "placed his hands to his face" implying Kennedy himself viewed the threat as coming from in front of him. Witnesses Vincent DiPierro and Frank Burns also testified that Kennedy threw his hands to his face. Two witnesses, Freddy Plimpton and Lisa Urso, said RFK put his hands to the side of his face, perhaps reacting to a shot rather than protecting his face from a perceived threat in front.[729] Urso stated, "Kennedy grabbed his head behind the right ear and jerked forward about six inches before moving in the opposite direction and falling backward."[730]

The number of shots Sirhan fired before he was tackled is also inconsistent with the autopsy report of four point-blank shots from the rear and the right. According to Uecker, he tackled Sirhan onto the steam table after two shots. Uecker's partner, Eddie Minasian, corroborated Uecker's account that he tackled Sirhan after two shots. Sirhan kept firing once on the steam table, but he was at that point in no position to fire the point-blank shots into Kennedy.[731] When asked if the shots fired after Sirhan had been tackled were in the same direction as the first two, Minasian replied, "I doubt it, because ... we had him, and his arm was somewhere on this steam table here. And I doubt if it was in the same direction as the first two shots."[732] Witness Martin Patrusky indicated he thought Sirhan had been tackled after one shot.[733] The testimony of ear witnesses confirmed that Sirhan was likely tackled after two shots:

Witness Jack Gallivan: I heard a series of shots, maybe two, then a pause and the rest.

Witness Martin Patrusky: All of a sudden, there was like a firecracker going off; then there was another; then there was a pause. Then all of a sudden, there was rapid fire.

Witness Rafer Johnson: I thought it was a balloon going off, two poppings, and then I looked in that direction, and I heard some other popping.

Witness Angelo DiPierro: I heard the shot … I thought it was a prank or something … then a volley of shots.

Witness Ira Goldstein: There was about two of them at first.[734]

Witness Booker Griffin told police he heard two noises, a pause, and then more noises.[735] Not only does witness testimony indicate that Sirhan was tackled after two shots, but witness Vincent DiPierro further testified that Kennedy "hit the ground just prior to the third shot."[736] If Vince is correct, then how could Sirhan have put four point-blank shots into Kennedy if he was tackled after two shots and Kennedy had fallen after Sirhan's second shot?

Not a single witness placed Sirhan in a position to fire the four point-blank, sharply upward-angle shots from the back right of Kennedy. Even those witnesses who felt Kennedy was still turned to his left did not have Sirhan close enough to fire at a point-blank distance, nor did they have him firing at a sharp upward angle or firing from behind Kennedy. Some witnesses had Kennedy spinning to his left as he fell.[737] RFK ended up lying down in a position that indicates he had turned forward and then spun to his left as he fell, or he had still been facing left and had only very slightly turned forward before falling without spinning. If he was shot from the back and right, his natural reaction to the shots may have been to turn left, away from the shots, hence the spinning to the left as he fell.

The coroner himself noted years later,

Eyewitnesses are notoriously unreliable, but this time sheer unanimity was too phenomenal to dismiss. Not a single witness in that crowded kitchen had seen him fire behind Kennedy's ear at point-blank range. There are lessons to be learned from this case: Do not take for granted that the one who is in custody is the one who committed the crime. Until more is positively known of what happened that night, the existence of a second gunman remains a possibility. Thus, I have never said that Sirhan Sirhan killed Robert Kennedy.[738]

Another problem with the official narrative of the crime is that there were more bullet entry points than possible bullets in Sirhan's gun. In the John Kennedy assassination, a "magic bullet" was used to explain the number of injuries found in Kennedy and Connally. Similarly, the police used "magic bullets" to explain away the documented bullet entry points in the Robert Kennedy assassination. There were twelve official bullet entry points. Sirhan's gun could hold at most eight bullets. One bullet lodged in each of the five non-fatal shooting victims. Kennedy had one bullet lodged in his spine in the back of his neck. One bullet entered his head. One bullet passed through his chest and exited. And one shot passed through his jacket without hitting RFK. There were also three bullet holes photographed in the ceiling. There were seven bullets recovered from the six shooting victims.[739] According to the official narrative, the eighth bullet penetrated a ceiling tile and became lost in the ceiling.[740]

So, how were the twelve documented entry points officially accounted for? According to criminalist DeWayne Wolfer, one bullet bounced off the ceiling and hit victim Elizabeth Evans in the head. However, Evans's medical report describes the bullet as entering in an upward direction. Would not a bullet ricocheting off the ceiling have hit her at a downward angle? Furthermore, to iron out the possible trajectories of the ricochet, Wolfer placed Sirhan much further back just for the shot that allegedly hit the ceiling and then Evans. But not a single witness ever placed Sirhan in that position, and certainly not for just one shot.[741] Lastly, three-quarters of the bullet's original weight was recovered from Evans even though the bullet allegedly shot through a one-inch-thick plaster ceiling tile, ricocheted off the inner ceiling, and re-entered through the tile.[742] The most implausible explanation given for a victim injury was the explanation given for Paul Schrade's wound. Wolfer concluded that the bullet which passed through RFK's jacket hit Schrade. The problem with this conclusion is that the bullet passed from back to front at an eighty-degree upward angle through RFK's coat, but Schrade was four to five feet behind RFK. Years later, Schrade angrily asked at a police commission hearing, "I want you to explain to me how a bullet traveling up and away from me can make a ninety-degree turn and end up in my head?"[743] As for the eighty-degree upward angle, Schrade commented, "I would have to be around nine feet tall—and to have somehow put my head on Bob's shoulder—for that to be possible. It was completely absurd." He concluded, "What's certain is that the bullet which passed through Bob's jacket could not have been the one which hit me. And that makes me believe there was more than one gun fired."[744]

In addition to the twelve official bullet entry points, there is evidence that Wolfer did not include additional bullet entry points in the official count. The police could not admit to more than twelve bullet entry points because even with twelve, they struggled greatly to describe the crime and arguably failed. Any more would have been almost impossible to explain. Nevertheless, there are photos of police and others pointing to additional bullet holes in the early hours and days after the shooting. So soon after the crime, no one yet knew that they were dealing with an eight-shot revolver and that anything more than eight bullets would be problematic as it would imply conspiracy. In one photograph, criminalist DeWayne Wolfer is pointing to an apparent bullet mark in front of the pantry doorway. In another, the chief medical examiner for Los Angeles County, the man who performed RFK's autopsy, Dr. Thomas Noguchi, is seen pointing at the doorframes. When asked later about the photograph, Noguchi stated that he had requested Wolfer to show him all the bullet holes, and Wolfer "pointed … to several holes in the doorframes of the swinging doors leading into the pantry."[745]

An Associated Press photograph showed Los Angeles police officers Robert

Rozzi and Charles Wright pointing to holes in the doorway. The photo's caption read, "Police technician inspects a bullet hole discovered in a door frame. … Bullet is still in the wood." In 1975 Rozzi confirmed he had indeed seen a bullet in the doorframe. When Rozzi's partner Charles Wright was later asked by a journalist how certain he was, on a scale of one to ten, that there was a bullet in the doorframe, he replied, "as close to ten as I'd ever want to go without ever pulling it out."[746]

FBI agent William Bailey was in the pantry within hours of the shooting. He stated:

> As I toured the pantry area I noticed in a wood doorframe, a center divider between the two swinging doors, two bullet holes. I've inspected quite a few crime scenes in my day. These were clearly bullet holes; the wood around them was freshly broken away and I could see the base of a bullet in each one.[747]

Other police officers also saw the extra bullet holes. Patrolman Al Lamoreaux stated, "seeing one or two holes in the door. … It was just obvious. Just being a dumb cop, you look and see where the bullets went." Sergeant Raymond Rolon stated, "One of the investigators pointed to a hole in the doorframe and said, 'We just pulled a bullet out of here.'" LAPD photographer Charles Collier stated, "A bullet hole looks like a bullet hole—if you've photographed enough of them." Detective Sergeant J. R. MacArthur said he had seen "quite a few" bullet holes. When asked if the hole might have had a nail in it instead of a bullet, Deputy Sheriff Thomas Beringer replied, "It wasn't a nail. It was a definite bullet hole."[748]

Wolfer's subordinate, David Butler, stated that he saw Wolfer remove two bullets from the wall. He made the statement not understanding the implications of what he was saying. He later changed his statement.[749] In the early days, not even Wolfer understood the significance raised by the bullets in the doorframe. In 1975, the FBI released certain documents from its files on the RFK case. In those documents were close-up photographs of the doorframes. Four of the pictures were labeled as "bullet holes." One was labeled "Close-up view of two bullet holes."[750]

Did any witnesses hear more than eight shots? Witness Nina Rhodes stated,

> There were 12-14 shots in all. I was 6-7 feet from the Senator when I saw him and a number of others fall. Rosey Grier and Rafer Johnson charged towards someone ahead and to the left of me. This surprised me because it was my impression that some of the shots had come from ahead of me and to my right. ... not from where I saw Sirhan. ... The shots were to the left and right from where I was.

Another witness, Joe LaHive, told a radio interviewer on the night of the shooting that the shots "went off like a staccato burst, and it was almost like rapid fire. The guy must have just squeezed them off as fast as he possibly could, and if there were two people, that would account for the seeming sequence of shots."[751] Witness Estelyn Duffy told police on the night of the shooting, "I thought I heard at least ten shots. ... It wasn't one or two, it was a lot of shots."[752]

In the spring of 2005, Brad Johnson, a senior writer at *CNN*, found an obscure audiotape in the California State Archives. The tape had been made on a cassette recorder owned by journalist Stanislaw Pruszynski, who had taped Robert Kennedy's victory speech at the Ambassador Hotel and then followed RFK into the pantry, not realizing his recorder was still on. Johnson contacted electrical engineer Philip Van Praag to see if he could use the recording to determine the number of shots. Van Praag found thirteen shot sounds spread over a little more than five seconds. He stated two shots were fired at first, then there was a pause of about 1.33 seconds, then a flurry of shots. This supports witness statements as well as Uecker's claim that he tackled Sirhan after two shots. Praag also described some shots as "double shots." These were shots that occurred almost simultaneously and could not have come from the same gun. This corroborates the many witness statements of the shots sounding like the uneven staccato of firecrackers.

A *Discovery Times* documentary covered Van Praag's findings. The documentary also hired its own experts, who attested that they heard ten shots, not thirteen. However, they still heard more than the eight held by Sirhan's gun, even though they spent far less time analyzing the tape than Van Praag did. Van Praag was not surprised that they only heard ten. He stated, "If it were as simple as putting on a good set of earphones, you wouldn't need an audio expert." *Discovery Times* also brought on an expert who argued against the possibility of a conspiracy, and this expert claimed there were only seven gunshots heard. However, he did not spend much time with the audio tape. And he started with the assumption that there was only one gun. For example, he discounted the double shots Van Praag counted by stating, "The higher frequency content is different, and the auditory quality is not consistent with the other shots. Also, it would require the trigger to be pulled in a very short space of time." So, he started with the belief that there was only one gun and analyzed the audio according to that presumption.[753]

On February 21, 2008, Van Praag presented his findings at the American Academy of Forensic Sciences Annual Scientific Meeting. In his presentation, he stated that the Pruszynski tape revealed that eight shots came from one type of gun firing in an east-to-west direction, and five shots came from another kind of gun firing from a west-to-east direction.[754]

The FBI then examined the Pruszynski tape and reported on May 13, 2013, that "The designated area recorded on the specimen [tape] was of insufficient quality to definitely classify the impulse events as gunshots."[755]

The bullet holes and the audio evidence suggest that perhaps there was more than one shooter in the pantry that night. The next question to ask then is, did any witnesses see other guns? Based on their statements, witnesses saw three, perhaps four, guns in the pantry. The security guard, Thane Eugene Cesar, has been brought up most often as a potential second gunman. At the very least, Cesar failed horribly at his job. He was supposed to watch over the pantry area, ensure no unauthorized individuals entered, and safely escort Robert Kennedy through the pantry. However, there are indications that Cesar not only failed miserably at his job but also that he fired his gun at Kennedy. He was in a perfect position to do so, holding Kennedy closely from the back and the right. Indeed, several witnesses saw Cesar pull his gun.[756]

Cesar was the only witness interviewed immediately after the shooting to accurately describe RFK's wounds:

> Interviewer: Officer, can you confirm the fact that the senator has been shot?
>
> Cesar: Yes. I was there holding his arm when they shot him.
>
> Interviewer: What happened?
>
> Cesar: I don't know. … As he walked up, the guy pulled a gun and shot at him.
>
> Interviewer: Was it just one man?
>
> Cesar: No. Yeah, one man.
>
> Interviewer: And what sort of wound did the senator receive?
>
> Cesar: Well, from where I could see, it looked like he was shot in the head and the chest and the shoulder.[757]

In a famous photograph showing Kennedy lying on the floor after being shot, his hand was next to Cesar's clip-on tie, implying Kennedy may have grabbed at it and pulled it off as he was fired at or falling. In his initial statement, Cesar claimed that he had pulled RFK down as he himself fell.[758]

Cesar admitted to police that he had a gun on him, but police asked him no questions about it, even though he was in a perfect position to fire the shots as described in the autopsy, point-blank at a steep upward trajectory from the back and the right.[759]

When witness Don Schulman told the police what he had seen, they were disinterested. In describing his interview with DA Thomas Kranz, Schulman stated:

> They said, "Anything else?" and I said, "Yeah, I saw other guns pulled and possibly fired." They said, "Why do you say that?" I said, "Well, because there was just like firecrackers, a whole bunch of shots." They said, "There were no other guns." I said, "I thought I saw them." They said, "No, you didn't." I said, "OK."[760]

Schulman later stated, "I saw a guard pull his gun, and I'm pretty sure he fired. I'm pretty cotton-picken' sure he did." Cesar admitted in a later interview that he pulled his gun but claimed he did not fire. When asked when he pulled his weapon, he stated, "When I saw the gun [Sirhan's] go off, I pulled it … just as soon as the shots were fired." Cesar also mentioned that he got powder burns in his eyes from Sirhan's gun. However, ballistics expert William Harper stated that Cesar was not close enough to Sirhan to get gunpowder in his eyes but that the powder could have been blowback from his own gun. In the interview, Cesar stated, "I definitely wouldn't have voted for Bobby Kennedy because he had the same ideas as John [Kennedy] did, and I think John sold the country down the road. … He literally gave it to the Commies, the minorities, the Black."[761] While it is certainly possible that Cesar could have accidentally fired his gun once, it is improbable that he would have accidentally fired multiple times.

As mentioned previously, Schulman was not the only one who saw Cesar pull his gun. Witness Richard Lubic was three feet to the right of Kennedy when the shooting happened. Lubic stated, "I was kneeling at Senator Kennedy's right side after he fell to the floor. I saw a man in a guard's uniform standing a couple of feet to my left behind Senator Kennedy. He had a gun in his hand and was pointing it downward."[762] Lubic later recounted to author David Talbot what was crossing his mind as he saw the guard, "Why would a security guard have his gun pointed towards the floor [where Robert Kennedy was] instead of at Sirhan?"[763] Witness Bill Barry saw a guard with his gun out and told him to put it back in his holster. Karl Uecker said he shouted at the guard, "Are you crazy! Pulling your gun … you could have killed me."[764]

Witness Lisa Urso said she saw someone who she assumed to be a security guard pull his gun. She said the guard was standing "by Kennedy." When she told investigators about this guard, "they reacted with disinterest on one occasion; hostility, on another."[765]

While Cesar is a prime suspect for having fired at least some of the shots into Kennedy, particularly the ones in the shoulder, which he was perfectly positioned to do without being noticed, other witness accounts mention other potential shooters, including another as potentially inflicting the fatal headshot.

Witness Joseph Klein told the LAPD he thought he saw a man with a gun running out of the pantry as Sirhan was being subdued. Dr. Marcus McBroom stated that he had the distinct impression of a second gunman brushing past him as Sirhan was being tackled. McBroom told the police that while he did not see the face of the gunman during the shooting, he saw the gun was in someone's left hand. Sirhan was right-handed and shooting with his right hand.[766]

Witness Frank Burns described what may have been different shooters to his right and left: "I was standing behind Mr. Kennedy when I heard the noise. It sounded like a string of firecrackers. I focused on an arm and a gun just to my right. It seemed to be close to Senator Kennedy. I felt a burning sensation on my left cheek, then I saw Senator Kennedy falling, turning to his left and holding his arms up."[767]

If Burns saw a gun to his right, why did he feel a burning sensation on his left cheek? Witness Boris Yoro was also behind Kennedy. He stated, "The Senator was backing up and putting both of his hands and arms in front of him in what would be best described as a protective effort. ... I felt powder from the weapon strike my face." If Yoro was nowhere near Sirhan, how did he get gunpowder on his face?[768]

Thirteen-year-old witness Ronald Panda, who was behind Kennedy, stated that he "saw a man with a gun in his right hand step from behind a wall." This was likely the dividing wall between the west side of the ice machine and the west entrance to the pantry. Sirhan was seen on the east side of the ice machine, so this could not have been Sirhan. Panda also told the police that he saw Sirhan but did not see a gun in his hand. So, in whose hand did he see the gun?[769]

Witness Freddy Plimpton saw a man with his hand right up to Kennedy's head at the time of the shooting. She did not see a gun, but she said it looked like the man shot Kennedy: "I saw his hand up next to Robert Kennedy's head. ... I just looked at him and from his position and his posture, just assumed he was the guy who fired. ... All I can say is I knew this guy was shooting Senator Kennedy. I just can't say I saw the gun, no."[770]

Is it possible that Plimpton saw a man using a hidden weapon? She assumed it was Sirhan as she stated the man was similar in appearance, but the man was dressed in white and looked like a waiter. Sirhan was in a blue shirt, and according to witnesses who were near him, he never got close enough to Kennedy to point a gun point-blank at his head. Another man at the hotel that night told researcher Lisa Pease that he had seen Sirhan, dressed in a white busboy uniform, shoot Kennedy. The man was convinced this was Sirhan.[771] But, again, Sirhan was in a blue shirt and jeans. Indeed, several additional witnesses had seen a man they thought was Sirhan dressed as a busboy that night at the Ambassador Hotel. Was a look-a-like used to confuse witnesses? Recall the potential use of an Oswald look-a-like in the John Kennedy assassination. When witnesses see someone for a few seconds, not expecting anything out of the ordinary to occur, the two individuals do not need to look that similar, just similar enough to allow witnesses to assume that they saw the person in question. Recall also the man who looked like Sirhan, who tried to get a job as a waiter at the hotel a couple of weeks before the assassination, and the men who had asked on June 2 how to obtain white kitchen staff jackets. Recall also the three men in white kitchen staff jackets lurking in the hallway that Robert Kennedy was to walk through at the Ambassador Hotel on June 2, one of whom witnesses identified as Sirhan. Sirhan, however, claimed he was never in that area nor dressed as a busboy. Was the person seen on June 2 in the busboy uniform the same person seen in the busboy uniform shooting at Kennedy's head on the night of June 4? Recall also that a girl in a polka dot dress was seen at the Kennedy event at the hotel on the night of June 2. Was June 2 perhaps either a dry run or an initial assassination attempt that failed?

If there were other gunmen in the pantry, then why would they have taken the job if an unskilled Sirhan was to fire his gun haphazardly? There would be no guarantee as to where Sirhan's bullets would land. And if one or more of these gunmen had been placed directly behind and to the right of Kennedy, then they would have been placed directly in Sirhan's line of fire, which was towards Robert Kennedy. Who would agree to be in the line of fire? And, if Sirhan was firing at Robert Kennedy, as witnesses claim, then why did none of his bullets hit Kennedy? Kennedy had no injuries from the front, no injuries at a parallel angle, and no injuries from more than a few inches away. But if Sirhan pointed his gun at Kennedy, why did his bullets not hit Kennedy? That begs the question: Was Sirhan firing bullets or blanks?

When a blank is fired, a wad of paper burns quickly and produces paper ash residue. The paper is the "cap" that seals in the gunpowder. When a cap gun fires, a flame of burning paper is visible.[772] Is there any evidence that Sirhan fired blanks? Karl Uecker, the man closest to Sirhan when Sirhan fired at Robert Kennedy, stated that at the first shot, he did not realize Sirhan had a gun. He said, "Then I saw something white, either paper or something."[773] He explained, "I heard a pop, I saw what looked like bits of paper flying."[774] Witness Rafer Johnson, an Olympic decathlon champion, knew well what a cap gun sounded like. He told police, "I saw smoke, and I saw like something from a—like a—the residue from a bullet or cap, looked like a cap gun throwing off the residue." He then told the police he saw "these particles flying in the air like, you know, expended—" but before he could say "caps," the police cut him off.[775] Witness Harold Burba testified that the "gunshots sounded like a cap pistol" to him.[776] Witness Norbert Schlei told a local news station soon after the shooting, "It didn't sound like gunshots to me, and I've heard a lot of gunshots. It sounded like a cap pistol or somebody cracking a balloon." Witness Dick Aubry stated, "I just saw this blue … like a flash, like maybe something from a firecracker … flash, like a little spark from a … it was just the flashes I saw; I thought somebody threw a firecracker right at him."[777] Busboy Juan Romero stated, "I felt something like burning, like, you know, like when you throw out firecrackers … I see it burn there. I see it all."[778] Richard Lubic told police he heard two shots "which sounded like shots from a starter pistol at a track meet." Witness Dick Truck stated he heard "what sounded like cap pistols or firecrackers." Various other witnesses also attested to Sirhan's gun sounding like a cap gun.[779]

If Sirhan was firing blanks, then who shot at the other five pantry victims? They were all behind RFK and RFK was shot from behind, those bullets going in the opposite direction of the other five victims. Was there anyone in a position to hit the other victims? Multiple witnesses stated that they saw Sirhan firing while standing on the steam table or with his knee on it. They said he was firing from an elevated position downwards. But all witnesses near Sirhan said he was standing on the ground when he started firing. Witness Nina Rhodes stated that the man standing and firing from the table wore a blue suit. Sirhan was wearing a blue shirt with a zipper at the neck and jeans, not a suit. However, one of the three men seen with Sirhan and the lady in the polka dot dress wore a blue suit. Rhodes stated years later that, at the time, she had just assumed the man was Sirhan. She had not seen his face. However, in her initial FBI interview, she said that the man was firing from an elevated position. The FBI and police should have known that this could not have been Sirhan, even if the witness did not realize this.[780]

Witness Richard Lubic gave a similar statement to the FBI, saying the shooter "had his knee on a small table or air conditioning vent and had lifted himself up on this knee to obtain elevation while shooting." He also assumed that the person he saw was Sirhan. He never saw the shooter's face. Lubic told the police, "He seemed to be higher than anybody else, and he had a perfect view of everything." Witness Harold Burba revealed to the FBI, "I had the impression of someone standing on a table and firing a gun at a downward angle." Yet another witness, George Green, in a live on-camera television interview for CBS shortly after the shooting, stated that he saw the shooter standing on the table while firing. Witness Ronald Panda also told the LAPD that he thought the shooter "was standing on something and pointing down." Years later, Panda stated that the person next to him had been shot in the upper part of their body, but because that person was surrounded, the shot could only have hit the person if it was coming via a downward angle. Multiple witnesses attested to a man jumping off the table.[781] If these witnesses are correct, then their testimony supports the notion that Sirhan was firing blanks. A shooter would be needed to account for the east to west shooting direction that Sirhan was positioned at. And a shooter at an elevated position makes sense because it would be easy for that shooter to then avoid the area of Robert Kennedy and hence avoid any shooters firing point-blank at RFK.

The assassination was over in just a few seconds. However, Sirhan was exerting great strength, and it took over forty seconds to separate him from his gun.[782] Somehow, Sirhan had the strength to hold off Rosey Grier, a former professional football player, Rafer Johnson, an Olympic athlete, and many others taller and bigger than him.[783] As Sirhan was being tackled, witness George Plimpton noticed that he had "enormously peaceful eyes." Plimpton stated, "In the middle of a hurricane of sound and feeling, he seemed peaceful."[784] Patrolman Randolph Adair observed, "He had a blank, glassed-over look on his face—like he wasn't in complete control of his mind." The unusual degree of strength and the peaceful state are both signs of Sirhan perhaps being in a state of hypnosis.[785]

As almost everyone focused on Sirhan, others made their exits but did not go completely unnoticed. Witness Evan Freed told police that he saw two men and a woman leave the pantry in a hurry after the shooting. He described the woman as "possibly wearing a polka dot dress" and one of the men as wearing a blue sports coat. He said the two exited via different doors, and the third man chased after the man in the blue sports coat, yelling, "Get him! Get him!"[786] The two men were running from "the vicinity of the second steam table."[787] This is the location where several witnesses had seen a man in a blue sports coat firing a gun while either standing or perched up on the table. Ace Security guard Jack Merritt gives some corroboration to Freed's statements. He heard a woman coming out of the pantry yelling, "We need a doctor!" He ran towards the pantry, entering from the east side, where Freed was standing.

Merritt stated that upon entering, he "observed two men and a woman walking away from him and out of the kitchen. They seemed to be smiling." He said the woman wore a polka-dot dress.[788] Witness Booker Griffin further corroborates these statements. He said he had seen Sirhan throughout the evening with a woman in a "predominantly white dress" that had "colorations" on it and with a tall Caucasian man. Griffin had just started to enter the pantry at the east end when the shooting began. He stated, "I distinctly saw the other man and the girl flee a side corridor heading out of the hotel as I raced to the feet of the senator. There is no doubt in my mind that on several trips past the trio that they were together." Griffin tried to pursue them down the corridor but could not get through. He stated he kept yelling, "They're getting away!" but no one seemed to pay attention.[789] Could Griffin have been the man that Freed had seen chasing and shouting after the man in the blue sports coat? Griffin further told police that "it sounded as though there was more than one gun being used."[790] Another witness, George Green, told the FBI that he saw a man and a woman in a polka-dot dress run out of the pantry after the shooting. He noticed them because everyone else was trying to get into the room, and they were rushing out of the room.[791]

Darnell Johnson, the witness who had seen Sirhan with the girl in the polka-dot dress and three other men, stated that he saw the girl and the three men leave after the shooting. He said as Sirhan was being subdued, the girl in the polka-dot dress and the man in the blue sport coat came back and looked, then left again. Witness Jose Carvajal stated he saw a girl in a polka-dot dress "run straight into a dead-end hallway." Perhaps this explains why Johnson saw her return. It may be that she realized she could not exit via the original path she attempted.[792]

Witness Richard Houston, who was outside of the pantry at the time of the shooting, told the police that shortly after, he saw a woman who wore a polka-dot dress run out of the pantry, and he overheard her say, "We killed him!" after which she "ran out onto a terrace area."[793]

Within minutes of the shooting, an elderly couple ran up to Sergeant Paul Sharaga, who was standing in the hotel's rear parking lot. The couple was distraught and told Sharaga that they had been "just outside the Embassy room, on the balcony" when a young couple in their early twenties ran by them from the direction of the Embassy Room, shouting, "We shot him! We shot him!" in a state of glee. When the couple asked, "Shot who?" the young woman replied, "Kennedy, we shot him! We killed him!" They described the young woman as wearing a polka-dot dress and the man as wearing a tan shirt. Sergeant Sharaga stated of the elderly couple, "They were excited, but their statements were rational … not hysterical. They just didn't have time to dream up a story. … It was too spontaneous."[794]

Fourteen-year-old witness Katie Keir told police she was standing on the "platform" of a stairway immediately after the shooting when a girl in a polka dot dress ran out of the building and down a stairway, yelling, "We shot Kennedy!" *Washington Post* reporter Mary Ann Wiegers told the FBI she was in the Kennedys' fifth-floor suite after the shooting when a young girl, about fifteen years of age, was brought in by two policemen. The young girl stated she saw a woman in a polka-dot dress rush by, yelling, "We killed him, we killed him!" Wiegers said the teenage girl was hysterical. Was the teenage girl she saw Katie Keir?[795]

The parking lot where Sergeant Sharaga met the elderly couple was directly below the stairway Kennedy campaign volunteer Sandra Serrano was sitting on. Recall that Serrano had seen Sirhan, a girl in a polka-dot dress, and a man in a gold sweater go up the stairway shortly before the shooting. Serrano was still sitting on the stairs when she heard what she thought were six backfires from a vehicle. A few seconds later, two of the three people who had passed her earlier—the girl in the polka-dot dress and the man in the gold sweater—came running down the stairs. The girl was shouting ecstatically, "We shot him! We shot him!" Serrano asked, "Who did you shoot?" The girl replied, "Senator Kennedy!"[796]

There are five different witnesses (Richard Houston, the elderly couple, Katie Keir, and Sandra Serrano) who heard and saw a young woman in a polka-dot dress run out of the hotel, onto a terrace, and down the stairs, yelling, "We shot him!" or "We killed him!" What are the odds that all five witnesses would randomly make up such a story, especially given these witnesses did not know each other or each other's stories? The question is, then, why would the girl in the polka-dot dress have yelled such a statement? Recall that other witnesses had stated they saw a man with a radio watching the exit door and that the man had "a sense of urgency" to him. It is possible that this man was watching the exit to ensure the culprits had an escape and that the girl in the polka-dot dress was letting him know, "We shot him!" When Serrano and the elderly couple replied, "Shot who?" the girl in the polka dot dress and her companion had already escaped; perhaps in her excitement, she replied, "Kennedy!" She was already out of the building. Once she was down the stairs, she was in the clear. As for the vehicle backfires that Serrano says she heard, she was too far from the pantry to hear gunshots, but perhaps she heard them through the radio of the man by the door, or maybe they were just what she initially thought they were, vehicle backfires.

After speaking with the elderly couple, Sergeant Sharaga radioed in a description of the male suspect; however, soon after, his broadcast was discarded, and another broadcast came over the police radio, "Disregard [Sharaga's] broadcast. We got Rafer Johnson and Jesse Unruh, who were right next to him, and they have only one man and don't want them to get anything started on a big conspiracy. This could be somebody that was getting out of the way so they wouldn't get shot. But the people that were right next to Kennedy say there was just one man."[797]

And that was it. The police had solved the murder within mere minutes. Sirhan was going to be the one and only culprit. Did Rafer Johnson ever tell the police there was only one man? No, he simply told them he did not look elsewhere after he saw Sirhan. His exact words were, "I didn't notice what was around. I was just trying to get to him [Sirhan]. ... I really ... couldn't tell you anything about the people around at that point. I just wasn't looking."[798]

Sirhan was quickly apprehended and taken to the downtown Los Angeles police station. When asked in the vehicle why he did it, Sirhan allegedly replied, "I did it for my country."[799] Police officer Arthur Palencia took Sirhan into custody and checked to see if his pupils reacted to light. They did not, which told Palencia that the prisoner was under the influence of something. Sirhan could not answer basic questions, such as what his name was or where he lived. For a while, Sirhan said almost nothing, but when he found out that the deputy district attorney interrogating him was with the DA's office, he began chatting with him and philosophizing about a well-publicized murder. Deputy DA John Howard lost his patience and asked Sirhan, "Do you know where you are now? I've told you you've been booked." Sirhan replied, "I don't know." Howard repeated, "You're in custody. You've been booked. You understand what I've been—." Sirhan cut him off, "I have been before a magistrate, have I or have I not?" Howard replied, "No, you have not. You will be taken before a magistrate as soon as possible. ... You're downtown Los Angeles in central jail. ... We're not communicating very well up to now, but you are downtown Los Angeles, OK? This is the main jail for the LA Police Department. You'll be booked into a cell. ... Do you understand that? Do you understand where you are?"[800] When asked if he was married, Sirhan replied that he did not know.[801]

By 4 a.m., the prisoner had still not revealed his name, nor had the cops been able to get him to speak about what had happened that night. Instead, he brought up such random topics as the types of books the police officers liked to read and their knowledge of the stock market. He then began philosophizing about the definition of justice. The prisoner stated, "Treat others as you would want them to treat you—that's what Jesus said. Beautiful thing." When the cops asked Sirhan if he agreed with the statement, he replied, "Very much so, sir. Very much."[802] Sergeant Bill Jordan stated about the prisoner, "He appeared less upset to me than individuals arrested for a traffic violation."[803] Police chief Thomas Reddin commented about Sirhan, "He was very relaxed and wanted to talk about everything except the events last night. If I were to judge him strictly on the basis of our conversation

… I would say he was a gentleman."[804]

By daybreak, the police still had no idea who the prisoner was. Finally, at around 9:30 a.m., Sirhan's brother, Adel, walked into the police station carrying a newspaper with the suspect's photo in it and told the police that it was his brother.[805] At around the same time, Sirhan was examined by the jail's medical director, Dr. Marcus Crahan. As Crahan asked him questions, Sirhan replied, "no comment" to queries about his age, nationality, family background, education, occupation, and medical history. Otherwise, he was very chatty. Toward the end he began to go into shivers in front of the doctor, even though it was very hot. Later, every time psychiatrists brought Sirhan out of a hypnotic trance, he would shiver. Soon after meeting with the doctor, Sirhan met with an attorney and finally revealed his name.[806]

The LAPD constructed a special unit to investigate the Robert Kennedy assassination. They titled it Special Unit Senator (SUS) and placed Chief of Detectives Robert A. Houghton in charge of it. He stated that SUS was "a unit completely detached from any organizational branch of the Los Angeles Police Department." Lieutenant Manuel Pena was placed in charge of the daily flow and direction of the investigation. Houghton boasted that Pena "had connections with various intelligence agencies in several countries." Working underneath Pena on what was called the Background/Conspiracy team tasked with investigating Sirhan's past and any potential conspiracy was Sergeant Enrique "Hank" Hernandez. Both Pena and Hernandez had ties to the CIA. Pena had left the police force to work for the Office of Public Safety of the Agency for International Development (AID) in the training and advising of foreign police forces. This office has long served as a cover for the CIA's program of supplying advisors for national police and intelligence services in Southeast Asia and Latin America. Pena's brother casually told a television reporter how proud Manuel was of his services to the CIA. Hernandez had also worked for AID's Office of Public Safety. He boasted on his resume that he had played a key role in "Unified Police Command" training for the CIA in Latin America.[807]

Despite Hernandez being tasked with investigating any potential conspiracies, it is clear from his behavior that his goal was to quell any possible conspiracies. Hernandez was in charge of determining witness credibility and performed questionable lie detector tests.[808] The witnesses themselves did not understand what they had seen and how it related to the bigger picture. Each witness was isolated and made to feel they were mistaken and that no one else was reporting similar information.[809] There was one witness in particular that the police could not ignore and that Hernandez gave special attention to, and that was Sandra Serrano. She had gone on national TV the night of the assassination and recounted her story of seeing the girl in the polka-dot dress run past her on the stairs, excitedly yelling, "We shot him!" The police had to discredit Serrano in the public eye. She is the only witness who had made public her sighting of the girl in the polka-dot dress. Police would not declassify and make available to the public many of the other witness statements for decades. Serrano had no idea that others corroborated her story, and the authorities tried to mess with her mind.

FBI agent Richard Burris pressed Serrano,

> On television … you didn't say anything about seeing a girl and two men going up the fire stairs. You only said you saw a girl and a man coming down. And later, you told the police you saw two men and a girl going up together, and one of them was Sirhan Sirhan. That was the most significant thing you had to tell the police, and yet you didn't say anything about this in your first interview, your interview on television.

A confused Serrano replied, "I can't explain why. You're trying to trick me. You're lying, and you're trying to trick me."[810] Serrano was right. Although she could not recall it in her FBI interview, at the time she gave the TV interview, it was moments after the shooting, and she had not yet seen a picture of the suspect. Hence, what would have been significant to her at that moment was the polka-dot dress girl running down the stairs excitedly

179

yelling, "We shot him!" not that she had earlier been with Sirhan, as Serrano had no idea who Sirhan was at the time nor that he was the suspect. Serrano faced a brutal interrogation by the police and held up better than most would have, but with time, even she wore down. Below is a small excerpt:

Sergeant Hernandez: Nobody told you, "We have shot Kennedy."

Serrano: Yes, somebody told me that, "We have shot Kennedy."

Sergeant Hernandez: No, Sandy.

Serrano: I'm sorry, but that's true. That is true.

Sergeant Hernandez: One of these days, you're gonna be a mother. … You know that you can't live a life of shame, knowing what you're doing right now is wrong.

Serrano: But I seen those people.

Sergeant Hernandez: Sandy, you know that is wrong.

Serrano: I know what I saw. … I remember seeing the girl!

Sergeant Hernandez: No, no. I am talking about what you have told here about seeing a person tell you, "We have shot Kennedy." And that's wrong.

Serrano: That's what she said.

Sergeant Hernandez: No, it isn't Sandy. Please don't.

Serrano: No, that's what she said.

Sergeant Hernandez: Look it, I love this man [RFK].

Serrano: So do I.

Sergeant Hernandez: And you're shaming ...

Serrano: Don't shout at me.

Sergeant Hernandez: ... You don't know, and I don't know if he's a witness right now in this room watching what we're doing in here. Please, in the name of Kennedy ... don't shame his death.

After endless interrogation, Serrano cried, "Why don't you leave me alone!" Hernandez replied, "The only time you will be left alone is when you tell me the truth about what happened outside the staircase."[811] As can be seen, the police treated Serrano like a criminal, not a witness. Hernandez never informed her that other witnesses corroborated her story. Instead, he wore her down until she, to some extent, recanted and admitted she could not remember what she saw or heard, just so she could get away from him. The press then informed the public that Serrano admitted to making up her story. Serrano, to the end of her life, stood by her story. It is worth mentioning that the original district attorney, John Ambrose, whom Serrano spoke to on the night of the assassination, stated about her, "Serrano impressed me as a sincere girl ... not interested in publicity."[812]

So, what happened at the trial, and how was all of this confusing evidence that appears to point to more than one culprit addressed? The simple answer is that it was not addressed. Both the prosecution and the defense completely shunned any notion of conspiracy and avoided any analysis of the evidence as a result. Sirhan was found with the smoking gun. The prosecution wanted to get a conviction and did not want to open a can of worms. Assuming Sirhan was guilty, the defense wanted to save his life and argue his mental capacity. Any conspiracy implied premeditation, therefore the defense felt it hurt their case and their chances of saving Sirhan from the death penalty. As a result, the evidence of the case was essentially completely ignored, and the trial focused mainly on Sirhan's mental state. The public is unaware that the case was essentially never tried before a jury. Only Sirhan's mental state was tried. During jury selection, Sirhan's lawyer, Grant Cooper, told prospective jurors that "there will be no denial of the fact that our client, Sirhan Sirhan, fired the shot that killed Senator Kennedy." Cooper told the prospective jurors that in order for an act to be considered murder, in addition to the act, there must be a requisite state of mind. He was looking for jurors that would be open to assessing mental state in the act of a crime.[813]

Opening arguments were made in the trial on February 13, 1969.[814] During opening statements, another of Sirhan's lawyers, Emile Berman, told the jurors, "There is no doubt ... that he did, in fact, fire the shot that killed Senator Kennedy. The killing was unplanned and undeliberate, impulsive, and without premeditation or malice, totally a product of a sick, obsessed mind and personality. ... Sirhan was out of contact with reality, in a trance in which he had no voluntary control over his will, his judgment, his feelings or his actions."[815]

It is difficult to know why Sirhan's defense team took this approach rather than looking at the evidence to assess whether their client was actually guilty. There are various possibilities. The most innocent is simply that they believed their client was guilty. There is no doubt he fired a gun in Robert Kennedy's direction. Sirhan himself had no memory of the event and could give no clarity to his attorneys. His defense team may have simply figured there was no benefit to exploring the evidence; it would not change the fact that Sirhan fired a gun at Robert Kennedy. And as mentioned previously, any co-conspirators would have made a reduced mental capacity defense harder to argue, as co-conspirators would have implied premeditation. Another possibility is that his defense team was co-opted, at least to some extent. Sirhan had high-priced lawyers who took on the case pro bono. His lead attorney, Grant Cooper, was the object of a federal investigation for allegedly bribing a court clerk for documentation and then lying to a judge about how he had secured the documentation. This bribery case took up much of Cooper's time, which took away from the time he could dedicate to Sirhan's case.[816] Cooper's own legal troubles could have potentially been used to keep him in line regarding what sort of defense he offered to Sirhan. Regardless of why Sirhan's attorneys never looked at the evidence concerning the events of that evening in the pantry, their decision to take at face value that Sirhan had killed Robert Kennedy ultimately caused great harm to Sirhan and to any chance at justice for Robert Kennedy. Sirhan likely would have been better off with a public defender. It is understandable why they thought he was guilty and why they did not want to open the can of worms that potential co-conspirators would have brought. However, their decision ensured there would never be an opportunity for truth to come out in this case. It also gave the public the false impression that Sirhan had been convicted based on the evidence. The opening statements, however, make clear that the evidence never came into the picture.

During coroner Thomas Noguchi's brief testimony, the defense had no interest in the details of the autopsy. Sirhan's attorney, Cooper, stated, "Is all this detail necessary? This witness can certainly testify to the cause of death, but I don't think it's necessary to go into the details. I think he can express an opinion that death was due to a gunshot wound."[817] A defense that was dedicated to uncovering the truth would have explained to the jury the drastic differences between the autopsy report and the witness statements. It is unclear if Cooper was even cognizant of these discrepancies. In addition to paying no attention to the autopsy, the defense also paid no attention to the ballistics evidence. The number of bullet holes and the improbability of the official bullet trajectories were never brought up. The defense team was top-heavy with psychologists and psychiatrists but had no expertise in forensics.[818] All witness testimony pointing to the involvement of other parties was ignored.

Much has been made about the fact that Sirhan admitted he killed Robert Kennedy. But it is not wholly accurate to state that Sirhan confessed. Sirhan has always claimed he did not remember. However, he accepted that he killed Kennedy, as everyone told him he did. He did claim in court once that he was guilty, but that outburst was clearly not a genuine confession but rather a desire to stave off embarrassment. His defense counsel wanted to call a couple of young females to the stand that Sirhan had had a crush on to testify to his mental state, and he asked his defense not to out of embarrassment. Sirhan then asked the judge if he could plead guilty. He told the judge that he had killed Robert Kennedy with twenty years of malice aforethought. This means he would have been planning the killing since he was four years old, which is clearly not possible. Sirhan was a young, self-conscious man whose mental well-being was being questioned by his attorneys in a very public atmosphere for the whole world to see.[819]

The defense hired Dr. Bernard Diamond to analyze Sirhan's mental state. Diamond ultimately concluded that Sirhan had been in a hypnotic state when he shot at Robert Kennedy. However, Diamond concluded that Sirhan had hypnotized himself to shoot Kennedy and then to forget he shot Kennedy. Diamond had repeatedly asked Sirhan under hypnosis if anyone had put him into a trance, and Sirhan replied, "No."[820] Diamond did not, however, make a note of the delays in Sirhan's responses when he asked him if anyone had hypnotized him. The term "blocking" is used to describe what happens when a person has a conflict between what they want to do and what a hypnotic command tells them to do. These delays in Sirhan's responses indicate he may have been programmed to answer such questions with a "no."[821] Diamond was also unaware of the physical evidence and witness statements.[822] Had he been aware, would he have come to a different conclusion about who hypnotized Sirhan?

Diamond concluded that Sirhan had also been in a hypnotic trance when he made the repeated writings in his notebook, "RFK must die, RFK must die." Diamond put Sirhan under hypnosis and asked him to write various statements in a notebook. Sirhan wrote in the same repetitive handwriting as had been found in the notebooks at his house. When Diamond asked him who killed Kennedy, Sirhan wrote in his notebook, "Who Killed Kennedy?" Diamond then asked him to answer the question rather than repeat it, and Sirhan wrote, "I don't know. I don't know." Diamond then asked Sirhan if anyone was with him when he shot Kennedy. Sirhan wrote down, "Girl the girl the girl."[823] During one hypnosis session, Diamond instructed Sirhan that when he came out of the trance, and Diamond blew his nose, Sirhan should climb the bars of his prison cell like a monkey. Once out of hypnosis, Sirhan indeed climbed the bars of his cell. When asked why he was climbing the bars, Sirhan replied matter-of-factly, "For exercise."[824]

According to Dr. Herbert Spiegel, a world authority on hypnosis and professor of psychiatry at Columbia University, approximately 80 to 85 percent of the population is susceptible to hypnosis, but to varying degrees. About five to ten percent of people are extremely hypnotizable. Dr. Spiegel felt that Sirhan was on the high side but stated, "The judge would not permit me to examine him at all."[825] Unlike Dr. Diamond, Dr. Spiegel felt others had hypnotized Sirhan. He thought that "one senior programmer and many accessories" were involved. The girl in the polka-dot dress would have been an accessory. Dr. Spiegel stated that he believed that the whole project was "very carefully designed by people who were expert in brainwashing victims … finding him, training him, then having this man and woman develop a comradeship with him so they got used to the idea of being together; and placing him there in the right spot, with a gun to use, as instructed."[826]

When asked at his trial what he thought of John F. Kennedy, Sirhan replied,

> I loved him, sir. More than any American could have. … He was working, sir, with the leaders of the Arab government, the Arab countries, to bring a solution, sir, to the Palestinian refugee problem, and he promised these Arab leaders that he would do his utmost and his best to force or to put some pressure on Israel, sir,

to comply with the 1948 United Nations Resolution, sir; to either repatriate those Arab refugees or give them back, give them the right to return to their homes. And when he was killed, sir, that never happened.[827]

The jury convicted Sirhan, and he was given the death penalty, which was later commuted to life in prison when California changed its death penalty law.[828] Ultimately, the defense argument that Sirhan killed Robert Kennedy but did so after hypnotizing himself was too much to take in. Had the jury been given the evidence of the case, they may very well have rendered a different verdict. But no one had mentioned to them that the evidence strongly implied that someone else fired the fatal bullets at Kennedy and that it was not certain that Sirhan fired any bullets at all. No one mentioned that a young female, whose own behavior was suspicious, accompanied him. Had the jury understood this, and had it been explained to them that perhaps someone else hypnotized Sirhan, would the case have had a different outcome? Regardless, if Robert Kennedy's assassination was indeed an intelligence operation, that would have been difficult for a jury of laypersons to understand and comprehend. Schools do not teach the inner workings of intelligence operations. It would have required an incredibly specialized and brave team of attorneys to properly investigate and explain the case to jurors.

Those who supported the official thesis of Sirhan's guilt experienced career growth as a result of the case, and those who did not encountered difficulties. Sergeant Hernandez was promoted to lieutenant a month after getting Sandra Serrano to back off her story about the girl in the polka-dot dress.[829] Sirhan's attorney Grant Cooper received only a mild reprimand in his bribery case, receiving a $1,000 fine. The *LA Times* wrote, "It was the mildest form of discipline the court could impose. Other choices available were disbarment and suspension."[830] DeWayne Wolfer was appointed as chief forensic chemist of the Los Angeles Police Department, the director of the entire crime laboratory.[831]

The coroner, Dr. Thomas Noguchi, faced tremendous attacks because of his autopsy report. Lin Hollinger, the chief administrative officer of the county coroner's office, tried to transfer Noguchi to another hospital. When Noguchi refused, Hollinger demanded his resignation, threatening him with charges he was ready to file against him. Noguchi described the smear campaign against him as "perhaps the most lurid ever brought against a public servant." He stated, "The implication was that I was mentally disturbed—crazy." Hollinger fired Noguchi and filed charges against him. Former chairman of the pathology section of the American Academy of Forensic Sciences, Dr. William Eckert, testified in Noguchi's defense, stating that the RFK autopsy was "probably the best, most thorough and most minutely handled forensic case I've ever seen." Noguchi was ultimately cleared of all charges and reinstated.[832]

On May 23, 1969, a month after Sirhan's trial had ended, an article was published in the *Los Angeles Free Press*, "Ten Shots from an Eight-Shot Revolver." This was the first public mention of more shots fired in the pantry than could have been held by Sirhan's gun. The article did not receive much attention, but three weeks later, the police destroyed the pantry doorframes and ceiling tiles.[833]

At Sirhan's trial, DeWayne Wolfer had claimed that he had made a match between all the victims' bullets and those test-fired from Sirhan's gun. However, he offered no supporting evidence for his statement. It was later uncovered that the gun that Wolfer used to test-fire the bullets was not Sirhan's gun. In 1975 a judge ordered an independent panel to examine the Sirhan firearms evidence. The panel was requested to examine the gun and bullets but was not to investigate bullet trajectories, eyewitness data, or the issue of possible extra bullets. After two weeks of analysis, the panel issued a statement that it could not be concluded that the victim bullets were fired by Sirhan's gun. It stated, "The reasons for this are that there are insufficient corresponding individual characteristics to make an identification." The panel also concluded that the evidence was not sufficient to indicate whether the three victim bullets examined came from more than one gun. The media misinterpreted these findings and reported that the panel concluded that the three victim bullets, including one from RFK, came from only one gun. As a result, panelist Lowell Bradford issued the following clarification:

> The findings of the firearms examiners is [sic] being improperly interpreted by the news media. 1.) The examiners found that the Sirhan gun cannot be identified with the bullets from the crime scene. 2.) The firearms evidence does not in and of itself establish a basis for a two-gun proposition; likewise, this same proposition, on a basis of other evidence, is not precluded either.[834]

In later years, Sirhan's new attorney, William Pepper, approached Dr. Daniel P. Brown, a professor of psychology at Harvard Medical School who had written four books on hypnosis and was an expert in the field. Pepper asked Brown to help Sirhan recover his memory. Over a period of five years, Dr. Brown interviewed and tested Sirhan on sixteen different occasions for a total of more than ninety hours. Brown stated, "I've hypnotized thousands of people over a 40-year professional career. Mr. Sirhan is one of the most hypnotizable individuals I've ever met. He is also exactly the type of person who could have been induced by others to engage in uncharacteristic action for which he would subsequently become amnesiac." While he was not able to recover Sirhan's memory in full, he was able to recover pieces of his memory through hypnosis. Dr. Brown stated that he believed the woman in the polka-dot dress was Sirhan's handler, and it was "her cue, a pinch on the arm, that sent Sirhan forward with his gun to shoot at Robert Kennedy." Witness statements corroborate this recovered memory. Vincent DiPierro had told police that it looked like the girl in the polka-dot dress was holding Sirhan immediately before the shooting.

Dr. Brown was also able to recover a memory of Sirhan being in some sort of hospital for two weeks and a memory of being brought to a gun firing range and taught to shoot on command. According to Sirhan's recovered memory through the diligent work of Dr. Brown, after the girl had pinched Sirhan, he entered "range mode" and believed he was back at the firing range shooting at a target and not at Robert Kennedy. Dr. Brown concluded:

> The tapes of his police interviews the night of the murder and the morning after appear to show a calm, reflective person with no knowledge that he had done something horrific. He had never done a violent thing in his life. Had no political or religious affiliations that might have led him to kill. ... In my opinion, Sirhan was trained through coercive persuasion to serve as a distractor, so that a second shooter could render the fatal shot.[835]

Is there any evidence as to who may have hypnotized Sirhan? A key suspect is Dr. William J. Bryan. Bryan called into a show on Culver City, California's KABC radio within hours of the assassination, before police had even identified Sirhan, and suggested the suspect had been hypnotized.[836] This was a strange observation to make, given no one knew anything about the murder at this point. Two prostitutes who regularly serviced Bryan claimed he had told them that he hypnotized Sirhan. Bryan had hypnotized Bryan Desalvo, the "Boston Strangler." In his notebook, Sirhan had written "Salvo Di Di Salvo Die S Salvo," and "DieSovo." Sirhan did not recognize what these writings meant.[837] Bryan told prostitutes that he worked for the CIA, but there is no documented evidence that he did.[838] In an interview on LA's KNX radio in 1972, Bryan claimed to be the "chief of all medical survival training for the United States Air Force during the Korean War ... which meant the brainwashing section." In a later interview, he stated, "You can brainwash a person to do just about anything."[839] The CIA had experimented in the 1950s extensively with both hypnosis and drugs as tools to control an individual's behavior.[840]

Similarly, the Mossad had also experimented with hypnosis. In his book *Rise and Kill First: The Secret History of Israel's Targeted Assassinations*, Israeli journalist Ronen Bergman revealed that in May 1968, the Israeli Intelligence

(AMAN) approved an assassination attempt on Yasser Arafat that entailed hypnotizing a Palestinian to shoot Arafat. Navy psychologist Binyamin Shalit proposed the idea. He claimed that "if he was given a Palestinian prisoner—one of thousands in Israeli jails—with the right characteristics, he could brainwash and hypnotize him into becoming a programmed killer." A twenty-eight-year-old Palestinian was selected, but the operation failed. However, it does show that Israel was experimenting with assassination methods in the spring of 1968 that involved using a hypnotized Palestinian shooting at the desired target.[841]

The next logical question to ask is, if Sirhan was not a lone assassin, then who orchestrated the murder? Some links, albeit tenuous, may give insight into the higher-level players who participated in the crime. As previously mentioned, the Special Unit Senator investigation team at LAPD had ties to the CIA. Sirhan's attorneys were, to at least some extent, tied to organized crime figures. Lead defense attorney Grant Cooper's bribery case was a result of his defense of Maurice Friedman in the Friars Club scandal. Friedman and four others had been charged in federal court with a five-year conspiracy to cheat wealthy members of the exclusive Beverly Hills Friars Club. They had rigged gin rummy games by sending signals to certain players from peepholes in the ceiling. One of the co-defendants was mobster Johnny Roselli. Years later, Roselli testified that the CIA had contacted him to oversee an assassination attempt on Castro. When Cooper took on Sirhan's case, he asked attorney Russell Parsons to take the lead until he completed his work on the Friars Club case. Parsons himself had defended members of the mob, including Mickey Cohen's henchmen, the Sica brothers.[842] These potential mob connections do not mean organized crime figures compromised Sirhan's lawyers, but they do raise the possibility.

In 1973, security guard Thane Eugene Cesar was hired by Hughes Aircraft Company, where he worked for seven years. Hughes Aircraft had close connections to the CIA.[843] Robert Maheu was Howard Hughes' right-hand man and acted as a liaison between the CIA, Johnny Roselli, and the Chicago mob during attempts to assassinate Castro.[844] Maheu, on behalf of Howard Hughes, offered shooting victim Paul Schrade a place at his ranch in Las Vegas to stay and recover from his head wound, an offer Schrade accepted.[845]

James Jesus Angleton, CIA chief of counterintelligence and head of the Israeli desk at the CIA, spoke at Hughes' small funeral service after his passing.[846] After Angleton retired, Robert Kennedy's gruesome color autopsy photos were found in his personal safe.[847] Why was Angleton, a man whose name is all over the JFK assassination, holding onto autopsy photos of Robert Kennedy?

It is difficult to know precisely what happened on that fateful night in the pantry. Based on the evidence, it is not unreasonable to formulate the hypothesis that Sirhan was merely a distractor. It appears he was accompanied that evening by a young woman in a white dress with black polka dots. The young woman pinched him as Robert Kennedy approached, causing Sirhan to go into "range mode" and start firing what were possibly, and perhaps likely, blanks at Robert Kennedy. As Sirhan fired and attracted the bulk of the attention on himself, several others committed the crime. It appears a man was standing on the table shooting downwards to account for the random firing of Sirhan. If Sirhan was firing blanks, then someone else nearby would have to have been firing real bullets. Standing on a table would place this man out of the peripheral vision of most witnesses. At this same time, it appears that a man, likely security guard Cesar, fired at the back and right shoulder area of Robert Kennedy. Cesar was in a perfect position to do so without being seen by others. Multiple witnesses saw him with his gun pulled after the fact, and one claimed he was pointing the weapon downwards at Robert Kennedy instead of at Sirhan as one would expect. It appears that possibly the fatal headshot did not come from Cesar but rather came from a man near him in a white busboy jacket. Had Cesar aimed his gun at Kennedy's head, he would have exposed his arm and would likely have been seen by at least one witness with his gun pointed at Kennedy's head. No witness saw this, but a few saw a man in a white busboy jacket pointing at Kennedy's head. They did not see a gun in the busboy's hand, but they had the distinct impression that he was shooting at Kennedy. Or did perhaps Cesar fire the fatal head shot as he was pulling Kennedy down? This he could have done without being noticed. Witnesses were inconsistent in how many shots they heard, but many described the sounds as firecrackers, happening in rapid succession, likely too quickly for a single gunman. It is also possible that one or more shooters used a silencer on his weapon. As everyone's attention was on Sirhan, the others quickly escaped the scene. It all happened in a matter of seconds. While we do not know definitively that this is what happened, it is a reasonable hypothesis based on the evidence and witness statements. However, even this hypothesis does not wholly fit the evidence. According to her medical report, a bullet struck victim Evans just below the hairline of her forehead and then traveled upward to just above the hairline. However, Evans stated she was bending downwards to retrieve her shoe when she was hit, so it is unclear how she could have been hit at an upward angle by anyone, let alone a man standing on a table. It is possible the bullet may have struck something else first and ricocheted before it hit her. She had no exit wound, which supports this possibility.[848] At the very least, the evidence calls for a thorough and genuine investigation.

If the interests that murdered John Kennedy also murdered Robert Kennedy, it would make sense that those interests wanted to send someone to prison for the murder after all the unanswered questions the death of Lee Harvey Oswald left behind. The crime appears to have been the action of sophisticated actors—a magic trick, indeed. Sirhan prosecutor John Howard stated, "If he isn't guilty, it's the sweetest frame in the world."[849]

8

New Investigations and Continuing Cover-ups

Those fellows on the Warren Commission were dead wrong. There's no way in the world that one man could have shot up Jack Kennedy that way. – Senator Russell Long

Speculation regarding John F. Kennedy's assassination and Oswald's role in it continued after the Warren Commission issued its report. Despite the commission's hope that the report would "lay the dust" and serve as the definitive word on the assassination, many refused to accept it.

In the late 1960s, New Orleans District Attorney Jim Garrison shook things up when he charged Clay Shaw, director of the International Trade Mart in New Orleans, with conspiracy to murder John F. Kennedy. On the afternoon of the assassination, Guy Banister was drinking heavily at a bar with Jack Martin, a hanger-on at Banister's office. Banister was the former FBI man who had the office at 544 Camp Street that Oswald had been hanging around in the summer of 1963. After Banister and Martin returned to Banister's office, the two got into a heated argument. During this argument, Martin informed Banister that he had not forgotten who had been going in and out of his office that past summer. This comment enraged Banister and caused him to whip out his .357 Magnum pistol and hit Martin over the head with it. Martin was then taken to the hospital by a police car. Within a day or so, Jack Martin then confided to a friend his suspicion that David Ferrie, another frequent visitor of Banister's and an associate of Oswald's, had driven to Dallas on the day of the assassination to serve as a "getaway" pilot for the assassins. As news spread in the media about Oswald's summer in New Orleans, Garrison felt it was his duty to check into any possible associates of Oswald's in the city. He quickly became aware that Oswald had spent time with David Ferrie that summer. Soon after Ferrie's name came up, one of Garrison's assistant DAs, Herman Kohlman, learned that Ferrie had made a trip to Texas on the day of the assassination. His source was the man Jack Martin had confided in after being pistol-whipped by Banister. Garrison then sent some of his investigators to Ferrie's apartment and found two men waiting there for Ferrie to return. They stated he had left for Texas in his car about an hour after the assassination. Others who had seen Ferrie still in New Orleans around midday verified that timing.

The timing confirmed to Garrison that Ferrie probably left for Texas not to serve as a getaway pilot but for another reason. However, he still felt that reason might have been related to the assassination. When Ferrie returned to New Orleans on Monday morning, November 25, Garrison brought him into his office for questioning. Ferrie denied knowing Oswald but admitted he drove to Houston early Friday afternoon, the day of the assassination. When Garrison asked him why he drove to Houston after the assassination, Ferrie replied that it was to go ice skating. Garrison then asked him why he took a long drive through a heavy thunderstorm to go ice skating, and Ferrie had no reply. Later, Garrison would learn that Ferrie did go to an ice-skating rink, but he never put on skates; he just stood by a pay phone, making and receiving calls. Garrison decided to hand over Ferrie to the FBI for questioning, assuming the FBI would investigate thoroughly. The FBI, however, quickly released Ferrie. Garrison accepted the FBI's decision, still having much trust in the institution then.[850]

For most of the next three years, Garrison assumed the Warren Commission had gotten it right. Then one day in the fall of 1966, he had a chance encounter with Russell Long, a United States senator from Louisiana. Long told Garrison, "Those fellows on the Warren Commission were dead wrong. There's no way in the world that one man could have shot up Jack Kennedy that way." As a result of this conversation, Garrison ordered a copy of the Warren Commission volumes. Upon reading them, he commented, "The number of promising leads that were never followed up offended my prosecutorial sensibility. And, perhaps worst of all, the conclusions in the report seemed to be based on an appallingly selective reading of the evidence, ignoring credible testimony from literally dozens of witnesses." Garrison was particularly shocked by the lack of explanation for the "Secret Service" men in Dealey Plaza shortly after the assassination when all Secret Service agents were accounted for elsewhere and by the decision by police not to record their interrogations of Oswald. He was further appalled at how quickly the FBI had come to a conclusion as to what happened that day.[851]

After reading through the Warren Commission volumes, Garrison began quietly investigating Oswald's activities in New Orleans during the summer of 1963 and the individuals that Oswald had associated with. Unfortunately, Banister had passed away in 1964, so Garrison could not question him. However, Garrison did manage to get the title cards to Banister's files, and in them were included: American Central Intelligence Agency, Civil Rights Program of JFK, Fair Play for Cuba Committee, International Trade Mart, and Shaw.[852] In late 1966, Garrison began surveilling Ferrie.[853]

Though Garrison tried to keep his investigation quiet, on February 17, 1967, the *New Orleans States-Item* published an article titled, "DA Here Launches Full JFK Death Plot Probe." Upon seeing this article, Ferrie contacted Garrison's chief investigator, Louis Ivon, and scolded him, "You know what this news story does to me, don't you? I'm a dead man. From here on, believe me, I'm a dead man." Ferrie then tried to denounce Garrison to the press, calling his inquiry a "big joke." Despite publicly attacking Garrison, Ferrie reached out to Ivon again on February 19, telling him he was fearful for his life. Ivon then checked Ferrie into a hotel room under an assumed name. According to Ivon, Ferrie now admitted to him that he had worked for the CIA and knew Oswald. He also admitted that he knew Clay Shaw and that Shaw had also worked for the CIA. He added that Shaw despised Kennedy. However, Ferrie did not admit to any involvement in the assassination. A few days later, on the morning of February 22, 1967, Ferrie was found dead in his apartment with two typed but unsigned suicide notes. On February 28, the coroner ruled that Ferrie had died of natural causes, an aneurysm. Garrison was skeptical of the coroner's report. The coroner may have wanted to be cautious with his conclusion given the heavy publicity surrounding Ferrie's death.[854]

On March 1, 1967, Garrison obtained a warrant for Clay Shaw's arrest and a search of his house. As a routine question, the police officer booking Shaw, Aloysius Habighorst, asked him if he used any aliases, and Shaw replied, "Clay Bertrand." Habighorst noted the alias on the booking form. Shaw's admission to use of this alias is crucial because it is under this alias that he called attorney Dean Andrews to represent Oswald after the assassination. One of the more interesting items found in Shaw's home was his address book. Among the names in his address book was Lee Odom, P.O. Box 19106, Dallas, Texas. Lee Harvey Oswald had this same post office box number in his address book. Shaw's attorneys explained that Odom had once met Shaw to discuss the possibility of promoting a bullfight in New Orleans. Garrison did not buy this explanation, as Shaw had never participated in any promotion before. Further, although Oswald had the post office box number written in his address book, Dallas had not issued a post office box number that high as of 1963, so Garrison could find no explanation for why it was in Oswald's address book. Shaw's entire address book consisted of addresses and phone numbers, with one exception. On one of the unused pages, written in Shaw's handwriting, were the words "Oct" and "Nov," and then, after an indecipherable scribble, was written the word "Dallas."

Upon the announcement of Shaw's arrest, US Attorney General Ramsey Clark announced that the federal government had already exonerated Shaw from any involvement in the Kennedy assassination. One reporter asked Clark if Shaw had been "checked out and found clear?" Clark replied, "Yes, that's right." The question to be asked then is why did the FBI have any reason to investigate Shaw in the first place? Clark quickly realized his mistake and labeled his previous statement as "erroneous."[855]

Shortly after arresting Shaw, Garrison filed a motion for a preliminary hearing. Typically, defense attorneys, not prosecutors, request a preliminary hearing. The purpose of such a hearing is to force the district attorney to demonstrate that there is solid enough evidence to bring the defendant to trial. The procedure was created to prevent prosecutors from sending defendants to trial over frivolous charges. Garrison said he filed the motion out of fairness to Shaw, given the seriousness of the charges he was levying against him. Shaw's four-day preliminary hearing began on March 14, 1967.[856] At the end of the preliminary hearing, on March 17, the three-judge panel ordered Clay Shaw to be held for jury trial.[857]

In an ideal world, Garrison would have waited longer before arresting Shaw, until he had built a stronger case. But with Ferrie now gone, and with Garrison knowing his office was to some extent infiltrated, he felt he could not hold off.[858]

At a September 20, 1967, CIA meeting, labeled the first meeting of the "Garrison Group," Ray Rocca, CIA Counterintelligence Chief James Angleton's chief lieutenant, stated that he felt that Garrison would indeed obtain a conviction if the CIA did not intervene.[859] It was suggested that the CIA use their press contacts to plant negative stories about Garrison in the press.[860] Shaw's lawyers told the Justice Department that if Shaw were convicted then the Warren Commission would be discredited and the American government would be undermined in the eyes of the rest of the world.[861]

It was later revealed by the House Select Committee on Assassinations through CIA documents that there were nine undercover agents at one time or another in Garrison's office. One infiltrator, William Gurvich, later worked for Shaw's defense. Another, Gordon Novel, admitted to often speaking with former CIA Director and Warren Commission member Allen Dulles about the Garrison probe and sent letters to then CIA Director Richard Helms regarding Garrison.[862] In addition to his office being infiltrated, Garrison was also heavily battered by the press. Some of the most egregious attacks came from Walter Sheridan and NBC. Indeed, Novel did paid work against Garrison for Sheridan and NBC.[863] Sheridan had earlier worked for the Office of Naval Intelligence and then the counterintelligence unit at the National Security Agency (NSA). It appears Sheridan was tipping off James Angleton, the CIA's chief of counterintelligence, regarding Garrison's case. The NBC president at the time was Robert Sarnoff, son of the TV network's founder and then chairman, David Sarnoff.[864] In the 1950s, David had offered his services to Israeli Prime Minister David Ben-Gurion in helping Israel in general and its military in particular, to establish its own national broadcasting system. In 1963, Sarnoff contributed to the book *The Mission of Israel*, a homage to Israel that included articles, statements, and speeches by many dedicated to the nation.[865] Sarnoff was also a member of the Rockefeller Brothers Fund panel and urged the United States to fight a more aggressive battle of psychological warfare against the Soviet Union. Sarnoff's company, Radio Corporation of America, served as a large part of the technological core of the NSA, and his son, Robert, worked in the broadcast arm of the Office of Strategic Services (OSS), the precursor to the CIA, during World War II.[866]

The media smear campaign against Garrison gave cover to governors and judges to deny Garrison his extradition and subpoena requests, weakening his case.[867] Despite all the obstacles, the case of *State of Louisiana v Clay Shaw* came to trial on January 29, 1969.[868] In addition to the media smear campaign and the infiltration of his investigation by the intelligence community, Garrison also had to deal with the prejudice of potential jurors by prominent figures. Back in 1967, Earl Warren, the figurative head of the Warren Commission, declared publicly that "absolutely nothing" that Garrison had uncovered contradicted the findings of the Warren Commission and that not "one fact" refuted the commission's claim that Lee Harvey Oswald was the lone assassin. Garrison complained that Warren's statement was "wholly inappropriate" and that "no witness was going to be eager, in front of all the world, to make the Chief Justice appear to be a liar, or at least mistaken."[869] In further attempts to prejudice jurors, Attorney General Ramsey Clark convened a panel of four experts to review the autopsy photos and x-rays. The panel met in February of 1968 and did less than a week of work. Clark then held onto the results for almost a year. In early 1969, on the eve of Garrison's trial, two days before jury selection, Clark announced that this panel had endorsed the findings of the Warren Report.[870] Jury selection took a few weeks, and the trial began in earnest on February 6, 1969. James Angleton performed background checks on all the jurors and some of the witnesses as well.[871]

Garrison began the trial by calling the witnesses from Clinton, Louisiana. These are the witnesses who saw Shaw, Ferrie, and Oswald wait all day as Oswald tried to register as a voter in the parish. They established a connection between the three men. Garrison then called two witnesses from the Louisiana State Hospital, where Oswald hoped to get employment. They testified that Oswald did come in and fill out an employment application.[872] Next, Garrison called Vernon Bundy. Bundy testified that he had seen Shaw and Oswald together at Lake Pontchartrain. Bundy had been a drug addict, which the defense used to question his credibility. He testified that he saw Shaw speak with Oswald and then hand him some money, and when Oswald placed his hand into his pockets, one of his pro-Castro leaflets fell out, after which Bundy used the paper as wrapping for his heroin kit. When questioned if he could have been mistaken about his identification of Shaw, Bundy asked if Shaw could walk towards him in the courtroom. The judge, perplexed, said OK. Shaw walked with an almost imperceptible limp. Bundy then testified, "See, that is how I am certain he is the person I saw. He walks with the same limp."[873]

After a decent start, Garrison then brought on a witness that turned out to be a disaster for him. Charles Spiesel was a New York accountant, and unlike many other witnesses, Garrison did not find him; instead, Spiesel reached out to him. Spiesel testified that he had been visiting his daughter in New Orleans when he met Ferrie at a bar. The two then went to see Clay Shaw. Ferrie, drinking alcohol, then started talking about a possible Kennedy assassination. Spiesel attributed Ferrie's comments to the alcohol. Once the cross-examination began, Garrison realized he had been had. The defense attorney, Irvin Dymond, asked Spiesel if he had tried to sell his story to the media. Spiesel admitted he had contacted CBS and asked them for money. Dymond then asked Spiesel if he had noticed anything unusual about Ferrie's appearance. Spiesel replied, "No." He said the only thing unusual about his appearance was his fairly thin eyebrows. Ferrie, however, was hairless and always wore a wig and pasted bushy eyebrows above his eyes. Dymond then asked Spiesel if he had ever been hypnotized, and Spiesel replied that he had been hypnotized many times. Dymond then asked him if he had fingerprinted his daughter in New York before she left for New Orleans and again when she returned. Spiesel replied that he had been hypnotized so often that he wanted to be sure it was her when she returned. Garrison recalled that at this moment, he was "swept by a feeling of nausea."[874]

Garrison tried to recover by calling Perry Russo to the stand. Russo testified that Ferrie had often talked about assassinating Kennedy. He assumed it was just talk at the time and did not think much of it until Garrison came out with his investigation. He also testified to one particular encounter at a party in the months prior to the assassination. Shaw and Ferrie were there, and an Oswald look-alike who referred to himself as "Leon." Russo testified that they were talking about the assassination of Castro, and then the conversation turned to the assassination of Kennedy. Russo said he went in and out of the room and did not hear the full conversation. Russo testified that Shaw stated he would be on the West Coast when it happened, and Ferrie said he would be at Southeastern Louisiana University. Indeed, on the day of the assassination, Shaw was in California, and Ferrie did stop at Southeastern Louisiana University on his way back from Texas.[875]

Garrison then called various witnesses who linked the "Bertrand" alias to Shaw to support his argument that Clay Shaw had called attorney Dean Andrews after the assassination asking him to represent Oswald. Garrison also called various witnesses to bolster his claim that the assassination was committed by multiple shooters. Those witnesses included individuals who had been in Dealey Plaza at the time of the shooting and forensics experts. Due to the strength of these witnesses, the defense decided to call Doctor Pierre Finck to the stand. Finck was one of the autopsy doctors who performed Kennedy's autopsy at Bethesda. Finck ended up being as much of a disaster for the defense as Spiesel had been for the prosecution. He was fine under direct examination. He repeated the Warren Commission line on the single bullet theory. However, he faltered under cross-examination. The prosecution asked the witness if he dissected the wound that entered the back to see if it exited the neck, a requirement for the single bullet theory to be true. Finck testified he did not dissect the wound. The prosecution then asked him why he did not dissect the wound, and Finck tried to deflect. Indeed, the prosecution had to ask the question eight times before they could get a response. Finck finally replied, "As I recall, I was told not to, but I don't remember by whom."[876] Finck admitted, "You must understand that in those circumstances, there were law enforcement officials, military people with various ranks, and you have to coordinate the operations according to directions."[877] Finck essentially admitted that the autopsy was not in the hands of the doctors but rather in the hands of higher ranked military personnel.

The defense also called Dean Andrews to the stand, who testified that Clay Shaw was not the "Clay Bertrand" who called him and asked him to represent Oswald. However, the jury was not informed that Dean Andrews had previously been found guilty of committing perjury when he gave similar testimony under oath before a grand jury. During the Shaw trial, his conviction was on appeal and could not be referenced. Andrews ultimately lost his appeal.[878] Garrison had taken Andrews to lunch before the grand jury proceedings and informed him that he would charge him with perjury if he did not respond truthfully. According to Garrison, Andrews replied, "Let me sum this up for you real quick. It's as simple as this. If I answer that question you keep asking me, if I give you the name you keep trying to get, then it's goodbye, Dean Andrews; It's bon voyage, Deano. I mean like permanent. I mean like a bullet in my head."[879]

When Andrews was asked at the trial why he gave the name Clay Bertrand to the FBI after he initially received the phone call asking him to represent Oswald, Andrews replied, "It dawned on me that if I revealed the real name, I would bring a lot of heat and a lot of trouble to somebody that it didn't belong to. I fumbled around for a cover name." The prosecution replied, "In other words, you lied to the FBI?" Andrews replied, "No, sir ... I used a cover name." Andrews responded to many questions posed by the prosecution with the following statement, "I decline to answer that question on the ground that it may, might, could, would, or will tend to link me with a chain of circumstances that would incriminate me." Andrews had testified under oath to the Warren Commission that a man named Clay Bertrand had called him after the assassination asking him to represent Oswald. At the Shaw trial, Andrews denied that anyone had asked him to represent Oswald after the murder of Kennedy, contradicting his previous testimony under oath. In his Warren Commission testimony, he stated that because he was ill, he had contacted another man, Monk Zelden, to see if he would be interested in going to Dallas to represent Oswald. At the Shaw trial, when asked why he called Zelden since he was now denying that anyone had asked him to represent Oswald, Andrews replied, "No explanation. ... I would like to be famous too, other than as a perjurer."[880]

After all the testimony had been completed, the jurors rendered their verdict:

not guilty. Alternate juror Bob Burlet commented, "He [Shaw] was definitely involved with Oswald and Ferrie ... maybe the man is guilty, but they didn't prove it in the courtroom though—beyond a reasonable doubt."[881] At the time of the trial, Garrison did not have any evidence of Shaw's links to the CIA nor his links to Permindex and its de-facto head, Louis Bloomfield. Nor did Garrison have any knowledge of John F. Kennedy's intense battle with Israel over its nuclear weapons program, the program that Bloomfield had been financing and that was ultimately saved by Kennedy's removal from office. Had Garrison had evidence of these connections at the time of his trial, would he have gotten a conviction? Maybe. It is difficult to prove that Shaw was a witting participant in the assassination planning. The call made by Shaw to Andrews to seek legal assistance for Oswald after the assassination implies that perhaps he did not know. Same for Ferrie. Oswald's landlady in New Orleans testified that she saw Ferrie at Oswald's apartment shortly after the assassination. Ferrie was looking for his library card, which he thought he had left with Oswald.[882] It is not clear why Ferrie went to Oswald's apartment, whether he was actually looking for the library card or whether he made that up, but had he known about the assassination beforehand would he have not taken care of whatever he was trying to do earlier?

Nevertheless, there is no doubt that both Ferrie and Shaw are suspicious characters. Ferrie did travel to Texas in pouring rain after the assassination and then sat at a pay phone—odd behavior, but not proof of his witting involvement in the assassination. Regardless of whether Shaw and Ferrie were witting participants, Garrison was likely barking up the right tree, even if he had no idea what sat at the top of that tree. Furthermore, had he been able to complete his investigation quietly as he desired, had his extradition and subpoena requests not been denied, had his office not been infiltrated, and had the media not assassinated his character, prejudicing jurors, perhaps he would have had a shot at cracking the case wide open. The fact that Angleton's chief lieutenant, Ray Rocca, believed Shaw would be convicted unless the agency intervened speaks volumes. If for nothing else, Garrison should be given credit for attempting to do what virtually no one else dared: investigate John F. Kennedy's murder and hold those responsible accountable. He also uncovered a wealth of evidence that future researchers have been able to build upon.

While Garrison had shown the Zapruder film to the jurors, the public at the time of the trial had not yet seen it. The American people saw it for the first time on March 6, 1975, when Geraldo Rivera played it on his ABC talk show. Many were shocked because, to the naked eye, it seemed obvious that Kennedy had been shot from the front. The showing of this film, in combination with other government malfeasance that was being exposed during the 1970s, created a public desire for a reinvestigation of the Kennedy assassination. On September 8, 1975, Senator Richard Schweiker introduced a senate resolution calling for a re-opening of the Kennedy case. It took some time for the resolution to progress, but finally, on September 17, 1976, the bill passed, creating the House Select Committee on Assassinations. The committee was to review both the John F. Kennedy and the Martin Luther King assassinations. The Martin Luther King assassination was added to the bill to enlist the aid of the Black Caucus in the House in getting the bill passed.[883] It would have been more appropriate to include the assassination of Robert Kennedy so that the murders of the two brothers could have been investigated together.

While the HSCA was an improvement to the Warren Commission, it was, at the end of the day, still a quite limited investigation. The committee's chief counsel was Robert Blakey, a law professor from Cornell University whose focus was largely on organized crime. As such, Blakey, according to those who worked with him, focused mainly on the Mafia as the potential culprit.[884] Blakey put a two-year time limit on the inquiry, leaving only eighteen months of investigation as Blakey arrived six months in, which basically meant that other government agencies, such as the FBI and CIA, could merely stonewall until the investigation time limit ran out. Blakey replaced the original chief counsel, Richard Sprague, who was pushed out due to his desire to pursue a genuine inquiry.[885]

The HSCA issued its final report on July 17, 1979. The report was forced to concede that "scientific acoustical evidence established a high probability that two gunmen fired at President John F. Kennedy." Blakey had previously been planning to issue a final report in December of 1978 declaring that Oswald acted alone, but last-minute acoustic evidence, which has since been questioned, forced him to delay the report and ultimately issue a statement that the crime was likely a conspiracy.[886] As the report was originally written to put the full blame on Oswald, it still gave support to the single bullet theory and professed that the shot from the front missed.[887] The committee reached this conclusion even though JFK's White House doctor, Admiral George Burkley, wrote a letter to the HSCA, stating that he had information that more than one shooter was involved in Kennedy's assassination. There is no record of Burkley being deposed by the HSCA.[888]

The HSCA version of the single bullet theory differed from the Warren Commission version. The Warren Commission declared that the bullet entered Kennedy at a downward angle (since Oswald was allegedly shooting from the sixth floor); however, the HSCA version declared the bullet entered at a flat or upward angle. The HSCA did this because they had to correct the Warren Commission statement that the bullet entered the back of the neck and admit that it entered the back itself. However, if the bullet entered the back, it could not exit the neck unless it entered at an upward angle. So, by attempting to fix one invalid statement by the Warren Commission (that the bullet entered the neck), they created an even more implausible scenario, that a bullet shot downwards from the sixth floor towards Kennedy's vehicle entered Kennedy's back at an upward angle and then after exiting Kennedy's neck, hit Connally at a downward angle.[889] While the report did not state who was responsible besides Oswald, Blakey publicly declared that he thought it was the mob who assisted Oswald.[890] And while the government had to reluctantly admit to a "probable conspiracy" in the murder of JFK, it was too little too late. They still blamed Oswald. They suggested the conspiracy was minimal.

Furthermore, by 1979, the press had done a thorough trashing of JFK's character, with salacious stories about endless affairs, mob dealings, stolen elections, and Castro assassination attempts. This made it easier for the public to accept that Kennedy had been killed not by powerful forces who desired to change his policies but rather by some angry Mafia men seeking revenge for a mob deal gone bad. Political philosopher Noam Chomsky stated, "Who cares [who killed JFK]. Plenty of people get killed all the time, why does it matter that one of them had to be John F. Kennedy? ... If it happened to be a jealous husband or the Mafia, what difference does it make? It's just taking energy away from serious issues to the ones that don't matter."[891] Media slander had essentially made the JFK assassination irrelevant for many. It is important to note that there is no law protecting the deceased against defamation. So, it was open season on JFK. Nevertheless, despite the character attacks, there were still many in the public who cared about seeking justice for John F. Kennedy's murder. Not everyone believed Blakey's claims of the Mafia assisting Oswald.

A few months before the HSCA issued their report, a bizarre, alleged assassination plot against then-President Jimmy Carter was uncovered and reported in the major papers. In May of 1979, two men, Raymond Lee Harvey and Osvaldo (Spanish for "Oswald") Espionza-Ortiz, were arrested for participating in a plot to assassinate President Carter. As part of the plot, Harvey claimed he was planning to fire blanks from a gun as a distraction while others carried out the assassination. This author does not know what, if anything, these bizarre arrests mean, but thought it was worth mentioning since the two names put together contain the phrase Lee Harvey Oswald, and the claim is that Raymond Lee Harvey planned to shoot blanks as a distraction while the real assassins committed the crime, which many believe is exactly how Robert Kennedy was killed.[892] Raymond also happened to be the first name of the programmed assassin in *The Manchurian Candidate*. Many believe Sirhan was programmed to fire blanks at Robert Kennedy.

Was a message being sent to Carter?

The next big event concerning the JFK assassination was the Oliver Stone film *JFK*, released in 1991. The film chronicled Garrison's investigation into the murder, with some creative license, like any Hollywood film. It brought the JFK assassination back to the forefront and was roundly trashed by the corporate press. However, the film created such an uproar amongst the American public that it propelled Congress to pass the JFK Assassination Records Collection Act of 1992, establishing the Assassination Records Review Board (ARRB). The goal of the ARRB was to collect all government records related to the murder of President Kennedy. It was not an investigatory committee; its only purpose was to gather all available documentation and take the testimony of anyone with relevant information regarding the murder and then prepare the collected information for public release. All records were supposed to have been released by October 26, 2017, but some took longer to release than initially promised. President Donald Trump signed an executive order on January 23, 2025 ordering that a plan for release of all files be formulated and the first file dump occurred on March 18, 2025.[893]

The film identified various parties as potential culprits, including the CIA, the military, the military-industrial complex, the Mafia, and even Lyndon Johnson. It mentioned numerous Kennedy policies, including his desire to end the Cold War and pull out of Vietnam. However, it did not reference John F. Kennedy's intense conflicts with Israel. Nor did it mention Shaw's connection via Permindex to Israel's nuclear weapons program. Little was publicly known about JFK's struggles with Israel at the time Stone made the film, and Stone did mention some of these conflicts in his later 2021 documentary, *JFK Revisited*. The executive producer and financer of the 1991 film was Arnon Milchan, who later admitted to serving as an Israeli spy, buying arms on Israel's behalf, and bolstering its nuclear weapons program. Milchan stated, "I did it for my country, and I'm proud of it." While in Hollywood, he continued his clandestine work and maintained close ties with Israeli leadership. Milchan was recruited in the 1960s by Shimon Peres into the Bureau of Science Liaison, known as the LAKAM. The LAKAM's mission was to secure nuclear materials and technology for Israel's nuclear weapons program "by any means necessary."[894] Shimon Peres was the Israeli deputy minister of defense and chief of its atomic program who lied to JFK's face in the spring of 1963 about Israel's development of nuclear weapons.

Why was someone with very close ties to Israel's nuclear program, a major beneficiary of JFK's assassination, funding a film about the murder, a film that placed the blame on the other beneficiaries? Is it credible to think that Milchan was unaware of the fact that JFK's removal from office saved Israel's nuclear ambitions and perhaps saved Israel itself? Milchan may not have given creative and content input into the film, but in the name of transparency, should he not have revealed this information and disclosed Shaw's ties to Louis Bloomfield and, hence, to Israel's nuclear program? Should he not have disclosed his own intimate relations to that same program? If the public understood Milchan's potential conflicts of interest in financing the film, would they have viewed the movie in the same light? If Israel was involved in the crime, it can be argued that Milchan got a lot of value for his money. The film established an "official" contrarian view of the assassination, one that satisfied the skeptics and kept Israel out of the picture. Whoever the culprit behind the JFK assassination was, it would behoove them to play both sides of the debate—to control not just the narrative, but also the counter-narrative. It would be vital for them to not only promote the "lone-nut" story but also to supply the skeptics with a more believable hypothesis—but, of course, one that kept the culprits safe. Relying solely on the "lone-nut" thesis would not effectively keep skeptics at bay. The film did lead to the creation of the ARRB, which was a great outcome, but is the United States the only country from which files need to be released? A whistleblower of Israel's nuclear weapons program, Mordechai Vanunu, whom Israel jailed for eighteen years for his revelations of the inner workings of Israel's nuclear reactor at Dimona, has publicly claimed that according to "near-certain indications," Israel was involved in the JFK assassination.[895]

While concerned citizens have made tremendous progress over the decades in getting closer to the truth, to this day there has still been no proper investigation into the murder of John F. Kennedy. And to this day, books and articles are published that smear his reputation and skew his policies. It is a sad fact of history that justice is not always served.

As for the Robert Kennedy assassination, Sirhan's lawyers have tried over the years to re-open the case and overturn Sirhan's conviction but have never succeeded. In a recent attempt, they argued for an evidentiary hearing where they could present evidence of Sirhan's "actual innocence." The respondent was the State of California, which submitted a brief signed by the state's attorney general and future United States Vice President Kamala Harris. The State of California said of Sirhan, "He was highly alert, conscious, and not surprised at all about what he had done and about his predicament immediately after the shooting." As a result, the judge denied the request for a hearing.[896]

At a 2016 parole hearing, victim Paul Schrade, who took a bullet to the head that evening but survived, spoke in favor of Sirhan's release: "I know that [Sirhan] did not kill Robert Kennedy. And I'm here because of that. And I wouldn't be here if I wasn't sure of that. I loved Robert Kennedy, and I would not defend somebody who killed him. Kennedy was a man of justice. Justice so far has not been served in this case." After the parole board denied Sirhan parole, Schrade said to him, "I'm sorry, Sirhan. It's my fault. I should have come sooner. I didn't know. I'm sorry, Sirhan."[897]

On December 19, 2017, Robert F. Kennedy Jr. visited Sirhan for three hours, hugged him, and, according to researcher Lisa Pease, told him he knew he had not killed his father and that he considered him to be as much a victim of that night as his father.[898] Sirhan was granted parole in 2021, in part due to statements made by Robert F. Kennedy Jr. and his brother Douglas Kennedy.

Other members of the Kennedy family vehemently opposed Sirhan's parole. California Governor Gavin Newsom overturned the parole board's decision, preventing Sirhan's release.

9

The Son

In the U.S. we pride ourselves on being a country where political change occurs without violence. ... Yet, an examination of history reveals a persistent thread of convenient tragedy linked to the turning points of the fates of nations. – Oliver Stone

There has been public speculation for decades about a "Kennedy curse." John F. Kennedy and Robert F. Kennedy were not the only members of the family to suffer young and tragic deaths. John F. Kennedy's son and namesake, John F. Kennedy Jr., also passed away at far too young an age. He perished in a terrible plane crash on July 16, 1999, at the youthful age of thirty-eight. The crash was officially ruled an accident. There is certainly a great possibility that it was just that, an accident; however, given the murder of his father and uncle, it is worth at least exploring the possibility of foul play.

John F. Kennedy Jr. was perhaps the last person with any realistic chance of obtaining justice for his father's murder. Likely the only platform from which he could have enforced a rigorous investigation was the presidency of the United States. The question then becomes, were there any indications that he was interested in his father's murder and any signs of him having political aspirations? If the answer to both questions can be determined as yes, then that establishes a potential motive for foul play. It would be logical that any assassination attempt would occur before JFK Jr. made public his aspirations of reaching the presidency and bringing his father's murderers to justice. After the assassination of JFK's younger brother on his road to the presidency, the murder of JFK's son on that same road would likely have been too much for Americans to swallow. Thus, it is not illogical to assume that, were there a desire to prevent JFK Jr. from reaching a position where he could expose his father's murderers, then that desire would need to be acted upon at the point of any inkling of action on JFK Jr.'s part.

As such, it is important to include JFK Jr. in any analysis of the Kennedy murders. If it can be shown that the entities responsible for JFK's murder had a motive to murder his son and that, indeed, the plane crash was not an accident, that evidence would imply that such entities, if responsible for the plane crash, had power that reached across generations. This would thus limit the suspect list. For example, the power of Lee Harvey Oswald was clearly not multi-generational. While the evidence of foul play in JFK Jr.'s plane crash may not be strong, it is still worth exploring.

JFK Jr. was born on November 25, 1960, just a few weeks after his father had been elected president of the United States. Thus, Americans watched him grow from his first day on Earth. According to his uncle Ted Kennedy, "The whole world knew his name before he did."[899] John was his father's delightful sidekick and was adored by the American public. From a young age, he was fascinated with airplanes and helicopters. Anytime JFK had to leave the White House and take the helicopter to Andrew's Airforce Base, where the presidential plane awaited him, JFK Jr. wanted to take the helicopter ride with him. When he heard the helicopter return, he would excitedly yell, "Daddy's hebrecop!"[900] It is difficult to know how much John understood about his father's death, which happened just three days short of John's third birthday. He told his nanny in the months after the assassination, "My poor mommy's crying ... because my daddy's gone away."[901] He asked his nanny if his father took his airplane with him to heaven. When she replied, "Yes," he pondered, "I wonder when he's coming back."[902] As John grew older, his mother tearfully asked a priest, "Maybe, sometime, you will get the chance to answer the question that comes to John: 'Why did they kill him?'"[903]

Jackie Kennedy put great effort into making sure her son knew his father. She surrounded him with people who were close to JFK. In 1972 she asked JFK's press secretary, Pierre Salinger, to spend a month with her and her children and teach them daily what their father did. According to author Christopher Anderson, "Whenever another child was visiting, [John] would inevitably ask, 'Would you like to hear my father?' Then he turned towards a small stack of records and selected one to play."[904] A high school girlfriend of John's, Meg Azzoni, wrote, "His heartfelt quest was to expose and bring to trial who killed his father and who covered it up."[905] JFK Jr. gave his first private airplane the registration number N529JK, after his father's birthday, May 29, and his father's initials. He gave his second airplane, the one he died in, the registration number N9253N, which included his father's birthday written in reverse. He may have included the number three to reflect that he attended his father's funeral on his third birthday. Perhaps it was his desire to return to that day and reverse it. The meaning of the registration number is pure speculation on the author's part.

In 1995, after working several years in the New York district attorney's office, JFK Jr. founded *George*, a magazine mixing popular culture and politics. It was non-partisan and featured writers from various political persuasions. According to Azzoni, *George* was "a presidential platform magazine."[906] Friend Robert Littell expressed similar views; he felt the magazine "was an opportunity for John to build a platform from which he might possibly move into political life."[907] Indeed, John's father had dabbled in journalism before running for Congress in 1946.

On the surface, the magazine had a certain air of superficiality, displaying endless celebrities on its covers. But within its pages, it did not shy away from covering controversial subjects avoided by other publishing outlets.

Nor did the magazine shy away from John's own family, though he did address rumors surrounding his father in his own way. In one issue, John placed a young Drew Barrymore posing as Marilyn Monroe on the cover. Some wondered why John chose a cover that was seemingly humiliating to his mother. Author Steven Gillon wrote, "The reality ... was that John never believed that his father had an affair with Monroe. He, therefore, did not view the cover as an attempt to play with the truth but rather to toy with public perceptions of his family."[908]

John wanted articles that were unconventional. According to editor Ned Martel, John found articles in other political magazines "tedious and overbaked."[909] In October 1996, John sat down for an interview with the controversial Louis Farrakhan of the Nation of Islam.[910] In December 1996, *George* covered TWA flight 800, which had exploded on July 17, 1996, shortly after taking off from JFK International Airport. The National Transportation Safety Board (NTSB) concluded that the plane crashed due to a short-circuit near the central fuel tank; however, *George* explored the possibility of foul play.[911] JFK's press secretary, Pierre Salinger, the man whom Jackie had asked to teach her children about their father, publicly stated that he believed a missile had downed the plane.[912]

In March 1997, JFK Jr. published an article written by the mother of Yigal Amir, who had assassinated Israeli Prime Minister Yitzhak Rabin in November 1995. Many of his top editors cautioned him not to publish the story, but John went against their advice. Amir's mother wrote that her son belonged to a right-wing conspiracy within the Israeli government that opposed Rabin's peace overtures to the Palestinians. She stated that members of the Israeli secret service manipulated her son into killing Rabin. John hired investigators in Israel and fact-checked the story for months before agreeing to publish it. Rabin's widow responded with harsh remarks towards JFK Jr., "I would expect John Kennedy, who lost his father to an assassin's bullet when he was a mere child and grew up in the shadow of that horrible tragedy, to adopt a higher moral standard in his paper."[913]

Nitsana Darshan-Leitner, an attorney for the Amir family, stated about JFK Jr.'s interest in the Rabin case, "He called me several times, and said he personally felt a type of connection because of his father's case. Because of the passage of time since his father's assassination, he said the family could not resolve the questions surrounding it. He encouraged the Amir family to look further into the Rabin case, as quickly as possible, to see if there was possibly [something amiss]."[914] Ironically, Rabin's widow wrote in a book chronicling her life with her husband that she and Rabin had learned about JFK's 1963 assassination upon returning to Tel Aviv from a trip across the United States. She wrote that they had just been in Dallas "hours before."[915] It should be noted that everyone and their mother visited the Dallas area in the weeks leading up to the assassination—from Allen Dulles to George Bush to Richard Nixon—giving much fodder for speculation.

In the fall of 1997 JFK Jr. traveled to Cuba to interview Fidel Castro.[916] In October 1998, JFK Jr. published an article by Oliver Stone titled "Our Counterfeit History." He introduced it on the cover as "Paranoid and Proud of it." In the article, Stone wrote:

> In the U.S. we pride ourselves on being a country where political change occurs without violence—through a peaceful democratic process. ... The deaths of our leaders are tragic acts of faith, accidents, the work of unbalanced madmen, who, once destroyed, can no longer harm us. In such a view, tragedy becomes a random event, an act of God that could not have been prevented. ... Yet, an examination of history reveals a persistent thread of convenient tragedy linked to the turning points of the fates of nations. And in the smoke of the funeral pyre, not all the faces are crying. ...
>
> Paranoia in moderation, like red wine, is healthy precisely because conspiracy does not sleep. Our failure of perception is the reason we rarely see it. Why? "Treason doth never prosper," an English poet once wrote. "What's the reason? For if it prosper, none dare

call it treason."[917]

As can be seen, JFK Jr. was not afraid to cover touchy or controversial subjects in his magazine. While this is far from definitive evidence that he would have pursued an in-depth investigation into his father's assassination, it does imply that he may have, under the right circumstances. And his interest in his father did not wane as an adult. While running *George*, he hired Jacques Lowe, his father's official photographer, and questioned him about his father for hours.[918]

The next question to ask is, are there any indications that JFK Jr. had political ambitions? According to those close to him, yes. John's assistant, RoseMarie Terenzio, revealed that she and John's wife, Carolyn, often spoke of John running for office, "We talked about it as though it was inevitable."[919] After spending the day ice-skating with underprivileged children in Harlem, JFK Jr. told author Steven Gillon, "What they need is hope. They need to know that tomorrow will be better than today. I can do that. I can give them that hope." Gillon interpreted this as a desire to enter the political arena.[920] In November 1998, New York Senator Daniel Patrick Moynihan announced that he would not be seeking another term in 2000. There was much speculation about whether John would vie for the senate seat. According to Susan Doyle, who worked on Hilary Clinton's 2000 New York senate campaign, "We were scared shitless that John F. Kennedy Jr. would run. [He] would be serious competition and the one person she would not be able to beat in the primary."[921] According to Gillon, JFK Jr. stated to him, "Somebody [meaning Gillon] should write an article about this carpetbagger Clinton moving to New York solely to run for a Senate seat."[922] Friend Billy Noonan stated that during his last conversation with John, he tried to rib him about the press pushing for Hillary to win the senate seat. John replied, "Wait until she gets here. She's gonna get her head handed to her." Noonan concluded, "He was in."[923] Indeed, the cover of the April 1999 issue of *George* ran the headline, "Why Hillary won't be senator."

Other friends of John's felt he would run for governor of New York rather than a senator. John told his friend Gary Ginsberg that he was eyeing the New York governor's race in 2002. He confided, "I'm intellectually and temperamentally better suited to be an executive than a legislator. My dad didn't like it either."[924] Friend Robert Littell wrote that JFK Jr. had "begun to put a team together to develop a road map for his political future."[925]

And what about the presidency? In 1989, while watching television coverage of George H. W. Bush's inauguration, John told Littell that he wanted to go home someday—home being the White House. When a friend kept badgering him about running for Congress, he replied, "How many members of Congress ever became President?"[926] It should be noted that JFK was a congressman for six years before he became a senator. John made similar statements to his assistant, RoseMarie Terenzio. After New York Senator Al D'Amato suggested to JFK Jr. that he run for mayor of New York, John laughed it off and later confided to RoseMarie, "Well, Rosie, how many mayors do you know that become President?"[927] Friend Gustavo Paredes revealed, "Absolutely, he felt it was expected that he run for president someday. He was trying to figure out the road to get there."[928] Pierre Salinger stated that he felt JFK Jr. would run directly for the presidency, saying on a French radio show, "I felt that in the coming year John Jr. would also enter politics. ... We thought he was going to be a Democratic candidate for the next presidential election."[929]

It is evident from the statements of those who knew John that he was looking at various options for launching a political career. Which avenue he would have ultimately pursued is unclear, but many felt his ultimate aim was the presidency. His cousin, Robert F. Kennedy Jr., stated in 2022 about John's desire to reach the presidency, "He wanted to run because he was capable, he had great ideas, he was interesting, and he was charismatic."[930]

Given John's interest in controversial subjects, including potentially his father's assassination, and John's desire to run for office—and ultimately the highest office—it is not inconceivable that there would be motive on the part of his father's assassins to remove John. If anyone could have achieved justice for JFK, it was his son. The next question to ask then is, is there any evidence of potential foul play? What exactly happened on the fateful night of July 16, 1999?

John F. Kennedy Jr. took off from New Jersey's Essex County Airport with his wife, Carolyn Bessette, and her sister, Lauren Bessette. The plan was to drop Lauren off at Martha's Vineyard and then continue that evening to Hyannis Port, where JFK Jr. and his wife were to attend his cousin's wedding. It is worth noting that if anyone wanted to make an assassination attempt on JFK Jr., they would have known well in advance that he would likely be flying that weekend to Cape Cod. He flew to the Cape often during the summer months, but the wedding gave further assurance that he would fly that weekend.

The plane never made it to Martha's Vineyard. The NTSB report listed the probable cause of death as: "The Pilot's failure to maintain control of the airplane during a descent over water at night, which was a result of spatial disorientation. Factors in the accident were haze and the dark night." Spatial disorientation is the inability to correctly perceive one's body position, motion, and altitude relative to the Earth or the surrounding environment. It can occur in conditions with poor visibility, such as fog, clouds, or darkness, which remove visual cues for the body. Shortly before 9:41 p.m., the plane nose-dived into the water at a rapid speed.[931]

There is controversy over when the last communication from JFK Jr. occurred. Early news accounts reported a 9:39 p.m. phone call,[932] but this phone call was later erased from the official version of the crash. The potential occurrence of this phone call is critical as on the initially reported call, JFK Jr. indicated everything was OK. The FAA radar showed the plane going into a nosedive moments after the presumed call. The alleged reason for the crash was bad weather, but if that 9:39 p.m. phone call occurred, then JFK Jr. made no mention of having any difficulties.

The local television station interviewed Coast Guard Petty Officer Todd Burgun, the public information officer for the Boston Coast Guard station, who claimed that Kennedy radioed in at 9:39 p.m. According to initial reports, Kennedy stated that he was thirteen miles from the airport and ten miles from the coast. He said he was making his final approach and told controllers that he planned to drop off his sister-in-law and then take off again between 11 p.m. and 11:30 p.m. for Hyannis Port. Burgun claimed he got his information from the FAA but the FAA later denied this phone call ever happened. Why the local Coast Guard would send its public information officer to speak to the local television station and give a detailed account of a phone call that did not occur has never been explained.[933] A controller at the airport "declined comment" on whether he had radio contact with the airplane though later denied that radio contact was made.[934]

It took some time before a search for the plane began, despite family members reporting almost immediately after the expected landing time that the plane had not arrived. Even the *Boston Herald* reported, "Time Gaps in Early Hours of Search are Beyond Explanation." The Coast Guard began a search around 3:30 a.m. but Senator Ted Kennedy had to call President Bill Clinton's chief of staff, John Podesta, to try to get a more thorough search started, which Clinton ordered immediately, though it still took some hours for it to begin. The Pentagon then took command of the communication and reporting regarding the crash even though JFK Jr. had never been in the military and was flying a civilian aircraft.[935] President Clinton was busy during the days before and after the crash with Israeli Prime Minister Ehud Barak, who was visiting from July 14 to July 20.[936] During a joint press conference on July 19, the two expressed their sympathies for the loss.[937]

The plane wreckage was found on the night of July 20 and recovered on July 21. Despite the local Coast Guard office claiming JFK Jr. dialed in at

9:39 p.m. informing air traffic control that he was approaching Martha's Vineyard, the original search canvassed a massive area spreading from Long Island to the Cape' which perhaps delayed the amount of time it took to find the plane. The plane was ultimately discovered in the location it would have been expected to be found based on the alleged 9:39 p.m. phone call, near the coast of Martha's Vineyard.[938]

When the NTSB report was finally released, the media ran with stories claiming JFK Jr. was a reckless and inexperienced pilot since the report listed the crash's probable cause as the "pilot's failure to maintain control of the airplane." However, the NTSB report also detailed statements from JFK Jr.'s flight instructors, whose comments implied he was more than capable of safely managing the flight. He received his first flight instruction in 1982. He flew with six different flight instructors for the next six years, logging 47 hours. Then it appears he took a break until 1997, when he enrolled in a training program at Flight Safety International (FSI) to obtain a private pilot certificate. Between December 1997 and April 1998, he flew about 53 hours, of which 43 were flown with a flight instructor on board. The certified flight instructor (CFI) who prepared him for his private pilot check ride stated that JFK Jr. had "very good" flying skills. On April 22, 1998, JFK Jr. passed his private pilot flight test. During the calendar year 1998, he flew approximately 179 hours, including 65 without a CFI on board. On March 22, 1999, he completed the FAA's written airplane instrument examination. On April 5, 1999, he returned to FSI to begin an airplane instrument rating course. He was halfway through the training course at the time of his death, satisfactorily completing twelve of twenty-five lessons. The CFI stated that JFK Jr.'s basic instrument flying skills and simulator work were "excellent." During this training, he accumulated 13.3 hours of flight time with a CFI on board and 16.9 hours of simulation time. His last training at FSI was on April 24, 1999. He continued, however, to receive flight instruction from CFIs in New Jersey, flying with his newly purchased Piper Saratoga, the accident airplane.

Of the multiple CFIs that flew with JFK Jr. in the last months of his life, one stated that his aeronautical abilities and ability to handle multiple tasks while flying were average for his experience level. A second CFI accumulated 57 hours of flight time with JFK Jr. between May 1998 and July 1999, including 17 hours of night flight and 8 hours flown in instrument meteorological conditions (IMC). This CFI had conducted a "complex airplane" evaluation on the pilot and signed him off in the accident airplane in May 1999. The CFI had made six or seven flights to Martha's Vineyard Airport with JFK Jr. in the accident airplane. The CFI stated that most of the flights were conducted at night and that, during the flights, JFK Jr. did not have any trouble flying the airplane. The instructor stated that JFK Jr. was methodical in his flight planning and very cautious about his aviation decision-making. The CFI noted that JFK Jr. had the capability to conduct a night flight to Martha's Vineyard Airport as long as a visible horizon existed.

A third CFI, who accumulated 39 hours of flight time with JFK Jr., including 21 at night, stated that JFK Jr. used and seemed competent with the autopilot and could fly the airplane without a visible horizon. The CFI was unaware of JFK Jr. conducting any flight in the accident plane without an instructor on board.

JFK Jr.'s estimated total flight experience was about 310 hours, of which 55 hours were at night. His estimated flight time in the accident airplane was about 36 hours, of which about 9.4 hours were at night. About 3 hours of that time was without a certified flight instructor (CFI) on board, and about 0.8 hours of that was flown at night and included a night landing. In the 15 months before the crash, he had flown to or from the destination area about 35 times. He flew at least 17 of these flight legs without a CFI on board, of which 5 were at night.[939]

John McColgan, JFK Jr.'s federal licensing instructor, stated, "He was an excellent pilot. I put him through the paces, and he passed everything with flying colors." McColgan further said, "He flew a lot. In fact, by now, he probably has enough hours to be a commercial pilot."[940] Edward Gacio, a pilot who had befriended Kennedy, said, "If the weather was questionable, Kennedy would cancel a flight. He didn't appear to be a risk-taker."[941]

The media ran with the narrative that JFK Jr. was a reckless daredevil. After the NTSB issued its report, this narrative went into overdrive since, according to the report, one of JFK Jr.'s flight instructors claimed that he had spoken to JFK Jr. on the day of the accident and offered to fly with him. He stated that JFK Jr. replied that "he wanted to do it alone."[942] No one, however, questioned the authenticity of this statement. In the early days after the crash, much speculation existed about whether a flight instructor had been on board. This flight instructor was interviewed and mentioned nothing about such a conversation with JFK Jr., which would have clarified the many questions swirling in the media. What he did say is that, as far as he was aware, JFK Jr. never flew without a flight instructor and that their conversation that morning centered around dropping off some keys, which JFK Jr. replied he did not need. His attorney then wrote a letter to the NTSB stating that, according to his client, "John F. Kennedy Jr. never indicated that time that he intended to depart on the day or evening in question."[943] Furthermore, the alleged statement makes little sense. JFK Jr. could have easily brought the flight instructor with him and simply asked him not to intervene unless there was an emergency. A flight instructor being on board does not mean he could not have "done it alone."

Indeed, *George* magazine coeditor Richard Blow stated that during his last lunch with him, JFK Jr. indicated he was taking a flight instructor with him.[944]

The NTSB report claimed that JFK Jr. lost control of the aircraft due to "adverse weather conditions." The question to ask then is, what exactly were the weather conditions on that night? According to the NTSB report, the tower manager at Martha's Vineyard Airport stated, "The visibility, present weather, and sky condition at the approximate time of the accident was probably a little better than what was being reported. I say this because I remember aircraft on visual approaches saying they had the airport in sight between 10 and 12 miles out. I do recall being able to see those aircraft, and I do remember seeing the stars out that night." The ASOS (Automated Surface Observing System) reading at 9:53 p.m. at Martha's Vineyard Airport was "Clear at or below 12,000 feet; visibility 10 miles." JFK Jr.'s plane was found seven miles from the shore, and as such, based on the statement of the tower manager and the ASOS reading, he should have seen the island at the time he crashed, weakening the argument that he crashed due to spatial disorientation. The NTSB report included statements from three unnamed pilots who flew that night. They stated that their flight path was hazy at times, particularly over the water. One pilot made a particularly concerning statement, seemingly contradicting the tower manager at Martha's Vineyard Airport and the ASOS reading. He stated, "There was no horizon and no light. ... I turned left toward Martha's Vineyard to see if it was visible but could see no lights of any kind nor any evidence of the island. ... I thought the island might [have] suffered a power failure."[945] While the NTSB report did not include the name of this pilot, this statement was likely given by private pilot Dr. Bob Arnot, who appeared in the documentary *The Last Days of JFK Jr.* Dr. Arnot was a journalist, author, former host of the *Dr. Danger* reality TV series, and previous medical and foreign correspondent for NBC and CBS. He told *Newsweek* in the days after the crash that he flew approximately the same route as JFK Jr. approximately fifteen minutes earlier and that while looking down at Martha's Vineyard, "I couldn't see anything at all. It was murky black."[946] Local news reports that evening indicated the weather was clear.[947]

FAA Flight Specialist Edward Meyer prepared the FAA's special report on weather conditions the night JFK Jr.'s plane crashed. He was so disturbed by media reports that he issued a statement on it, "Nothing of what I have heard on mainstream media makes any sense to me. ... The weather along his flight was just fine. A little haze over eastern Connecticut. ... Any mention of 'daring' or 'inexperience' is absolute nonsense. I don't know why the airplane crashed, but what I heard on the media was nothing but garbage."[948] Jeb Burnside, editor-in-chief of *Aviation Safety Magazine*, wrote, "On paper, this accident shouldn't have happened. Despite most of his time being in a training environment, a typical 310-hour instrument-rating student in a well-equipped airplane should have had no problem with this flight." However, Burnside acknowledged that if there was no visual horizon, that could lead to the onset of spatial disorientation, which could explain the crash.[949]

One last question to ask regarding the weather is, even if the haze was as bad as alleged by some, why did JFK Jr. not turn on his autopilot? It appears JFK Jr. had been flying on autopilot but at some point the autopilot was disengaged.[950] Why did he not reengage it? According to researcher Scott Meyers, "The fact that Kennedy knew how to use the plane's navigational instruments casts serious doubt on the official explanation for the crash because even if he had gotten lost, his knowledge of the plane's instruments would have allowed him to flip a switch and allow the autopilot to guide him to a short distance from his runway destination. A little haze should have never stopped him from landing safely."[951] According to *The Boston Globe*, even engine failure or running out of gas should not have caused the plane to nosedive: "Even if the engine died, a federal aviation source said, it is unlikely that the plane would reach such a high rate of descent because the plane is designed to glide without power at a much slower rate for several miles. And if Kennedy had run out of fuel, it is likely he would have made a distress call."[952]

Despite the probable cause of the crash being listed as the "pilot's failure to maintain control of the airplane," there were details listed in the NTSB report that are worth further exploration. According to the report, JFK Jr. did not file a flight plan for his flight.[953] It should be noted, however, that filing a flight plan was not required and was often skipped by many pilots. His flight log was missing as well,[954] making it impossible to definitively determine whether a flight instructor was on board during the fatal flight.

There were six seats in the plane, two in each of three rows. Only five were recovered from the wreckage. One of the two front seats was missing,[955] leading to further speculation of a possible flight instructor on board.

The airplane was equipped with a voice recorder; however, when the wreckage was found the voice recorder was missing its battery and hence retained no data. The voice recorder had a nonvolatile speech memory that required a 9-volt battery to preserve the speech data. Another potentially concerning item in the NTSB report was the statement that the fuel selector valve was found in the OFF position.[956] The fuel selector valve cannot be accidentally shut off. It requires the pilot to hit another switch before he can move the valve to an OFF position. According to Google, "The primary role of this valve is to serve as a fuel shut off valve. This is essential to allow the crew to prevent fuel from reaching the engine in the event of a fire." Did JFK Jr.'s plane perhaps catch fire, causing him to turn off the fuel selector valve? According to the NTSB report, there was no evidence of a fire. However, several witnesses reported either hearing or seeing an explosion, but these witness accounts were never properly followed up to assess their accuracy.[957]

There was another plane crash that occurred a few months after JFK Jr.'s and only approximately fifty miles away from his crash. In that crash, the plane, a large Boeing 767 aircraft, was also found with the fuel selector valve turned off. The flight was Egypt Air 990. According to the NTSB report, that crash's probable cause was listed as "the relief first officer's flight control inputs." According to flight recorder information, the captain had left the cockpit to use the restroom, at which point the first officer stated, "I rely on God," and began to drive the plane downwards in an apparent suicide attempt. The captain managed to get back into the cockpit and tried to regain control. However, the first officer shut off the fuel selector valve, cutting off the fuel supply to the engines. Hence the captain could not regain control of the aircraft, and it nosedived into the ocean.[958] Some suspected foul play, as more than thirty Egyptian military officers, some high ranking, were on the flight.[959]

Both Egypt Air flight 990 and JFK Jr.'s flight, only a few months and a few miles apart, nosedived into the ocean at night and were found with the fuel selector valve turned off. Why, then, did the NTSB come to different conclusions concerning the two crashes? First, the NTSB had the flight recorder information from the Egypt Air flight, but the battery was missing from the flight recorder on JFK Jr.'s airplane, so no one knows what communications occurred in his airplane. Second, the flight log and one of the front seats were missing from JFK Jr.'s flight, so there was no definitive knowledge of whether a flight instructor was on board his aircraft. Hence, for these reasons, among others, the NTSB concluded that the JFK Jr. crash must have been due to bad weather and an inexperienced pilot. This author has brought up Egypt Air flight 990 not to argue that the same occurred on JFK Jr.'s flight but to stress that missing information, such as a missing flight log or an inoperable flight recorder, can alter the way we perceive a crash.

The fuel selector valve being in an OFF position is not a small detail to be overlooked, as it cannot be accidentally shut off, though it is always possible that the crash's impact somehow pushed the valve into an OFF position. According to the NTSB report, the bottom of the valve was missing, perhaps supporting this possibility.

After the bodies were recovered, there was a very cursory autopsy—less than four hours for all three bodies combined—and then the bodies were quickly cremated despite the deceased being Catholics. Catholics traditionally are buried. The former deputy chief medical examiner for Cook County, Illinois, was quoted in *The Boston Globe* as saying, "The haste [of the autopsies] in this case could lead to questions about the investigation's thoroughness."[960]

As can be seen, there are many unanswered questions regarding the JFK Jr. plane crash. Did he make a phone call at 9:39 p.m.? If he did not, why did the local Coast Guard send their information officer to the local TV station to give an account of a phone call that never occurred? And if the Coast Guard officer was mistaken somehow, where did he get his details from, and did he just by luck manage to get the location to match just right with the eventual information discovered about the crash? Why was JFK Jr.'s flight log missing? Why was one of the front seats missing from the wreckage? Why was the battery missing from his flight recorder? Any one of these three items would have definitively confirmed whether or not a flight instructor was onboard, but with these items missing, it can never be known with 100 percent certainty who was on the aircraft. Why were media pundits speaking incessantly about horrible weather conditions when others stated the weather conditions were just fine? Why were the media insisting JFK Jr. was a reckless and inexperienced pilot when many indicated he was quite cautious and experienced? Why did JFK Jr. not turn on his autopilot? Why was the fuel selector valve set to an OFF position? Why were the autopsies rushed and the bodies cremated?

This author is by no means saying that the plane crash definitively involved foul play. Statistics show that between five to ten percent of all general aviation accidents are attributed to spatial disorientation, and the JFK Jr. crash, as described in the NTSB report, seems to fit the trajectory of a typical spatial disorientation graveyard spiral, with his plane allegedly banking right as it dived into the ocean.[961] JFK Jr. was also experiencing both personal and professional stress in the weeks prior to the accident and had arrived approximately two hours later than expected at the departing airport due to traffic. So, it is possible he was more distracted than usual. The "probable cause" listed in the NTSB report may very well have been the actual cause. But it is important to keep in mind that the NTSB listed the conclusion as "probable," not definitive. As such, it is fair to explore other possibilities, particularly when there are motives for foul play and many unanswered questions. What is clear, however, is that if foul play was involved, then the crime was committed by sophisticated and well-connected actors.

It will never be known what might have been. Would JFK Jr. have run for office? Would he have reached the presidency? If he had been in office at the time of the September 11 attacks, how would he have responded? Would he have asked questions? Would he have pushed for a thorough investigation? Would he have opposed the Iraq war like his uncle Ted Kennedy did? Would opposition coming from an elected official with close ties to New York City have had a greater impact? Would he have achieved the justice he desired for his father? Whatever the reason that his life was cut short, the American people suffered yet another great tragedy from the loss of yet another Kennedy.

10

Conclusion

I want to make sure ... we hear all the alternatives and listen to all the criticisms. ... We need to keep our minds open to criticism and to new ideas—to dissent and alternatives—to reconsideration and reflection. – John F. Kennedy

There are two histories in America, the official history—coined in John F. Kennedy Jr.'s *George* magazine as the "counterfeit history"—and the authentic history. How closely these two align is in question. True history is complicated to decipher. Much of the information we know is disseminated over decades by parties with agendas—with institutions and interests to protect and promote. It is slanted. It is misleading. It leaves out vital pieces of data. Official history—like all propaganda—is narrative maintenance. Every empire throughout time has had some form of narrative control—greatly impacting how we interpret our past. As JFK once said, "We subject all facts to a prefabricated set of interpretations. We enjoy the comfort of opinion without the discomfort of thought. Mythology distracts us everywhere—in government, as in business, in politics as in economics, in foreign affairs as in domestic affairs."[962]

We are taught in school that a "lone nut" murdered John F. Kennedy. We are taught in school that a second "lone nut" then killed the first "lone nut." Who needs rigorous courtroom trials when we have the setting of official

229

narrative to determine guilt or innocence for us? We are then taught that a third "lone nut" came along and killed the brother of JFK. Then a few decades later, the son of John F. Kennedy died in a tragic accident. This is official history.

Schools do not teach the change in policy and power that resulted from these three tragedies. They do not teach who benefited from these deaths and who lost—who is still benefiting and who is still suffering. Nor do schools ask their students to ponder the connections between the three Kennedy deaths. They are treated as three distinct and random tragedies, not as a continuation of the same crime—the same ongoing coup d'état. This author does not know if JFK Jr.'s death was an accident or an assassination, but assassination should not be ruled out as a possibility.

Studying the three Kennedy deaths can be overwhelming. It is easy to get lost in the myriad details. This author has tried to share the most relevant publicly available facts—evidence uncovered over the years by tireless researchers. We only know some of the puzzle pieces. It is up to us as citizens to fit together those puzzle pieces as best we can into a coherent whole.

The assassination of John F. Kennedy is a complicated web. It is difficult to assess who knew what. But I hope this book has given readers food for thought. It is important to be open to all possibilities and to acknowledge that each of the various theories purported over the years likely holds a piece of the truth. We should always remain open to exploring all avenues and listening to all perspectives. That is the only way the full truth can be uncovered. As John F. Kennedy once said, "I want to make sure ... we hear all the alternatives and listen to all the criticisms. ... We need to keep our minds open to criticism and to new ideas—to dissent and alternatives—to reconsideration and reflection."[963] We should not be afraid to explore history through a different lens than the one we were taught.

It is a sad reality that John F. Kennedy's murderers will never be held accountable for their crime. But that does not mean it is not essential to understand what happened to JFK, his brother, and his son. For starters, understanding who killed the Kennedys can give us a better understanding of today and where the power really lies. A genuine recognition of how these deaths occurred can also help ensure that similar crimes are not repeated. By acknowledging what we lost and how we lost it, we can better prepare to recreate it—and, this time, ensure we do not lose it. There is no reason the world that John F. Kennedy envisioned cannot still come to light. We can fix the structures and the systems that allowed these murders to be perpetrated and covered up—but only if we first understand them.

The president of the United States was brutally murdered, and a massive and broad policy change ensued. The public has a right to question if powerful players were involved. It is up to the government to prove that Oswald was a lone assassin—while giving him a proper defense—and that has never been done. For decades the community of skeptics has been forced to be on the defensive to try to prove that a conspiracy occurred. But the onus should be on those who claim Oswald acted alone. Oswald never had a fair trial. Short of definitive proof of his sole guilt, the default position should be that Oswald was innocent. The fundamental basis of our criminal justice system is the concept of innocent until proven guilty. It is true that a court of law convicted Sirhan Sirhan of the murder of Robert Kennedy. But as has been shown, the case was never tried—only Sirhan's mental state was on trial. In essence, neither of the arguably two most monumental murders of the twentieth century has ever been adequately tried in a courtroom. Despite this fact we have been asked to believe—without question—the official narratives of these crimes.

The removal of JFK was not something that just happened on the fateful day of November 22, 1963. It was a process that involved months of planning—and additional crimes after the fact to cover up the initial crime. This author does not pretend to know who ordered the assassination, but there are credible suspects who were *not* named Lee Harvey Oswald. This author has tried to link the beneficiaries of the crime to those involved in it. Not all the individuals mentioned throughout this book were witting participants in the assassination, but hopefully the information shared gives the reader an idea of what may have happened and, at the very least, a basis from which to ask questions and continue researching. There is much evidence that a coup d'état occurred in America, but deliberate character assassination has allowed people like Noam Chomsky to declare, "Who cares [if a] jealous husband or the mafia [killed Kennedy]?" That is the level of discourse in America. Most Americans have no idea what was lost on that grisly day and who was responsible for that loss. Such is the power of propaganda.

Robert Kennedy once said, "Justice delayed is democracy denied."[964] I hope this book has contributed a step along the long and arduous path toward truth, justice, redemption, and a return to genuine democracy in America—the restoration of a nation of the people, by the people, for the people. We owe it not only to John F. Kennedy but to ourselves.

11

Why JFK Still Matters

Man holds in his mortal hands the power to abolish all forms of human poverty and all forms of human life. – John F. Kennedy

It has been more than sixty years since John F. Kennedy was assassinated. Why does his death still matter? After all, JFK was merely one man. Why did I take the time and effort to write this book despite not wanting to? Because our world would look very different today had JFK lived.

Could the life or death of a single individual change the course of history? JFK thought so. According to his wife, Jackie Kennedy, "He believed that one person can make a difference—and everyone should try."[965] Clearly, JFK's assassins felt the same, or else they would not have expended massive effort and energy into removing him from power. Indeed, this may be the only conviction he and his assassins shared.

What would the world look like today had JFK lived and had his policies been pursued? Would the US government work for its people rather than special interests? Would the United States have a robust production-based economy rather than a service-based one that could easily collapse with the dollar? Would the border crisis be non-existent, with those in poorer nations no longer desperate to flee in search of a better life? Would the horrors in the

Middle East have been avoided with a resolution to the Palestinian refugee issue, a nuclear-disarmed Israel, and no lobby in America to push Israeli interests over American interests? Would the U.S. be less involved in Middle East wars, wars that drain American lives and trillions in tax dollars[966] and offer little benefit to the average American? Would censorship be less prevalent? Would food be free from toxic pesticides? Would consumer rights be respected? Would the economy be more decentralized with a larger volume of small businesses? Would a more decentralized economy make enforcing arbitrary government dictates on the population more difficult? Would the power of the intelligence community be more limited? Would war be less rampant? Would the chances of nuclear conflict be smaller? These are just some of the possibilities.

Nothing is guaranteed. However, there is no doubt that America, under the leadership of JFK, would have gone down a far more positive path than it ultimately did. Furthermore, if we settle on the assumption that no single man can make a difference, then why should anyone try? If we permit JFK's assassination to be forgotten and we never achieve genuine truth and reconciliation, then why should anyone else risk pursuing his policies? Should we forever suffer at the hands of his assassins? By allowing his murder to be swept under the rug, we are, in effect, saying that it is permissible for powerful interests to assassinate our elected leaders. Essentially, we are saying it is OK if those representing us are violently removed and replaced by individuals representing narrower interests. Our implicit acceptance of this sad reality has led us to where we are today: a society where very few trust the government and most feel powerless to affect change.

But according to JFK, we are not helpless. In his January 20, 1961, inaugural address, he spoke of humanity's potential, declaring, "Man holds in his mortal hands the power to abolish all forms of human poverty and all forms of human life." He proclaimed that all on earth should join together in a "struggle against the common enemies of man: tyranny, poverty, disease, and war itself." He asked, "Can we forge against these enemies a grand and global alliance, north and south, east and west, that can assure a more fruitful life for mankind? Will you join in that historic effort?" It was a call for unity, not global governance, as JFK believed strongly in decentralized power and professed, "The rights of man come not from the generosity of the state but from the hand of God."[967]

JFK understood that such goals would be challenging, but he often said we must always begin no matter how difficult the journey is. Indeed, in his inaugural address, he proclaimed, "All this will not be finished in the first one hundred days. Nor will it be finished in the first one thousand days, nor in the life of this administration, nor even perhaps in our lifetime on this planet. But let us begin." There is no doubt that JFK made significant progress on that journey and that he understood the risks he was taking in pursuing such laudable goals, sharing that a "good conscience" would be the only "sure reward" and that history would be the "final judge of our deeds."[968] Indeed, his good conscience is the only thing he took with him when he was murdered on November 22, 1963. Let us not allow his efforts to have been in vain. It is up to us now to continue his quest.

Notes

PREFACE

1   Scott Campbell, "A Nightmare on Elm Street has an interesting Connection to the JFK Assassination," *We Got This Covered*, September 1, 2020, https://wegotthiscovered.com/movies/nightmare-elm-street-connection-jfk-assassination/ .

2   "Presidential Approval Ratings—Gallup Historical Statistics and Trends," *Gallup*, accessed December 5, 2022, https://news.gallup.com/poll/116677/Presidential-Approval-Ratings-Gallup-Historical-Statistics-Trends.aspx.

CUI BONO

3   Robert F. Kennedy Memo to John F. Kennedy, January 10, 1963, https://www.justice.gov/sites/default/files/ag/legacy/2011/01/20/01-10-1963.pdf.

4   News Conference 17, October 11, 1961, John F. Kennedy Presidential Library and Museum, https://www.jfklibrary.org/archives/other-resources/john-f-kennedy-press-conferences/news-conference-17.

5   Remarks upon signing the foreign assistance act, August 1, 1962, John F. Kennedy Presidential Library and Museum, https://www.jfklibrary.org/asset-viewer/archives/JFKWHA/1962/JFKWHA-117-001/JFKWHA-117-001.

6   Arthur Schlesinger Jr., *A Thousand Days: John F. Kennedy in the White House* (Boston, MA: Houghton Mifflin Harcourt Publishing Company, 1965), 575.

7   Philip E. Muehlenbeck, *Betting on the Africans: John F. Kennedy's Courting of African Nationalist Leaders* (New York, NY: Oxford University Press, 2014), 92.

8   James Douglass, *JFK and the Unspeakable* (New York, NY: Touchstone, 2010), 177.

9   Ibid., 134.

10 Ibid., 121.

11 Ibid., 126.

12 Papers of John F. Kennedy. Presidential Papers. National Security Files. Meetings and Memoranda. National Security Action Memoranda [NSAM]: NSAM 263, South Vietnam. JFKNSF-342-007. John F. Kennedy Presidential Library and Museum, https://www.jfklibrary.org/asset-viewer/archives/JFKNSF/342/JFKNSF-342-007.

13 Douglass, *JFK and the Unspeakable*, 187.

14 American University Commencement Address, June 10, 1963, John F. Kennedy Presidential Library and Museum, https://www.jfklibrary.org/learn/about-jfk/historic-speeches/american-university-commencement-address.

15 Papers of John F. Kennedy. President's Office Files. Speech Files. Address at 18th UN General Assembly, September 20, 1963, https://www.jfklibrary.org/asset-viewer/archives/JFKPOF/046/JFKPOF-046-041.

16 News Conference 62, October 9, 1963, John F. Kennedy Presidential Library and Museum, https://www.jfklibrary.org/archives/other-resources/john-f-kennedy-press-conferences/news-conference-62.

17 *Jacqueline Kennedy: Historic Conversations on Life with John F. Kennedy*, narrated by Jacqueline Kennedy and Arthur M. Schlesinger Jr. (Hyperion Audiobooks, 2011), Audible audio ed., 9 hr., 14 min.

18 John M. Newman, *JFK and Vietnam: Deception, Intrigue, and the Struggle for Power* (New York, NY: Grand Central Publishing, 1992) 462–466.

19 Ellen Kershner, "How Many Americans were Killed in Vietnam War," *World Atlas*, June 10, 2020, https://www.worldatlas.com/articles/how-many-americans-were-killed-in-the-vietnam-war.html.

20 Donald Gibson, *Battling Wall Street: The Kennedy Presidency* (New York, NY: Sheridan Square Publications, 1994), 79.

21 Papers of John F. Kennedy. Presidential Papers. National Security Files. Meetings and Memoranda. National Security Action Memoranda [NSAM]: NSAM 179, U.S. Policy Toward Indonesia. JFKNSF-338-006. John F. Kennedy Presidential Library and Museum, https://www.jfklibrary.org/asset-viewer/archives/JFKNSF/338/JFKNSF-338-006.

22 Douglass, *JFK and the Unspeakable*, 376.

23 Ibid., 260.

24 Ibid., 376–377.

25 Greg Poulgrain, *JFK vs. Allen Dulles: Battleground Indonesia* (New York, NY: Skyhorse, 2020), 8.

26 Douglass, *JFK and the Unspeakable*, 376–377.

27 Richard D. Mahoney, *JFK: Ordeal in Africa* (New York, NY: Oxford University Press, 1983), 87.

28 Ibid., 40–41, 46.

29 Ibid., 52–55.

30 Ibid., 230-231 and Muehlenbeck, *Betting on the Africans*, 232.

31 Ted Sorensen, *Kennedy: The Classic Biography* (New York, NY: Konecky & Konecky, 1965), 295.

32 Schlesinger, *A Thousand Days*, 252-256, 267, 289.

33   *Jacqueline Kennedy: Historic Conversations.*

34   Robert F. Kennedy, *Robert Kennedy in His Own Words: The Unpublished Recollection of the Kennedy Years* (New York, NY: Bantam, 1988), 274.

35   Douglass, *JFK and the Unspeakable*, 103–104.

36   Ibid., 106–107.

37   Douglas P. Horne, *JFK's War with the National Security Establishment*, (Fairfax, VA: The Future of Freedom Foundation, 2014), 28–29.

38   Douglass, *JFK and the Unspeakable*, 109.

39   Ibid., xxii.

40   Kenneth P. O'Donnell and David F. Powers, *Johnny, We Hardly Knew Ye* (New York, NY: Little, Brown, 1972), 343.

41   Ibid., 156–169.

42   Douglass, *JFK and the Unspeakable*, 30.

43   David Talbot, *Brothers: The Hidden History of the Kennedy Years* (London: Pocket Books, 2008), 172.

44   Talbot, *Brothers*, 172–173.

45   Douglass, *JFK and the Unspeakable*, 30.

46   Oral History Transcript, Curtis LeMay, Interview 1, June 28, 1971, https://discoverlbj.or g/item/oh-lemayc-19710628-1-76-30.

47   *Jacqueline Kennedy: Historic Conversations.*

48   Ted Sorensen, *Kennedy*, 517.

49   Schlesinger, *A Thousand Days*, 502.

50   Papers of John F. Kennedy. Presidential Papers. National Security Files. Subjects. President's speeches: UN address, September 1961, September 1961: 25-26, https://ww w.jfklibrary.org/asset-viewer/archives/JFKNSF/305/JFKNSF-305-009.

51   State of the Union Address, January 11, 1962, John F. Kennedy Presidential Library and Museum, https://www.jfklibrary.org/asset-viewer/archives/JFKWHA/1962/JFKWHA-066A/JFKWHA-066A.

52   Papers of John F. Kennedy. Presidential Papers. National Security Files. Meetings and Memoranda. National Security Action Memoranda [NSAM]: NSAM 239, U.S. Disarmament Proposals. JFKNSF-340-027. John F. Kennedy Presidential Library and Museum, https://www.jfklibrary.org/asset-viewer/archives/JFKNSF/340/JFKNSF-340 -027.

53   American University Commencement Address, 10 June 1963, John F. Kennedy Presiden-tial Library and Museum, https://www.jfklibrary.org/learn/about-jfk/historic-speeches /american-university-commencement-address.

54   *Jacqueline Kennedy: Historic Conversations.*

55   Schlesinger, *A Thousand Days*, 894.

56   Ibid., 296.

57   Arthur Schlesinger Jr. memo to JFK, CIA Reorganization, June 30, 1961, https://www.ar
      chives.gov/files/research/jfk/releases/2025/0318/176-10030-10422.pdf.

58   Tom Wicker, John W. Finney, Max Frankel, and E. W. Kenworthy, "C.I.A.: Maker of Policy,
      or Tool?" *New York Times*, April 25, 1966, 20.

59   Papers of John F. Kennedy. Presidential Papers. National Security Files. Meetings and
      Memoranda. National Security Action Memoranda [NSAM]: NSAM 55, Relations of the
      Joint Chiefs of Staff to the President in Cold War Operations. JFKNSF-330-005. John F.
      Kennedy Presidential Library and Museum, https://www.jfklibrary.org/asset-viewer/ar
      chives/JFKNSF/330/JFKNSF-330-005.

60   Papers of John F. Kennedy. Presidential Papers. National Security Files. Meetings and
      Memoranda. National Security Action Memoranda [NSAM]: NSAM 57, Responsibility
      for Paramilitary Operations. JFKNSF-330-007. John F. Kennedy Presidential Library
      and Museum, https://www.jfklibrary.org/asset-viewer/archives/JFKNSF/330/JFKNSF-
      330-007.

61   James DiEugenio, *Destiny Betrayed: JFK, Cuba and the Garrison Case* (New York, NY:
      Skyhorse Publishing, 2012), 48.

62   Schlesinger, *A Thousand Days*, 428.

63   Ibid., 427–428.

64   Mark Lane, *Plausible Denial: Was the CIA Involved in the Assassination of John F. Kennedy?*
      (New York, NY: Thunder's Mouth Press: 1991), 98.

65   "John F. Kennedy Administration: Memorandum on Palestinian Refugee Item in UN,
      Relations with Arabs (November 21, 1963)," Jewish Virtual Library, https://www.jewishv
      irtuallibrary.org/memorandum-on-palestinian-refugee-item-in-un-relations-with-arab
      s-november-1963.

66   George W. Ball and Douglas B. Ball, *The Passionate Attachment: America's Involvement with
      Israel, 1947 to the Present* (New York, NY: W. W. Norton & Co., 1992), 51.

67   Papers of John F. Kennedy. Presidential Papers. National Security Files. Robert W. Komer
      Files. Arab Refugees, 1961-1963 (3 of 3 folders). JFKNSF-408-003. John F. Kennedy
      Presidential Library and Museum, https://www.jfklibrary.org/asset-viewer/archives/JF
      KNSF/408/JFKNSF-408-003.

68   Ibid.

69   Papers of John F. Kennedy. Presidential Papers. National Security Files. Robert W. Komer
      Files. Arab Refugees, 1961-1963 (2 of 3 folders). JFKNSF-408-002. John F. Kennedy
      Presidential Library and Museum, https://www.jfklibrary.org/asset-viewer/archives/JF
      KNSF/408/JFKNSF-408-002.

70   "John F. Kennedy: Memorandum on Palestinian Refugee Item," Jewish Virtual Library.

71   Prime Minister Ben-Gurion to President Kennedy, 12 May 1963, with State Department memo attached, 14 May 1963, Secret, National Security Archive, https://nsarchive.gwu.e du/document/18724-national-security-archive-doc-25-prime-minister.

72   Muehlenbeck, *Betting on the Africans*, 128.

73   "John F. Kennedy Administration: Meeting with Israeli Foreign Minister Golda Meir (December 27, 1962)," Jewish Virtual Library, https://www.jewishvirtuallibrary.org/pres ident-kennedy-meeting-with-israeli-foreign-minister-golda-meir-december-1962.

74   "John F. Kennedy Administration: Memorandum on Palestinian Refugee Item," Jewish Virtual Library.

75   Seymour M. Hersh, *The Samson Option: Israel's Nuclear Arsenal and American Foreign Policy* (New York, NY: Random House, 1991) 93, 97.

76   Department of Justice letter to American Zionist council (dated November 21, 1962), The Israel Lobby Archive, https://www.israellobby.org/azcdoj/P6100127redorder/defa ult.asp.

77   Certificate of Incorporation, AIPAC, The Israel Lobby Archive, https://www.israellobby. org/AIPAC/01021963_AIPAC_Articles_of_Incorporation.pdf.

78   August 16, 1963, DOJ memo on AZC, The Israel Lobby Archive, https://www.israellobb y.org/azcdoj/p6100042-48/default.asp.

79   DOJ October 11 letter to Rifkind, The Israel Lobby Archive, https://www.israellobby.or g/azcdoj/P6100033_72hr/default.asp.

80   October 17, 1963, DOJ memo on AZC, The Israel Lobby Archive, https://www.israellob by.org/azcdoj/P6100028-29azcobligate/default.asp.

81   May 20, 1965, DOJ memo, The Israel Lobby Archive, https://www.israellobby.org/azcd oj/p6100006/default.asp.

82   Hersh, *The Samson Option*, 111.

83   "State Department telegram 658 to U.S. Embassy, Israel, 27 March 1963, Secret," National Security Archive, https://nsarchive.gwu.edu/document/18713-national-security-archiv e-doc-14-state.

84   "State Department telegram 800 to US Embassy, May 10, 1963, Secret," National Security Archive, https://nsarchive.gwu.edu/document/18722-national-security-archive-doc-23-state.

85   "John F. Kennedy Administration: Memorandum Responding to Israeli Security Guaran-tee Requests (May 16, 1963)," Jewish Virtual Library, https://www.jewishvirtuallibrary.o rg/memorandum-responding-to-israeli-security-guarantee-requests-may-1963.

86   "State Department telegram 780 to U.S. Embassy, Israel [transmitting letter from President Kennedy to Prime Minister Ben-Gurion], 4 May 1963, with State Department memo attached, Secret," National Security Archive, https://nsarchive.gwu.edu/document/1871 9-national-security-archive-doc-20-state.

87 "Prime Minister Ben-Gurion to President Kennedy, May 12, 1963, with State Department memo attached, May 14, 1963, Secret" National Security Archive, https://nsarchive.gwu.edu/document/18724-national-security-archive-doc-25-prime-minister.

88 "Department of State telegram 835 to U.S. Embassy Tel Aviv, 18 May 1963, Secret" National Security Archive, https://nsarchive.gwu.edu/document/18727-national-security-archive-doc-28-department.

89 "U.S. Embassy Israel Airgram A-746 to State Department, 'Visits to Dimona; Prime Minister Ben-Gurion's Letter of May 27 to President Kennedy,' 29 May 1963, Secret," National Security Archive, https://nsarchive.gwu.edu/document/18729-national-security-archive-doc-30-u-s-embassy.

90 "State Department telegram 938 to U.S. Embassy Israel, 15 June 1963, Secret," National Security Archive, https://nsarchive.gwu.edu/document/18732-national-security-archive-doc-33-state.

91 Ibid.

92 Avner Cohen, *Israel and the Bomb* (New York, NY: Columbia University Press, 1998), 13.

93 Jefferson Morley, *The Ghost: The Secret Life of CIA Spymaster James Jesus Angleton* (New York, NY: St. Martin's Press, 2018), 176–178.

94 Ibid., 171, 261–265.

95 "State Department telegram 938 to U.S. Embassy Israel, July 4, 1963, Secret," National Security Archive, https://nsarchive.gwu.edu/document/18734-national-security-archive-doc-35-state.

96 "U.S. Embassy Israel telegram 74 to State Department, July 17, 1963, Secret," National Security Archive, https://nsarchive.gwu.edu/document/18735-national-security-archive-doc-36-u-s-embassy.

97 "Memorandum of Conversation, 'McCloy's Near East Arms Limitation Probe; Security Guarantee for Israel,' July 23, 1963, Top Secret," National Security Archive, https://nsarchive.gwu.edu/document/18736-national-security-archive-doc-37-memorandum.

98 "U.S. Embassy Israel telegram 204 to State Department, August 19, 1963, Secret," National Security Archive, https://nsarchive.gwu.edu/document/18739-national-security-archive-doc-40-u-s-embassy.

99 I. L. Kenen, *Israel's Defense Line: Her Friends and Foes in Washington* (Buffalo, NY: Prometheus Books, 1981), 166.

100 Ibid., 173.

101 Laurent Guyénot, *The Unspoken Kennedy Truth* (self-published, 2021), 38.

102 Ibid., 39.

103 Ibid., 42.

104 Jim DiEugenio, "Nasser, Kennedy, and the Middle East," *Kennedys and King*, October 22,

2020, https://www.kennedysandking.com/john-f-kennedy-articles/nasser-kennedy-the
-middle-east-and-israel.

105 Komer, Robert W.: Oral History Interview – JFK #2, 07/16/1964, John F. Kennedy
Presidential Library and Museum, https://www.jfklibrary.org/asset-viewer/archives/JF
KOH/Komer%2C%20Robert%20W/JFKOH-ROWK-02/JFKOH-ROWK-02.

106 Ibid., 42.

107 Ibid., 25.

108 Stephen J. Green, *Taking Sides: America's Secret Relations with Militant Israel* (New York,
NY: William Morrow & Co., 1984), 166.

109 "Telephone Conversation #6862, Lyndon Johnson and Abe Feinberg, February 20, 1965,"
Discover LBJ, https://www.discoverlbj.org/item/tel-06862.

110 Alan Hart, *Zionism: The Real Enemy of the Jews, Volume Two: David Becomes Goliath* (Kent,
England: World Focus Publishing, 2007), 30.

111 David Nasaw, *The Patriarch: The Remarkable Life and Turbulent Times of Joseph P. Kennedy*
(New York, NY: Penguin Books, 2013), 403–406.

112 Alan Hart, *Zionism: The Real Enemy of the Jews, Volume One: The False Messiah* (Atlanta,
GA: Clarity Press Inc, 2009), 165.

113 Memo to FBI Director, March 23, 1961, Israel Lobby, https://www.israellobby.org/Fein
berg/03271963rfk.pdf, FBI Response to Attorney General Re Abraham Feinberg, March
31, 1961, Israel Lobby, https://www.israellobby.org/Feinberg/03311961fbi_rfk.pdf and
"Abraham Feinberg's FBI File," Israel Lobby, https://www.israellobby.org/Feinberg/defa
ult.asp.

114 Hersh, *The Samson Option*, 93, 97.

115 Roger J. Mattson, Stealing the Atom Bomb: How Denial and Deception Armed Israel
(CreateSpace, 2016), 33.

116 "How Israel Made AIPAC, Episode 3: AIPAC's Founder," podcast, August 1, 2022, The
Institute for Research Middle Eastern Policy (IRmep), https://howisraelmadeaipac.podb
ean.com/e/aipac-s-founder/.

117 Morley, *The Ghost*, 271–273.

118 "How Israel Made AIPAC, Episode 4: Lobbying for a Country," podcast, August 1, 2022,
The Institute for Research Middle Eastern Policy (IRmep), https://howisraelmadeaipac.p
odbean.com/e/episode-4-lobbying-for-a-country/.

119 "How Israel Made AIPAC, Episode 11: Fighting Justice, podcast, September 5, 2022, The
Institute for Research Middle Eastern Policy (IRmep), https:117//howisraelmadeaipac.p
odbean.com/e/episode-11-fighting-justice/.

120 Hersh, *The Sampson Option*, 192.

121 JTA and Ron Kampeas, "Israel Has Had No Better Friend," May 9, 2018, *Haaretz*, https://w

ww.haaretz.com/us-news/2018-05-09/ty-article/lyndon-johnson-no-better-friend/000
0017f-e356-d9aa-afff-fb5ea2b60000.

122 J. Correspondent, "Friend, ally, savior: Revealing LBJ's Jewish Ties," *The Jewish News of
Northern California*, November 28, 2008, https://jweekly.com/2008/11/28/friend-ally-s
avior-revealing-lbj-s-jewish-ties/.

123 Gibson, *Battling Wall Street*, 19.

124 News Conference 44, September 26, 1962, John F. Kennedy Presidential Library and
Museum, Press Conference, https://www.jfklibrary.org/archives/other-resources/john-
f-kennedy-press-conferences/news-conference-44.

125 John F. Kennedy, Special Message to the Congress on Tax Reduction and Reform. Online
by Gerhard Peters and John T. Woolley, The American Presidency Project, https://www.
presidency.ucsb.edu/node/237353.

126 John F. Kennedy, Message to the Congress Presenting the President's First Economic
Report Online by Gerhard Peters and John T. Woolley, The American Presidency Project,
https://www.presidency.ucsb.edu/node/236490.

127 Gibson, *Battling Wall Street*, 30.

128 "Are Banks Behind the Times? The Case for Broad Changes," *U.S. News and World Report*,
November 23, 1963, https://archive.org/details/InterviewWithJamesSaxonCurrencyCo
mptrollerForPresidentKennedy/mode/2up.

129 John F. Kennedy, Message to the Congress Presenting the President's First Economic
Report Online by Gerhard Peters and John T. Woolley, The American Presidency Project
https://www.presidency.ucsb.edu/node/236490.

130 Remarks at the National Advisory Council of the Small Business Administration, 16 May
1963, John F. Kennedy Presidential Library and Museum, https://www.jfklibrary.org/ass
et-viewer/archives/JFKWHA/1963/JFKWHA-184-007/JFKWHA-184-007.

131 News Conference 6, March 8, 1961, John F. Kennedy Presidential Library and Museum,
https://www.jfklibrary.org/archives/other-resources/john-f-kennedy-press-conference
s/news-conference-6.

132 John Newman, *Into the Storm: The Assassination of President Kennedy, Volume 3*, (CreateS-
pace, 2019), 51–52.

133 Ibid., 55.

134 Legislative Summary, Social Security, John F. Kennedy Presidential Library and Museum,
https://www.jfklibrary.org/archives/other-resources/legislative-summary/social-securi
ty.

135 Sorensen, *Kennedy*, 435.

136 Ibid., 445–446.

137 Gibson, *Battling Wall Street*, 9–18.

138 Douglass, *JFK and the Unspeakable*, 138.

139 Kennedy, *Robert Kennedy in His Own Words*, 333–334.

140 Douglass, *JFK and the Unspeakable*, 139.

141 Ibid., 141.

142 Ibid.

143 Remarks at the New York Birthday Salute to the President, May 23, 1963, John F. Kennedy Presidential Library and Museum, https://www.jfklibrary.org/asset-viewer/archives/JF KWHA/1963/JFKWHA-187-006/JFKWHA-187-006.

144 Douglas Brinkley, "Rachel Carson and JFK, An Environmental Tag Team," *Audobon*, May–June 2012, https://www.audubon.org/magazine/may-june-2012/rachel-carson-a nd-jfk-environmental-tag-team and Papers of John F. Kennedy. Presidential Papers. President's Office Files. Departments and Agencies. President's Science Advisory Committee (PSAC): Pesticides report, 15 May 1963, https://www.jfklibrary.org/ass et-viewer/archives/JFKPOF/087/JFKPOF-087-003.

145 "Kefauver-Harris Amendments Revolutionized Drug Development," FDA Consumer Health Information, October 2012, https://www.gvsu.edu/cms4/asset/F51281F0-00AF-E25A-5BF632E8D4A243C7/kefauver-harris_amendments.fda.thalidomide.pdf.

146 Jeremy A. Greene and Scott H. Podolsky, "Reform, Regulation, and Pharmaceuticals—The Kefauver-Harris Amendments at 50," *The New England Journal of Medicine* 367, no. 16 (2012): 1481–1483, https://doi.org/10.1056/NEJMp1210007.

147 Remarks to the White House Conference on Narcotic and Drug Abuse, September 27, 1962, https://www.jfklibrary.org/asset-viewer/archives/JFKWHA/1962/JFKWHA-131-004/JFKWHA-131-004.

148 Executive Order 11076—Establishing the President's Advisory Commission on Narcotic and Drug Abuse, January 15, 1963, https://www.presidency.ucsb.edu/documents/execut ive-order-11076-establishing-the-presidents-advisory-commission-narcotic-and-drug# :~:text=States%3A%201961%20%E2%80%90%201963-,Executive%20Order%2011076% E2%80%94Establishing%20the%20President's%20Advisory,on%20Narcotic%20and%20 Drug%20Abuse.

149 Papers of John F. Kennedy. Presidential Papers. President's Office Files. Special Events Through the Years. Interim report of President's Advisory Commission on Narcotics and Drug Abuse, 3 April 1963, https://www.jfklibrary.org/asset-viewer/archives/jfkpof-138 -009#?image_identifier=JFKPOF-138-009-p0014.

150 Papers of John F. Kennedy. Presidential Papers. White House Staff Files of Lee C. White. General File, 1954-1964. Narcotics: Miscellaneous, undated (7 of 7 folders), https://ww w.jfklibrary.org/asset-viewer/archives/jfkwhsflcw-011-007#?image_identifier=JFKWH SFLCW-011-007-p0004.

151 Remarks of Senator John F. Kennedy, District Attorneys' Convention, Milwaukee, Wisconsin, July 31, 1959, https://www.jfklibrary.org/archives/other-resources/joh n-f-kennedy-speeches/milwaukee-wi-19590731.

152 Papers of John F. Kennedy. Presidential Papers. White House Staff Files of Lee C. White. General File, 1954-1964. Narcotics, 1963: 20 March-13 November (6 of 7 folders), https://www.jfklibrary.org/asset-viewer/archives/jfkwhsflcw-011-006#?image_identifier=JFKWHSFLCW-011-006-p0171.

153 Theodore C. Sorensen Personal Papers. Legislative Files, 1961-1964. Legislative program, 1964: Proposals for 1964. TCSPP-059-020. John F. Kennedy Presidential Library and Museum, https://www.jfklibrary.org/asset-viewer/archives/tcspp-059-020#?image_identifier=TCSPP-059-020-p0034.

154 Office of the White House Press Secretary Press Release, October 4, 1961, Papers of John F. Kennedy, Presidential Papers, President's Office Files, Departments and Agencies, Commission on Campaign Costs, https://www.jfklibrary.org/asset-viewer/archives/jfkpof-093-002#?image_identifier=JFKPOF-093-002-p0029.

155 News Conference 31, April 18, 1962, John F. Kennedy Presidential Library and Museum, https://www.jfklibrary.org/archives/other-resources/john-f-kennedy-press-conferences/news-conference-31.

156 Letter to the President of the Senate and to the Speaker of the House Transmitting Bills to Carry Out Recommendations of the Commission on Campaign Costs, May 29, 1962, online by Gerhard Peters and John T. Woolley, The American Presidency Project, https://www.presidency.ucsb.edu/documents/letter-the-president-the-senate-and-the-speaker-the-house-transmitting-bills-carry-out-0.

157 Letter to the President of the Senate and to the Speaker of the House Transmitting Bills to Carry Out Recommendations of the Commission on Campaign Costs, April 30, 1963, online by Gerhard Peters and John T. Woolley, The American Presidency Project, https://www.presidency.ucsb.edu/documents/letter-the-president-the-senate-and-the-speaker-the-house-transmitting-bills-carry-out.

158 Michael Levy, "Political Action Committee," *Encyclopedia Britannica*, updated June 7, 2024, https://www.britannica.com/topic/political-action-committee.

159 "How Does Campaign Funding Work?" *Caltech Science Exchange*, accessed July 9, 2024, https://scienceexchange.caltech.edu/topics/voting-elections/campaign-funding-finance-explained.

160 Report of the President's Commission on Campaign Costs, pg 17, Papers of John F. Kennedy, Presidential Papers, President's Office Files, Departments and Agencies, Commission on Campaign Costs, https://www.jfklibrary.org/asset-viewer/archives/jfkpof-093-002#?image_identifier=JFKPOF-093-002-p0018.

161 Letter to the President of the Senate and to the Speaker of the House Transmitting Bills to Carry Out Recommendations of the Commission on Campaign Costs, April 30, 1963, online by Gerhard Peters and John T. Woolley, The American Presidency Project, https://www.presidency.ucsb.edu/documents/letter-the-president-the-senate-and-the-speaker-the-house-transmitting-bills-carry-out.

162 Clifford A. Jones, "Federal Election Campaign Act," *Encyclopedia Britannica*, updated May 29, 2024, https://www.britannica.com/topic/Federal-Election-Campaign-Act.

163 News Conference 39, July 23, 1962, John F. Kennedy Presidential Library and Museum, https://www.jfklibrary.org/archives/other-resources/john-f-kennedy-press-conferences/news-conference-39.

164 Mahoney, *JFK: Ordeal in Africa*, 114.

165 Ibid., 139–149.

166 Gibson, *Battling Wall Street*, 65.

167 Address before the Florida State Chamber of Commerce, November 18, 1963, https://www.jfklibrary.org/asset-viewer/archives/JFKWHA/1963/JFKWHA-242/JFKWHA-242.

168 Morley, *The Ghost*, 201.

169 Guyénot, *The Unspoken Kennedy Truth*, 44.

170 Andrei Gromyko, *Memoirs* (New York, NY: Doubleday, 1990), 181–182.

THE ALLEGED ASSASSIN

171 DiEugenio, *Destiny Betrayed*, 121.

172 Ibid.

173 Ibid., 125.

174 "About Civil Air Patrol," *Civil Air Patrol*, accessed December 8, 2022, https://tnwg.cap.gov/about/about-civil-air-patrol.

175 DiEugenio, *Destiny Betrayed*, 125.

176 Ibid., 126.

177 Ibid., 127–8.

178 Jim Garrison, *On the Trail of the Assassins: One Man's Quest to Solve the Murder of President Kennedy* (New York, NY: Skyhorse Publishing, 2012), 47.

179 DiEugenio, *Destiny Betrayed*, 131–132.

180 Garrison, *On the Trail of the Assassins*, 47.

181 DiEugenio, *Destiny Betrayed*, 131–132.

182 Garrison, *On the Trail of the Assassins*, 45.

183 DiEugenio, *Destiny Betrayed*, 129.

184 Garrison, *On the Trail of the Assassins*, 45.

185 DiEugenio, *Destiny Betrayed*, 133.

186 Ibid., 134.

187 Ibid., 135–136.

188 Ibid., 137–138.

189 Ibid., 138–139.

190 DiEugenio, *Destiny Betrayed*, 140–141.

191 Ibid., 142.

192 Ibid., 142–144.

193 Jefferson Morley Interview, *JFK Facts*, March 21, 2025, https://jfkfacts.substack.com/p/from-the-new-jfk-files-theres-a-cia?r=1459&triedRedirect=true and NARA Record Number: 124-10273-10070, https://www.maryferrell.org/showDoc.html?docId=238089#relPageId=3&search=sole_purpose%20angleton.

194 John Newman, *Oswald and the CIA* (New York, NY: Skyhorse Publishing, 2008), 87–88.

195 Ibid., 49–51.

196 Newman, *Oswald and the CIA*, 176.

197 Peter Dale Scott, *Dallas '63: The First Deep State Revolt Against the White House* (New York, NY: Open Road Integrated Media, Inc, 2015), 58–59.

198 Morley, *The Ghost*, 89–90.

199 DiEugenio, *Destiny Betrayed*, 144.

200 Ibid., 147–148.

201 Ibid., 139–140.

202 Ibid., 149–150.

203 Garrison, *On the Trail of the Assassins*, 50–51.

204 Ibid., 49.

205 Newman, *Oswald and the CIA*, xx.

206 Ibid., 268–270.

207 Ibid., 273.

208 James P. Hosty Jr., *Assignment: Oswald* (Arcade Publishing: New York, NY, 1996), 52.

209 Garrison, *On the Trail of the Assassins*, 53.

210 Newman, *Oswald and the CIA*, 276–277.

211 Garrison, *On the Trail of the Assassins*, 53.

212 Dana Sloan, "Permindex, Mitterrand and the Schlumberger Connection," *EIR* (Executive Intelligence Review), 35, December 22, 1981, https://larouchepub.com/eiw/public/1981/eirv08n49-19811222/eirv08n49-19811222_035-permindex_mitterrand_and_the_sch.pdf.

213 Garrison, *On the Trail of the Assassins*, xi.

214 Michael Karpin, *The Bomb in the Basement* (New York, NY: Simon & Schuster, 2006), 57–73.

215 Ibid., 91.

216 Poulgrain, *JFK vs. Allen Dulles*, vii.

217 Ibid., 50.

218 DiEugenio, *Destiny Betrayed*, 153.

219 Garrison, *On the Trail of the Assassins*, 52–53.

220 George de Mohrenschildt, *I'm a Patsy*, 1978, https://archive.org/details/ImAPatsyImAPa tsy.

221 DiEugenio, *Destiny Betrayed*, 155.

222 Ibid., 338.

223 Ibid., 155.

224 Garrison, *On the Trail of the Assassins*, 56.

225 DiEugenio, *Destiny Betrayed*, 334.

226 Police Report on Suicide of George de Mohrenschildt, March 29, 1975, Case No. 77-117538, SCRIBD, https://www.scribd.com/document/258263723/Police-report-on-su cide-of-de-Mohrenschildt.

227 Garrison, *On the Trail of the Assassins*, 62.

228 DiEugenio, *Destiny Betrayed*, 197.

229 Ibid., 196.

230 Warren Commission Testimony of Ruth Hyde Paine, March 21, 1964, https://www.jfk-a ssassination.net/russ/testimony/paine_r3.htm.

231 "JCC Association Center for Israel Engagement," JCC Association of North America, accessed July 10, 2024, https://jcca.org/what-we-do/jcc-israel-center/.

232 Warren Commission Testimony of Ruth Hyde Paine, March 20, 1964, https://www.jfk-a ssassination.net/russ/testimony/paine_r2.htm.

233 Warren Commission Testimony of Ruth Hyde Paine, March 21, 1964, https://www.jfk-a ssassination.net/russ/testimony/paine_r3.htm.

THE LEAD UP TO THE CRIME

234 Newman, *Oswald and the CIA*, 274.

235 "The 6th Floor Museum at Dealey Plaza," *The Dallas Times Herald*, April 24, 1963, https://e museum.jfk.org/objects/11349/front-section-of-the-dallas-times-herald-with-stories-a bout;ctx=17211b63-c9d3-4671-92d7-e9d6a9c671f7&idx=10.

236 Garrison, *On the Trail of the Assassins*, 61.

237 Warren Commission Report, Chapter 2: Planning the Texas Trip, https://www.archives. gov/research/jfk/warren-commission-report/chapter-2.html

238 DiEugenio, *Destiny Betrayed*, 155–158.

239 Ibid., 158–159.

240 Gaeton Fonzi, *The Last Investigation: A Former Federal Investigator Reveals the Conspiracy to Kill JFK* (New York, NY: Thunder's Mouth Press, 1993), 141.

241 DiEugenio, *Destiny Betrayed*, 102.

242 Garrison, *On the Trail of the Assassins*, 4.

243 Ibid., 26.

244 Ibid., 41.

245 Ibid., 43.

246 DiEugenio, *Destiny Betrayed*, 111.

247 Garrison, *On the Trail of the Assassins*, 31–32.

248 Ibid., 41.

249 DiEugenio, *Destiny Betrayed*, 113.

250 Garrison, *On the Trail of the Assassins*, 40.

251 Ibid., 313.

252 DiEugenio, *Destiny Betrayed*, 159–160.

253 Newman, *Oswald and the CIA*, 325.

254 DiEugenio, *Destiny Betrayed*, 87.

255 Garrison, *On the Trail of the Assassins*, 157.

256 DiEugenio, *Destiny Betrayed*, 88–93.

257 "Clay Shaw Trial Transcript, 6 Feb 1969 (Testimony of Mr. MeGehee, Mr. Morgan ...," Mary Ferrell Foundation, https://www.maryferrell.org/showDoc.html?docId=1273#rel PageId=54.

258 "Clay Shaw Trial Transcript, 6 Feb 1969 (Testimony of Mr. MeGehee, Mr. Morgan ...," Mary Ferrell Foundation, https://www.maryferrell.org/showDoc.html?docId=1273#rel PageId=79.

259 Ibid.

260 Garrison, *On the Trail of the Assassins*, 108–109.

261 Ibid., 87.

262 Lane, *Plausible Denial*, 222–223.

263 Whitney Webb, *One Nation Under Blackmail* (Walterville, OR: Trine Day LLC, 2022), 87–88.

264 Ibid.

265 Bernard M. Bloomfield, *Israel Diary* (New York, NY: Crown Publishers, 1950), 5.

266 Roger J. Mattson, "The NUMEC Affair: Did Highly Enriched Uranium from the U.S. Aid Israel's Nuclear Weapon's Program?," National Security Archive, November 2, 2016, https://nsarchive.gwu.edu/briefing-book/nuclear-vault/2016-11-02/numec-affair-did-highly-enriched-uranium-us-aid-israels-nuclear-weapons-program.

267 Webb, *One Nation Under Blackmail*, 87–88.

268 "Balfour Declaration: Text of the Declaration (November 2, 1917)," Jewish Virtual Library, https://www.jewishvirtuallibrary.org/text-of-the-balfour-declaration.

269 Karpin, *The Bomb in the Basement*, 136–137.

270 Michele Metta, *Accomplishing Jim Garrison's Investigation on the Trail of the Assassins of JFK* (self-published, 2021), 237.

271 Webb, *One Nation Under Blackmail*, 91.

272 DiEugenio, *Destiny Betrayed*, 385.

273 Metta, *Accomplishing Jim Garrison's Investigation*, 235.

274 Webb, *One Nation Under Blackmail*, 92.

275 Garrison, *On the Trail of the Assassins*, 118.

276 DiEugenio, *Destiny Betrayed*, 161–162.

277 "Edgar Stern, Founder and Owner of WDSU, Dies," *WWLTV*, October 21, 2009, https://www.wwltv.com/article/news/local/edgar-stern-founder-owner-of-wdsu-dies/289-4129 06058.

278 Alonzo G. Ensenat, *The Story of International House and International Trade Mart*, 1974, http://wtcno.org/wp-content/uploads/2018/10/Story-of-International-House-and-International-Trade-Mart.pdf.

279 CIA Memorandum No. 9, Garrison and the Kennedy Assassination, June 5, 1968, 6, https://www.archives.gov/files/research/jfk/releases/2021/docid-32398261.pdf.

280 "Edgar B. Stern, American Jewish Leader, Dies; Was Active in J.D.C., Jewish Telegraphic Agency," August 27, 1959, *Jewish Telegraphic Agency*, https://www.jta.org/archive/edgar-b-stern-american-jewish-leader-dies-was-active-in-j-d-c.

281 Michael Collins Piper, *Final Judgment* (Washington, DC: American Free Press, 2017), introductory pages.

282 Newman, *Oswald and the CIA*, 351.

283 Ibid., 346–347.

284 Garrison, *On the Trail of the Assassins*, 62–63.

285 Ibid., 110–112.

286 Warren Commission Testimony of Lawrence V. Meyers, accessed July 10, 2024, https://www.jfk-assassination.net/russ/testimony/meyers_l.htm.

287 Garrison, *On the Trail of the Assassins*, 110–112.

288 Warren Commission Testimony of Lawrence V. Meyers.

289 "About Argonne," Argonne National Laboratory, accessed July 10, 2024, https://www.anl.gov/argonne-national-laboratory.

290 Mattson, *Stealing the Atom Bomb*, 26.

291 Dave Bukey, "Argonne to advance energy security and safety with funds from U.S.-Israel energy center," Argonne National Laboratory, June 30, 2020, https://www.anl.gov/articl e/argonne-to-advance-energy-security-and-safety-with-funds-from-usisrael-energy-ce nter.

292 "HSCA Report Volume IX, Current Section: x. Lawrence V. Meyers," Mary Ferrell Foundation, accessed July 10, 2024, https://www.maryferrell.org/showDoc.html?docId= 955#relPageId=859.

293 Webb, *One Nation Under Blackmail*, 440.

294 Karpin, *The Bomb in the Basement*, 136–137.

295 "Abraham Feinberg," Jewish Virtual Library, https://www.jewishvirtuallibrary.org/feinb erg-abraham.

296 Webb, *One Nation Under Blackmail*, 86–87.

297 Ibid., 440.

298 Remarks at the 50th Annual Meeting of the Anti-Defamation League of B'nai B'rith, January 31, 1963, audio, https://www.jfklibrary.org/asset-viewer/archives/jfkwha-161-004.

299 Newman, *Oswald and the CIA*, 354.

300 Ibid., 352.

301 Ibid., 375.

302 Ibid., 352.

303 Ibid., 375.

304 Newman, *Oswald and the CIA*, 615.

305 Morley, *The Ghost*, 130–131.

306 Richard Starnes, "'Spooks' make life miserable for Ambassador Lodge," *Washington Daily News*, October 2, 1963, https://www.blackopradio.com/starnes.htm.

307 Arthur Schlesinger, *Robert Kennedy and His Times* (New York, NY: Mariner Books, 2018), 450.

308 Arthur Krock, "The Intra-Administration War in Vietnam," *The New York Times*, October 3, 1963, http://www.maebrussell.com/Military/CIA%20War%20in%20Vietnam.html.

309 Kennedy, *Robert Kennedy in His Own Words*, 373–374.

310 *Jacqueline Kennedy: Historic Conversations.*

311 Garrison, *On the Trail of the Assassins*, 62–63.

312 "HSCA Report, Volume XII, Current Section: VI. Letters of CIA of September 1, 1978, and FBI of January 8, 1979," Mary Ferrell Foundation, accessed July 10, 2024, https://ww w.maryferrell.org/showDoc.html?docId=84#relPageId=570.

313 Newman, *Oswald and the CIA*, 630.

314 DiEugenio, *Destiny Betrayed*, 163.

315 Douglass, *JFK and the Unspeakable*, 200.

316 Ibid., 213.

317 Ibid., 203.

318 Ibid., 202.

319 Ibid., 205–206.

320 Ibid., 200.

321 Ibid., 201.

322 Abraham Bolden Interview, *Tom Meros*, June 29, 2023, https://www.youtube.com/watch?v=RpyGCrmoPRw.

323 "House Select Committee on Assassinations Final Report," Mary Ferrell Foundation, accessed July 10, 2024, https://www.maryferrell.org/showDoc.html?docId=800#relPageId=261.

324 "Former Agent: Kennedy assassination thwarted in Chicago," *ABC7 Chicago*, December 11, 2007, https://abc7chicago.com/archive/5787903/.

325 James DiEugenio and Oliver Stone, *JFK Revisited: Through the Looking Glass* (New York, NY: Skyhorse Publishing, 2022), 69.

326 Sylvia Meagher, *Accessories After the Fact: The Warren Commission, the Authorities, and the Report on the JFK Assassination* (New York, NY: MJF Books, 1967), 210–219.

327 Denis Morissette, "Testimonies of James Hosty, Gordon Shanklin and Nanny Fenner," video, accessed July 10, 2024, https://www.youtube.com/watch?v=ZCokPka5iSM.

328 Douglass, *JFK and the Unspeakable*, 223.

329 Garrison, *On the Trail of the Assassins*, 67.

330 Robert E. Baskin, "Kennedy to Visit Texas Nov. 21–22 Dallas Included," *The Dallas Morning News*, September 26, 1963.

331 Testimony of Mr. and Mrs. John B. Connally, Dallas, Texas, accessed July 10, 2024, https://www.jfk-assassination.net/russ/m_j_russ/hscacon.htm and Select Comm. on Assassinations, Politics and Presidential Protection: The Motorcade, https://www.jfk-online.com/cheramie-hsca.pdf (1979), https://www.jfk-assassination.net/russ/jfkinfo4/jfk11/hscv11c.htm.

332 Gerald J. "Jerry" Bruno Personal Papers, John F. Kennedy Administration, 1960–1963: Trips: Texas, November 1963: 21–22: Correspondence, https://www.jfklibrary.org/asset-viewer/archives/GJBPP/006/GJBPP-006-015.

333 Select Comm. on Assassinations, Politics and Presidential Protection.

334 Gerald J. "Jerry" Bruno Personal Papers, Correspondence.

335 Ibid.

336 "Twelve Who've Followed the Wet Road to Riches," *D Magazine*, May 1, 1984, https://ww
w.dmagazine.com/publications/d-magazine/1984/may/twelve-whove-traveled-the-wet
-road-to-riches/.

337 Karpin, *The Bomb in the Basement*, 136–137.

338 Remarks on the 50th Anniversary of the Children's Bureau, April 9, 1962, audio, https://w
ww.jfklibrary.org/asset-viewer/archives/JFKWHA/1962/JFKWHA-085-001/JFKWHA-
085-001.

339 Gerald J. "Jerry" Bruno Personal Papers, Correspondence.

340 American Beverage Membership List, https://www.americanbeverage.org/our-member
s/member-directory/?page=5#member_results#member_results.

341 Mattson, *Stealing the Atom Bomb*, 33.

342 Gerald J. "Jerry" Bruno Personal Papers, Correspondence.

343 Ibid.

344 Select Comm. on Assassinations, Politics and Presidential Protection.

345 Gerald J. "Jerry" Bruno Personal Papers, Correspondence.

346 Ibid.

347 Ibid.

348 Ibid.

349 Testimony of Kenneth P. O'Donnell, accessed July 10, 2024, https://www.jfk-assassinatio
n.net/russ/testimony/odonnell.htm.

350 Testimony of Mr. and Mrs. John B. Connally, Dallas, Texas, and Select Comm. on
Assassinations, Politics and Presidential Protection.

351 Ibid.

352 Elizabeth Harris, "Looking Back in Sorrow," *The Washington Post*, November 20, 1988,
https://www.washingtonpost.com/archive/lifestyle/magazine/1988/11/20/looking-bac
k-in-sorrow/d2ac9bfa-804f-4a31-baf0-34aeb2371215/.

353 David Ritz, "Remembering Bloom," *D Magazine*, July 1, 1975, https://www.dmagazine.co
m/publications/d-magazine/1975/july/remembering-bloom/.

354 "Sam R. Bloom Jr., Who Spent 50 Years with…," *UPI*, https://www.upi.com/Archives/19
83/07/18/Sam-R-Bloom-Jr-who-spent-50-years-with/2242427348800/.

355 "Our homeland of heart," Temple Emanu-El, accessed July 10, 2024, https://www.tedalla
s.org/connect/israel/.

356 Ritz, "Remembering Bloom."

357 Select Comm. on Assassinations, Politics and Presidential Protection.

358 "Warren Commission Hearings Volume XVII, Current Section CE 769 - Statement of
Special Agent Lawson concerning his official duties from November 4 to November 22,

1963," Mary Ferrell Foundation, accessed July 10, 2024, https://www.maryferrell.org/sh owDoc.html?docId=1134#relPageId=645.

359 Harris, "Looking Back in Sorrow."

360 "Warren Commission Hearings Volume XVII, Current Section CE 769 - Statement of Special Agent Lawson concerning his official duties from November 4 to November 22, 1963," Mary Ferrell Foundation, accessed July 10, 2024, https://www.maryferrell.org/sh owDoc.html?docId=1134#relPageId=645.

361 "Warren Commission Hearings Volume XVIII, Current Section CE 1022 - Letter from Secret Service to the Commission date March 26, 1964," Mary Ferrell Foundation, accessed July 10, 2024, https://www.maryferrell.org/showDoc.html?docId=1135#r elPageId=730.

362 "Warren Commission Hearings Volume XVII, Current Section CE 769 - Statement of Special Agent Lawson concerning his official duties from November 4 to November 22, 1963," Mary Ferrell Foundation, accessed July 10, 2024, https://www.maryferrell.org/sh owDoc.html?docId=1134#relPageId=649.

363 Vincent Michael Palamara, *Survivor's Guilt: The Secret Service and the Failure to Protect President Kennedy*, (Walterville, OR: Trine Day, LLC, 2013), 105.

364 Palamara, *Survivor's Guilt*, 139.

365 "Warren Commission Hearings, Volume VII, Current Section: CE 768 - Final survey report prepared by Special Agent Lawson concerning President Kennedy's trip to Dallas," Mary Ferrell Foundation, accessed July 10, 2024, https://www.maryferrell.org/showDoc. html?docId=1134#relPageId=634.

366 "Freedman is Opportunist," *Denton Record Chronicle*, December 9, 1955, https://i296.pho tobucket.com/albums/mm176/pleasestandby2/dallasurniumandoil_zpsfozwfkbc.jpg.

367 Bob Goodman, *Triangle of Fire*, (Laquerian Publishing Co.: San Jose, CA, 1993), 216–217 and John Delane Williams, "Why is Morris Jaffe Interesting?," *Dealey Plaza Echo*, Volume 7, Issue 2, 33, https://www.maryferrell.org/showDoc.html?docId=16251#relPageId=40 &search=morty_freidman.

368 Jefferson Morley, "From the new JFK Files: Dallas mayor in 1963 was a CIA asset," JFKFacts, https://jfkfacts.org/from-the-new-jfk-files-dallas-mayor-in-1963-was-a-cia-a sset/.

369 Russel Stites, "Dallas Citizens Council," *Texas State Historical Association*, updated June 11, 2021, https://www.tshaonline.org/handbook/entries/dallas-citizens-council.

370 Hosty, *Assignment: Oswald*, 54.

371 "Warren Commission Hearings Vol. IV - Page 169 (Testimony of Jesse Edward Curry)," The John F. Kennedy Assassination Homepage, accessed July 10, 2024, https://www.jfk-a ssassination.eu/warren/wch/vol4/page169.php.

372 FBI File DL 100-10461, December 12, 1963, http://jfk.hood.edu/Collection/FBI%20Rec ords%20Files/105-82555/105-82555%20Section%20057/105-57b.pdf.

373 Gerald J. "Jerry" Bruno Personal Papers, Correspondence.

374 FBI File DL 100-10461, December 12, 1963, http://jfk.hood.edu/Collection/FBI%20Rec
ords%20Files/105-82555/105-82555%20Section%20057/105-57b.pdf.

375 DiEugenio, *Destiny Betrayed*, 78.

376 Select Comm. on Assassinations, Rose Cheramie, H.R. Rep. 95-na (1979), accessed July
10, 2024, https://www.jfk-online.com/cheramie-hsca.pdf.

377 DiEugenio, *Destiny Betrayed*, 15.

378 Ibid., 182.

379 Lane, *Plausible Denial*, 295–303.

380 F. Peter Model, "Killing the Kennedys," *Argosy*, July 1975, 39, https://archive.org/details/
sim_argosy_1975-07_382_1/page/38/mode/2up?view=theater.

381 Lane, *Plausible Denial*, 295–303.

382 Carol J. Williams, "Watergate Plotter May Have a Last Tale," *The Los Angeles Times*, March
20, 2007, https://www.latimes.com/archives/la-xpm-2007-mar-20-na-hunt20-story.ht
ml

383 Aaron Good, "James Angleton, Mossad, the Syndicate, and the CIA's 'Cuban Business,'"
American Exception Substack, March 26, 2025, https://americanexception.substack.com/p
/james-angleton-mossad-the-syndicate.

384 Tom Mangold, *Cold Warrior: James Jesus Angleton, The CIA's Master Spy Hunter* (New York,
NY: Simon & Schuster, 1991), 132.

385 "John Souetre's expulsion from U.S., NARA Record Number 180-10001-10374," Mary
Ferrell Foundation, accessed July 10, 2024, https://www.maryferrell.org/showDoc.html?
docId=60443#relPageId=2&search=cia_632-796.

386 Mangold, *Cold Warrior*, 134.

387 Dan Raviv and Yossi Melman, *Every Spy a Prince* (Boston, MA: Houghton Mifflin Co.,
1990), 158–159.

388 Jefferson Morley Interview, *JFK Facts*, March 21, 2025, https://jfkfacts.substack.com/p/f
rom-the-new-jfk-files-theres-a-cia?r=1459&triedRedirect=true.

389 Meagher, *Accessories After the Fact*, 42–43.

390 Seymour M. Hersh, "Helms Disavows 'Illegal' Spying by the CIA in U.S.," December 25,
1974, *New York Times*, https://www.nytimes.com/1974/12/25/archives/helms-disavows
-illegal-spying-by-the-cia-in-us.html.

THE CRIME

391 Meagher, *Accessories After the Fact*, 37.

392 James DiEugenio, *The JFK Assassination: The Evidence Today* (New York NY: Skyhorse
Publishing, 2016), 200.

393 Mark Lane, *Rush to Judgment* (New York, NY: Holt, Rinehart & Winston, 1966), 142–147.

394 DiEugenio, *The JFK Assassination*, 200.

395 Lane, *Rush to Judgment*, 142–147.

396 Ibid., 29–30.

397 Garrison, *On the Trail of the Assassins*, 217–218.

398 Meagher, *Accessories After the Fact*, 37.

399 Ibid., 65–66.

400 Ibid., 225.

401 Ibid., 66–68.

402 Palamara, *Survivor's Guilt*, 9.

403 Ibid., 388–389.

404 Ibid., 131.

405 Warren Commission Testimony of Winston Lawson, April 23, 1964, https://www.govinf o.gov/content/pkg/GPO-WARRENCOMMISSIONHEARINGS-4/pdf/GPO-WARRE NCOMMISSIONHEARINGS-4.pdf.

406 Bill Sloan with Jean Hill, *JFK: The Last Dissenting Witness* (Gretna, LA: Pelican Publishing Company, 1992), 113.

407 Palamara, *Survivor's Guilt*, 389.

408 "Warren Commission Hearings Vol. IV - Page 169 (Testimony of Jesse Edward Curry)," The John F. Kennedy Assassination Homepage, accessed July 10, 2024, https://www.jfk-a ssassination.eu/warren/wch/vol4/page169.php.

409 "Emory P. Roberts Dies; Official in Secret Service," *The Washington Post*, October 11, 1973.

410 "Remarks to the Secret Service and Presentation of an Award to James J. Rowley, November 23, 1968," The American Presidency Project, https://www.presidency.ucsb.ed u/documents/remarks-the-secret-service-and-presentation-award-james-j-rowley.

411 Palamara, *Survivor's Guilt*, 388–389.

412 Lane, *Rush to Judgment*, 30–31.

413 Ibid., 261–262.

414 Ibid., 94–95.

415 Ibid., 102.

416 Ibid., 100–105.

417 "Testimony of Louie Steven Witt," accessed July 10, 2024, https://www.history-matters.c om/archive/jfk/hsca/reportvols/vol4/pdf/HSCA_Vol4_0925_7_Witt.pdf.

418 James W. Hilty, *Robert Kennedy: Brother Protector*, (Philadelphia, PA: Temple University Press), 151.

419 WWII Casualties by Country, https://www.worldatlas.com/articles/wwii-casualties-by-country.html.

420 "JFK Assassination Records, Chapter 2: The Assassination," National Archives, accessed July 10, 2024, https://www.archives.gov/research/jfk/warren-commission-report/chapter-2.html.

421 Palamara, *Survivor's Guilt*, 388–389.

422 Meagher, *Accessories After the Fact*, 5–7.

423 Lane, *Rush to Judgment*, 37–38.

424 Ibid., 30–32.

425 Meagher, *Accessories After the Fact*, 41.

426 Ibid., 57.

427 Lane, *Rush to Judgment*, 32–33.

428 Ibid., 33–34.

429 Ibid., 39–40.

430 Ibid., 41.

431 Ibid., 35.

432 Ibid., 43–44.

433 Meagher, *Accessories After the Fact*, 26.

434 Ibid.

435 CIA Memorandum from Sidney Gottlieb, Chief Technical Services Division to Carl E. Duckett, Director, Directorate of Science and Technology, May 8, 1973, CIA's "Family Jewels," pp. 215-218, https://nsarchive2.gwu.edu/NSAEBB/NSAEBB222/family_jewels_full_ocr.pdf.

436 Douglass, *JFK and the Unspeakable*, 262.

437 "Testimony Amos Lee Euins," accessed July 10, 2024, https://www.jfk-assassination.net/russ/testimony/euins.htm.

438 Meagher, *Accessories After the Fact*, 13.

439 "Testimony James Richard Worrell, Jr.," accessed July 10, 2024, https://www.jfk-assassination.net/russ/m_j_russ/worrell.htm.

440 "Testimony Amos Lee Euins," accessed July 10, 2024, https://www.jfk-assassination.net/russ/testimony/euins.htm.

441 "Testimony of Ronald Fischer," accessed July 10, 2024, https://www.history-matters.com/archive/jfk/wc/wcvols/wh6/pdf/WH6_Fischer.pdf and "Testimony of Robert Edwin Edwards," accessed July 10, 2024, https://www.history-matters.com/archive/jfk/wc/wcvols/wh6/pdf/WH6_Edwards.pdf.

442 Lane, *Rush to Judgment*, 100–106.

443 Meagher, *Accessories After the Fact*, 12.

444 Lane, *Rush to Judgment*, 100–106.

445 Barry Ernest, *The Girl on the Stairs* (Gretna, LA: Pelican Publishing Company Inc., 2012), 244.

446 Ibid., 266--268.

447 Meagher, *Accessories After the Fact*, 44–45.

448 Ibid., 72.

449 Ibid., 226.

450 DiEugenio, *The JFK Assassination: The Evidence Today*, 217–218.

451 Lane, *Rush to Judgment*, 159.

452 Meagher, *Accessories After the Fact*, 26.

453 "Oswald 201 File, Volume 3, Folder 9A, Part 1," Mary Ferrell Foundation, accessed July 10, 2024, November 22, 1963, https://www.maryferrell.org/showDoc.html?docId=95 614#relPageId=54&search=larry_florer and "Warren Commission Hearings, Volume XIX, Current Section: Decker Ex 5323 – Dallas County Sheriff's Office record of the evens surrounding the assassination," Mary Farrell Foundation, accessed July 10, 2024, https://www.maryferrell.org/showDoc.html?docId=1136#relPageId=487.

454 Goodman, *Triangle of Fire*, 214.

455 Jim Marrs, *Crossfire: The Plot That Killed Kennedy* (Basic Books: New York, NY, 2013), 327.

456 "Deposition of Jim Braden, NARA Record Number: 180-10103-10376," Mary Farrell Foundation, accessed July 10, 2024, https://www.maryferrell.org/showDoc.html?docId= 19907#relPageId=6&search=jim_braden.

457 "HSCA Report, Volume IX, Current Section: x. Lawrence V. Meyers," Mary Farrell Foundation, accessed July 10, 2024, https://www.maryferrell.org/showDoc.html?docId= 955#relPageId=891.

458 Lane, *Rush to Judgment*, 205.

459 Meagher, *Accessories After the Fact*, 260–266.

460 Ibid., 10.

461 Lane, *Rush to Judgment*, 83.

462 Ibid., 173.

463 November 22, 1963: Death of the President, John F. Kennedy Presidential Library and Museum, https://www.jfklibrary.org/learn/about-jfk/jfk-in-history/november-22-196 3-death-of-the-president.

464 Lane, *Rush to Judgment*, 46.

465 Ibid., 59–60.

466 Meagher, *Accessories After the Fact*, 162.

467 Lane, *Rush to Judgment*, 46–49.

468 Allen Public Library, "Dr. Robert McClelland - JFK's Last Doctor (11-12-15)," video, https://www.youtube.com/watch?v=ySO0pLcN5ww.

469 Lane, *Rush to Judgment*, 46–49.

470 Allen Public Library, "Dr. Robert McClelland."

471 Meagher, *Accessories After the Fact*, 10.

472 Ibid., 41.

473 Ibid., 43–45.

474 Douglass, *JFK and the Unspeakable*, 288.

475 Lane, *Rush to Judgment*, 168–171.

476 Meagher, *Accessories After the Fact*, 266.

477 Lane, *Rush to Judgment*, 168–171.

478 Ibid., 171–173.

479 Ibid., 191.

480 Ibid., 193–194.

481 Ibid., 177.

482 Douglass, *JFK and the Unspeakable*, 290–291.

483 Lane, *Rush to Judgment*, 114.

484 Ibid., 119–120.

485 Ibid., 203.

486 Douglass, *JFK and the Unspeakable*, 290–291.

487 Meagher, *Accessories After the Fact*, 88.

488 Ibid., 247.

489 Ibid., 85–88.

490 Lane, *Rush to Judgment*, 173–174.

491 Meagher, *Accessories After the Fact*, 309.

492 Lane, *Rush to Judgment*, 148–150.

493 Meagher, *Accessories After the Fact*, 305.

494 Ibid., 248.

495 Ibid., 306.

496 Lane, *Rush to Judgment*, 195–196.

497 Ibid., 90–91.

498 Meagher, *Accessories After the Fact*, 257.

499 Lane, *Rush to Judgment*, 193.

500 Ibid., 178.

501 Meagher, *Accessories After the Fact*, 279.

502 Lane, *Rush to Judgment*, 114.

503 Ibid., 122–123.

504 Meagher, *Accessories After the Fact*, 101.

505 Lane, *Rush to Judgment*, 153–154.

506 Meagher, *Accessories After the Fact*, 200–209.

507 Ibid., 234, 245.

508 Ibid., 200–209.

509 Ibid., 223.

510 Ibid., 193.

511 "JFK Assassination Records, Chapter 4: The Assassin," National Archives, accessed July 10, 2024, https://www.archives.gov/research/jfk/warren-commission-report/chapter-4. html.

512 Meagher, *Accessories After the Fact*, 111.

513 DiEugenio, *JFK Revisited*, 143.

514 Meagher, *Accessories After the Fact*, 49.

515 DiEugenio, *JFK Revisited*, 36.

516 Meagher, *Accessories After the Fact*, 114–115.

517 Garrison, *On the Trail of the Assassins*, 79–81.

518 Hosty, *Assignment: Oswald*, 54.

519 "Warren Commission Hearings, Volume XXII, Current Section: CE 1322 - FBI Report, Dated November 25, 1963, concerning inventory of items taken by Dallas Police Department from Jack…," Mary Ferrell Foundation, accessed July 10, 2024, https://www. maryferrell.org/showDoc.html?docId=1317#relPageId=546.

520 "Sam R. Bloom Jr. Who Spent 50 Years with…," *UPI*.

521 Meagher, *Accessories After the Fact*, 248.

THE ASSASSIN OF THE ALLEGED ASSASSIN

522 Peter Dale Scott, *Deep Politics and the Death of JFK* (Berkeley, CA: University of California Press, 1993), 141.

523 Scott, *Deep Politics*, 143.

524 "Warren Commission Hearings, Volume XXVI, Current Section: CE 3063 – FBI report of investigation of allegations that Jack Ruby dealt with illegal movement of arms to Cuba at …,"Mary Ferrell Foundation, accessed July 10, 2024, https://www.maryferrell.org/sho

wDoc.html?docId=1142#relPageId=670&search=warren_commission%20exibit%20Exh
ibit%203063.

525 Robert Lacey, *Little Man, Meyer Lansky and the Gangster Life* (Boston, MA: Little, Brown
and Company, 1991), 128.

526 Webb, *One Nation Under Blackmail*, 4.

527 Seth Kantor, *The Ruby Cover-Up* (New York, NY: Kensington Publishing Co., 1978), 39.

528 Webb, *One Nation Under Blackmail*, 2–5.

529 Kantor, *The Ruby Cover-Up*, 39.

530 Paul Jay Singer, "The Jewish Soul of Meyer Lansky," *JewishPress.com*, https://www.jewish
press.com/sections/features/features-on-jewish-world/the-jewish-soul-of-meyer-lansk
y/2019/08/21/.

531 Lacey, *Little Man, Meyer Lansky and the Gangster Life*, 203.

532 Mickey Cohen with John Peer Nugent, *Mickey Cohen: In My Own Words* (Englewood
Cliffs, NJ: Prentice Hall, Inc., 1975), 90–91.

533 Biography.com editors, "Mickey Cohen," *Biography*, November 28, 2023, https://www.bi
ography.com/crime/a45973387/mickey-cohen.

534 "Abraham Feinberg," Jewish Virtual Library.

535 Karpin, *The Bomb in the Basement*, 129.

536 Scott, *Deep Politics*, 70.

537 "House Select Committee on Assassinations, Final Report, Current Section: 4. The
Committee believes...," Mary Ferrell Foundation, accessed July 10, 2024, https://www.m
aryferrell.org/showDoc.html?docId=800#relPageId=186.

538 Donald Gibson, *The Kennedy Assassination Cover-Up* (self-published, 1999), 121–122.

539 "Warren Commission Hearings, Volume XXVI, Current Section: CE 3063 – FBI report
of investigation of allegations that Jack Ruby dealt with illegal movement of arms to Cuba
at ...,"Mary Ferrell Foundation, accessed July 10, 2024, https://www.maryferrell.org/sho
wDoc.html?docId=1142#relPageId=670&search=warren_commission%20exoibit%20Exh
ibit%203063.

540 "Warren Commission Hearings, Volume XXVI, Current Section: CE 3063 – FBI report
of investigation of allegations that Jack Ruby dealt with illegal movement of arms to Cuba
at ...," Mary Ferrell Foundation, accessed July 10, 2024, https://www.maryferrell.org/sho
wDoc.html?docId=1142#relPageId=670&search=warren_commission%20exoibit%20Exh
ibit%203063.

541 Kantor, *The Ruby Cover-Up*, 44.

542 "HSCA Report Volume IX, Current Section: Review by the Committee," Mary Ferrell
Foundation, accessed July 10, 2024, https://www.maryferrell.org/showDoc.html?docId=
955#relPageId=198.

543 Scott, *Deep Politics*, 143.

544 Kantor, *The Ruby Cover-Up*, 91.

545 Scott, *Deep Politics*, 143.

546 Kantor, *The Ruby Cover-Up*, 56–57.

547 Ibid., 60.

548 Ibid., 61.

549 Ibid., 252.

550 Ibid., 62.

551 Ibid., 48–49.

552 "HSCA Report Volume IX, Current Section: Review by the Committee," Mary Ferrell Foundation, accessed July 10, 2024, https://www.maryferrell.org/showDoc.html?docId=955#relPageId=198.

553 "Warren Commission Report, Current Section: Possible Conspiracy Involving Jack Ruby," Mary Ferrell Foundation, accessed July 10, 2024, https://www.maryferrell.org/showDoc.html?docId=946#relPageId=366 and Kantor, *The Ruby Cover-Up*, 97.

554 "Warren Commission Report, Current Section: Possible Conspiracy Involving Jack Ruby," Mary Ferrell Foundation, accessed July 10, 2024, https://www.maryferrell.org/showDoc.html?docId=946#relPageId=366.

555 Kantor, *The Ruby Cover-Up*, 100–101.

556 Ibid., 223.

557 "Warren Commission Report, Current Section: Possible Conspiracy Involving Jack Ruby," Mary Ferrell Foundation, accessed July 10, 2024, https://www.maryferrell.org/showDoc.html?docId=946#relPageId=366.

558 Kantor, *The Ruby Cover-Up*, 112–113.

559 Ibid., 116.

560 Ibid., 123–124.

561 Ibid., 131.

562 Ibid., 133–134.

563 Ibid., 139.

564 Lane, *Rush to Judgment*, 227.

565 Kantor, *The Ruby Cover-Up*, 140–143.

566 Ibid., 149.

567 Ibid., 221.

568 Meagher, *Accessories After the Fact*, 402.

569 Melvin M. Belli, *My Life on Trial* (New York, NY: William Morrow and Company, Inc., 1976), 12–13.

570 Belli, *My Life on Trial*, 232.

571 Melvin M. Belli, *Dallas Justice* (New York, NY: David McKay Company, 1964), 105.

572 Belli, *Dallas Justice*, 108.

573 Gerry May, "Retired Dallas Officer Billy Grammer Remembers the Call That Could Have Stopped Killing of JFK's Assassin," *KTBS3*, November 18, 2018, https://www.ktbs.com/c ommunity/hometown-patriot/retired-dallas-officer-billy-grammer-remembers-the-cal l-that-couldve-stopped-killing-of-jfks-assassin/article_f428d63e-e9ea-11e8-ac79-57eca 10df1f5.html.

574 Kantor, *The Ruby Cover-Up*, 276.

575 Steve North, "My History with the Family of Lee Harvey Oswald's Jewish Killer," *Jewish Telegraphic Agency*, November 11, 2013, https://www.jta.org/2013/11/11/united-states/ my-history-with-the-family-of-lee-harvey-oswalds-jewish-killer.

576 William M. Kunstler, *My Life as a Radical Lawyer* (New York, NY: Birch Lane Press, 1994), 158.

577 Kunstler, *My Life*, 158.

THE INITIAL COVER-UP

578 Warren Commission Testimony of Kenneth O'Donnell, May 18, 1964, https://ww w.aarclibrary.org/publib/jfk/wc/wcvols/wh7/pdf/WH7_ODonnell.pdf and Warren Commission Testimony of Lawrence O'Brien, May 26, 1964, https://history-matters.co m/archive/jfk/wc/wcvols/wh7/pdf/WH7_OBrien.pdf.

579 DiEugenio, *JFK Revisited*, 44–47.

580 Phillip F. Nelson, *LBJ: The Mastermind of the JFK Assassination* (New York, NY: Skyhorse Publishing, 2011), 526.

581 DiEugenio, *JFK Revisited*, 188.

582 Nelson, *LBJ*, 178.

583 *Sacrificing Liberty*, directed by Matthew Miller Skow (TruHistory, 2020), DVD.

584 Gibson, *The Kennedy Assassination Cover-Up*, 27–29.

585 Mal Hyman, *Burying the Lead: The Media and the JFK Assassination* (Walterville, OR: Trine Day LLC, 2019), 33.

586 Hyman, *Burying the Lead*, 35.

587 Gibson, *The Kennedy Assassination Cover-Up*, 33.

588 Ibid., 32.

589 Hyman, *Burying the Lead*, 38–39.

590 Gibson, *The Kennedy Assassination Cover-Up*, 32.

591 Harry Truman, "Limit CIA Role to Intelligence," *The Washington Post*, December 22, 1963, https://archive.org/details/LimitCIARoleToIntelligenceByHarrySTruman.

592 Gibson, *The Kennedy Assassination Cover-Up*, 43.

593 "Telephone Conversation Between Bill Moyers and Eugene Rostow Yale Law School ...,"
     Mary Ferrell Foundation, accessed July 10, 2024, https://www.maryferrell.org/showDoc.
     html?docId=831#relPageId=3 and https://www.maryferrell.org/audio/LbjLib/Audio_lb
     jlib_WCC1A_Moyers-Rostow_24-Nov-1963_2_1.mp3.

594 John Rosenberg, "The Quest Against Détente: Eugene Rostow, The October War, and the
     Origins of the Anti-Détente Movement, 1969-1976," *Diplomatic History*, Vol. 39, No. 4,
     September 2015, 728.

595 Ibid., 729.

596 Joan Mellen, *Blood in the Water* (Amherst, NY: Prometheus Books, 2018), 32.

597 Rosenberg, "The Quest Against Détente," 720–721.

598 Ibid., 722.

599 Ibid., 723.

600 Melvin Gurtov, "The National Security State and Soviet-American Relations," *The Journal
     of East Asian Affairs*, Vol. 2, No. 2, Fall/Winter 1982, 213–214.

601 Ali Wyne, "Greater Disorder Does Not Imply Greater Insecurity," *The Rand Blog*, January
     7, 2015, https://www.rand.org/blog/2015/01/greater-disorder-does-not-imply-greater-
     insecurity.html.

602 David Halberstam, *The Best and the Brightest* (New York, NY: Random House, 1969),
     156–162.

603 Gibson, *The Kennedy Assassination Cover-Up*, 56.

604 Ibid., 68.

605 Webb, *One Nation Under Blackmail*, 60.

606 Ibid.

607 Nelson, *LBJ*, 441.

608 Gerald D. McKnight, *Breach of Trust: How the Warren Commission Failed the Nation and
     Why* (Lawrence, KS: University Press of Kansas, 2005), 403.

609 May 20, 1965, DOJ memo, The Israel Lobby Archive, https://www.israellobby.org/azcd
     oj/p6100006/default.asp.

610 McKnight, *Breach of Trust*, 30.

611 Gibson, *The Kennedy Assassination Cover-Up*, 59–65, 128–129.

612 Guyénot, *The Unspoken Kennedy Truth*, 50.

613 Kennedy, *Robert Kennedy in His Own Words*, 421.

614 Alan Hart, *Zionism: The Real Enemy of the Jews, Volume Two*, 13.

615 Kennedy, *Robert Kennedy in His Own Words*, 20–21.

616 Gibson, *The Kennedy Assassination Cover-Up*, 67.

617 Ibid., 66.

618 Ibid., 59–65, 128–129.

619 Karpin, The Bomb in the Basement, 136–137.

620 Ibid.

621 Gibson, *The Kennedy Assassination Cover-Up*, 70–73, 79, 82–83.

622 Ibid., 49.

623 Ibid., 84.

624 *JFK: What the Doctors Saw*, directed by Barbara Shearer (Channel 5 Television, 2023) and Kenneth O'Donnell Warren Commission Testimony.

625 Jim DiEugenio, "The Nothingburgers? Nope.," *Kennedys and King*, April 24, 2025, https://www.kennedysandking.com/john-f-kennedy-articles/the-nothingburgers-nope.

626 Newman, *Oswald and the CIA*, 637.

627 David Talbot, *The Devil's Chessboard* (New York, NY: Harper Perennial, 2009), 8, 573.

628 McKnight, *Breach of Trust*, 34.

629 Gibson, *The Kennedy Assassination Cover-Up*, 91.

630 Ibid., 98–100.

631 Ibid., 100.

632 Ernest, *The Girl on the Stairs*, 34–35.

633 "Wednesday, March 25, 1964, Testimony of Marrion L. Baker, Mrs. Robert A. Reid, Luke Mooney, Eugene Bone, and M. N. McDonald," https://www.history-matters.com/archive/jfk/wc/wcvols/wh3/pdf/WH3_Baker.pdf.

634 Ernest, *The Girl on the Stairs*, 46.

635 "Vickie Adams: The Interview," *Mort Sahl Show*, November 25, 1966, video, https://rumble.com/v43w4sx-black-op-radio-1197.html.

636 *The American Media and the 2ⁿᵈ Assassination of President John F. Kennedy*, directed by John Barbour (John Barbour Productions, 2017).

637 DiEugenio, *JFK Revisited*, 45, 49.

638 Lane, *Rush to Judgment*, 12.

639 Meagher, *Accessories After the Fact*, 154.

640 DiEugenio, *The JFK Assassination: The Evidence Today*, 168.

641 McKnight, *Breach of Trust*, 5.

642 DiEugenio, *JFK Revisited*, 26.

643 McKnight, *Breach of Trust*, 5.

644 Ibid., 6–7.

645 Lane, *Rush to Judgment*, 71–73.

646 Ibid., 70.

647 Ibid., 126–130.

648 Meagher, *Accessories After the Fact*, 120–124.

649 Ibid., 43–45.

650 Lane, *Rush to Judgment, 119.*

651 Warren Commission Testimony of Eugene Boone, https://www.history-matters.com/ar chive/jfk/wc/wcvols/wh3/pdf/WH3_Boone.pdf.

652 Lane, *Rush to Judgment*, 195–200.

653 DiEugenio, *JFK Revisited*, 27–29.

654 McKnight, *Breach of Trust*, 6.

655 Meagher, *Accessories After the Fact*, 22.

656 Aaron Good, "James Angleton, Mossad, the Syndicate, and the CIA's 'Cuban Business,'" *American Exception Substack*, March 26, 2025, https://americanexception.substack.com/p /james-angleton-mossad-the-syndicate.

657 Lane, *Rush to Judgment*, 309–310.

658 Ibid., 315.

659 Ibid., 318.

660 "Marina Oswald-Porter's Statements of a Contradictory Nature," accessed July 10, 2024, https://docslib.org/doc/11287674/marina-oswald-porters-statements-of-a-contradicto ry-nature.

661 Meager, *Accessories After the Fact*, xxix–xxx.

662 McKnight, *Breach of Trust*, 48.

663 Gibson, *The Kennedy Assassination Cover-Up*, 84.

664 DiEugenio, *JFK Revisited*, 31.

THE LITTLE BROTHER

665 "Robert F. Kennedy Presidential Campaign Announcement," *C-SPAN*, March 16, 1968, video, https://www.c-span.org/video/?443225-1/robert-f-kennedy-presidential-campai gn-announcement.

666 Schlesinger, *Robert Kennedy and His Times*, 857.

667 Lisa Pease, *A Lie Too Big to Fail* (Port Townsend, WA: Feral House, 2018), 3.

668 Tim Tate and Brad Johnson, *The Assassination of Robert F. Kennedy* (Borough, SE1 OHS: Lume Books, 2020), vii.

669 William Klaber and Philip Melanson, *Shadow Play: The Unsolved Murder of Robert F. Kennedy* (New York, NY: St. Martin's Griffin, 2018), 5–7.

670 111 Cong. Rec. 14566-14568 (daily ed. June 23, 1965), https://www.congress.gov/boun d-congressional-record/1965/06/23.

671 "John F. Kennedy Administration: Memorandum on Palestinian Refugee Item in UN, Relations with Arabs (November 21, 1963)," Jewish Virtual Library, https://www.jewishv irtuallibrary.org/memorandum-on-palestinian-refugee-item-in-un-relations-with-arab s-november-1963.

672 Klaber and Melanson, *Shadow Play*, opening quote and Edward Curtin, "The Blatant Conspiracy Behind Senator Robert F. Kennedy's Assassination," *Covert Geopolitics*, June 13, 2020, https://geopolitics.co/2020/06/13/the-blatant-conspiracy-behind-senator-ro bert-f-kennedys-assassination/.

673 Tate and Johnson, *The Assassination of Robert F. Kennedy*, 83.

674 Shane O'Sullivan, *Who Killed Bobby?: The Unsolved Murder of Robert F. Kennedy* (New York, NY: Union Square Press, 2008), 85–88.

675 Ibid., 88–91.

676 Ibid., 91–92.

677 Tate and Johnson, *The Assassination of Robert F. Kennedy*, 85.

678 O'Sullivan, *Who Killed Bobby?* 91, 94–97.

679 Tate and Johnson, *The Assassination of Robert F. Kennedy*, 93.

680 O'Sullivan, *Who Killed Bobby?* 91.

681 Ibid., 98–101.

682 Ibid., 103.

683 Klaber and Melanson, *Shadow Play*, 137.

684 theCarbonFreeze, "Robert F. Kennedy and Eugene McCarthy Primary Debate (6-1-68), video, https://www.youtube.com/watch?v=NhYHK1CtPJc.

685 Pease, *A Lie Too Big to Fail*, 125.

686 Klaber and Melanson, *Shadow Play*, 137.

687 News Conference 53, April 3, 1963, John F. Kennedy Presidential Library and Museum, https://www.jfklibrary.org/archives/other-resources/john-f-kennedy-press-conference s/news-conference-53.

688 Klaber and Melanson, *Shadow Play*, 141.

689 Pease, *A Lie Too Big to Fail*, 334.

690 O'Sullivan, *Who Killed Bobby?* 114–116.

691 Pease, *A Lie Too Big to Fail*, 449–450.

692 O'Sullivan, *Who Killed Bobby?* 116–117.

693 Ibid., 117.

694 Ibid., 110–113.

695 Pease, *A Lie Too Big to Fail*, 340.

696 Pease, *A Lie Too Big to Fail*, 341.

697 Ibid., 342.

698 O'Sullivan, *Who Killed Bobby?* 217.

699 Pease, *A Lie Too Big to Fail*, 161–162.

700 Tate and Johnson, *The Assassination of Robert F. Kennedy*, 88.

701 Klaber and Melanson, *Shadow Play*, 158–159.

702 O'Sullivan, *Who Killed Bobby?* 114.

703 Klaber and Melanson, *Shadow Play*, 110.

704 Pease, *A Lie Too Big to Fail*, 11.

705 O'Sullivan, *Who Killed Bobby?* 10.

706 Pease, *A Lie Too Big to Fail*, 14.

707 Klaber and Melanson, *Shadow Play*, 108–109.

708 O'Sullivan, *Who Killed Bobby?*, 10.

709 Klaber and Melanson, *Shadow Play*, 116.

710 Pease, *A Lie Too Big to Fail*, 11.

711 James DiEugenio and Lisa Pease, eds., *The Assassinations: Probe Magazine on JFK, MLK, RFK and Malcom X* (Port Townsend, WA: Feral House, 2003), 603.

712 O'Sullivan, *Who Killed Bobby?* 312.

713 Ibid., 334–335.

714 Pease, *A Lie Too Big to Fail*, 350.

715 O'Sullivan, *Who Killed Bobby?* 13.

716 Klaber and Melanson, *Shadow Play*, 10, 117.

717 O'Sullivan, *Who Killed Bobby?* 124.

718 O'Sullivan, *Who Killed Bobby?* 13.

719 Pease, *A Lie Too Big to Fail*, 67–69.

720 Klaber and Melanson, *Shadow Play*, 110.

721 Ibid., 78.

722 Tate and Johnson, *The Assassination of Robert F. Kennedy*, 137.

723 Pease, *A Lie Too Big to Fail*, 213.

724 Tate and Johnson, *The Assassination of Robert F. Kennedy*, 137.

725 O'Sullivan, *Who Killed Bobby?* 63–64.

726 Ibid., 66.

727 Ibid., 71–77.

728 Ibid., 75–76.

729 Ibid., 71–77.

730 Ibid., 343.

731 Ibid., 72–74.

732 Klaber and Melanson, *Shadow Play*, 81.

733 O'Sullivan, *Who Killed Bobby?* 72–74.

734 Klaber and Melanson, *Shadow Play*, 81

735 "RFK LAPD Microfilm, Volume 51 (Interviews, I-70 thru I-134), Current Section: Griffin, Booker 25 Jul 1968," Mary Ferrell Foundation, accessed July 10, 2024, https://maryferrel l.org/showDoc.html?docId=99737#relPageId=24.

736 Pease, *A Lie Too Big to Fail*, 151.

737 O'Sullivan, *Who Killed Bobby?*, 75.

738 Ibid., 82.

739 Pease, *A Lie Too Big to Fail*, 256.

740 Klaber and Melanson, *Shadow Play*, 72.

741 Tate and Johnson, *The Assassination of Robert F. Kennedy*, 136.

742 O'Sullivan, *Who Killed Bobby?*, 69.

743 Klaber and Melanson, *Shadow Play*, 72-73.

744 Tate and Johnson, *The Assassination of Robert F. Kennedy*, 135–136.

745 Klaber and Melanson, *Shadow Play*, 66.

746 Ibid., 67.

747 Ibid., 69.

748 Ibid., 71.

749 Ibid., 74.

750 Ibid., 75.

751 O'Sullivan, *Who Killed Bobby?*, 343–344.

752 Pease, *A Lie Too Big to Fail*, 38.

753 Klaber and Melanson, *Shadow Play*, 292–295.

754 Ibid., 295–296.

755 Ibid., 304.

756 Pease, *A Lie Too Big to Fail*, 272.

757 O'Sullivan, *Who Killed Bobby?*, 315.

758 Ibid.

759 Ibid., 316–317.

760 Ibid., 320.

761 Ibid., 323–325.

762 Ibid., 336.

763 Pease, *A Lie Too Big to Fail*, 273.

764 O'Sullivan, *Who Killed Bobby?*, 336.

765 Ibid., 343.

766 Pease, *A Lie Too Big to Fail*, 273–274.

767 Ibid., 274.

768 Ibid., 275.

769 Ibid., 277.

770 Ibid., 334–335.

771 Ibid., 335.

772 Ibid., 288.

773 Ibid., 39–40.

774 Ibid., 56.

775 Ibid., 29–30.

776 Ibid., 77.

777 Ibid., 287–288.

778 Ibid., 51.

779 Ibid., 287–288.

780 Ibid., 278–279.

781 Ibid., 279–282.

782 Klaber and Melanson, *Shadow Play*, 106.

783 Pease, *A Lie Too Big to Fail*, 147.

784 Klaber and Melanson, *Shadow Play*, 106.

785 Ibid., 307.

786 Pease, *A Lie Too Big to Fail*, 351.

787 "RFK LAPD Microfilm, Volume 52 (Interviews, I-70 thru I-134), Current Section: Freed, Evan Phillip, 14 Jun 1968," Mary Ferrell Foundation, accessed July 10, 2024, https://mary ferrell.org/showDoc.html?docId=99738#relPageId=128.

788 Pease, *A Lie Too Big to Fail*, 352

789 Klaber and Melanson, *Shadow Play*, 109.

790 "RFK LAPD Microfilm, Volume 51 (Interviews, I-70 thru I-134), Current Section: Griffin, Booker 25 Jul 1968," Mary Ferrell Foundation, accessed July 10, 2024, https://maryferrel l.org/showDoc.html?docId=99737#relPageId=24.

791 Klaber and Melanson, *Shadow Play*, 109.

792 Pease, *A Lie Too Big to Fail*, 350–352.

793 Klaber and Melanson, *Shadow Play*, 109.

794 O'Sullivan, *Who Killed Bobby?*, 129.

795 Ibid., 132.

796 Pease, *A Lie Too Big to Fail*, 18.

797 O'Sullivan, *Who Killed Bobby?*, 131.

798 Pease, *A Lie Too Big to Fail*, 30.

799 Tate and Johnson, *The Assassination of Robert F. Kennedy*, 59.

800 Klaber and Melanson, *Shadow Play*, 1–2, 65.

801 Pease, *A Lie Too Big to Fail*, 54.

802 Klaber and Melanson, *Shadow Play*, 12–13.

803 Tate and Johnson, *The Assassination of Robert F. Kennedy*, 63.

804 O'Sullivan, *Who Killed Bobby?*, 39.

805 Klaber and Melanson, *Shadow Play, 13.*

806 Ibid., 42–43.

807 William Turner and Jonn Christian, *The Assassination of Robert F. Kennedy* (New York, NY: Thunder's Mouth Press, 1978), 61–67.

808 Pease, *A Lie Too Big to Fail*, 103.

809 Klaber and Melanson, *Shadow Play*, 113.

810 Ibid., 121.

811 Ibid., 123–125.

812 Ibid., 120.

813 Ibid., 39.

814 Ibid., 50.

815 Ibid., 64.

816 Ibid., 35, 38.

817 Tate and Johnson, *The Assassination of Robert F. Kennedy*, 99.

818 Klaber and Melanson, *Shadow Play*, 69.

819 Ibid., 150–151.

820 Ibid., 198–199.

821 Pease, *A Lie Too Big to Fail*, 418.

822 Klaber and Melanson, *Shadow Play*, 198–199.

823 O'Sullivan, *Who Killed Bobby?* 252–253.

824 Ibid., 257.

825 Ibid., 386.

826 Ibid., 393.

827 Klaber and Melanson, *Shadow Play*, 160.

828 O'Sullivan, *Who Killed Bobby?*, 305.

829 Ibid., 143.

830 Ibid., 351.

831 Klaber and Melanson, *Shadow Play*, 83–84.

832 O'Sullivan, *Who Killed Bobby?*, 349–350.

833 Klaber and Melanson, *Shadow Play*, 70.

834 Ibid., 85–91.

835 Ibid., 300–301.

836 O'Sullivan, *Who Killed Bobby?*, 398.

837 Pease, *A Lie Too Big to Fail*, 442–446.

838 Ibid., 410.

839 O'Sullivan, *Who Killed Bobby?* 399.

840 Pease, *A Lie Too Big to Fail*, 422.

841 Guyénot, *The Unspoken Kennedy Truth*, 15 and Ronen Bergman, *Rise and Kill First: The Secret History of Israel's Targeted Assassinations* (New York, NY: Random House, 2018), 117–119.

842 O'Sullivan, *Who Killed Bobby?*, 189–191.

843 Ibid., 334.

844 Ibid., 423.

845 Pease, *A Lie Too Big to Fail*, 64.

846 Ibid., 491.

847 O'Sullivan, *Who Killed Bobby?*, 424.

848 Ibid., 69, 54.

849 Ibid., 475.

NEW INVESTIGATIONS AND CONTINUING COVER-UPS

850 Garrison, *On the Trail of the Assassins*, 4–11.

851 Ibid., 12–14.

852 Garrison, *On the Trail of the Assassins*, 37–38 and DiEugenio, *Destiny Betrayed*, 179.

853 DiEugenio, *Destiny Betrayed*, 223.

854 Ibid., 220–226.

855 Garrison, *On the Trail of the Assassins*, 149–150.

856 Ibid., 150–151.

857 Ibid., 159.

858 Ibid., 144–148.

859 "Memo for: Garrison Group Meeting No. 1-20 September 1967, NARA Record Number: 104-10428-10023," Mary Ferrell Foundation, accessed July 10, 2024, https://www.maryf errell.org/showDoc.html?docId=6515#relPageId=2 and Jefferson Morley, "The Garrison Group: What one top CIA official said about Clay Shaw," JFKFacts, accessed July 10, 2024, https://jfkfacts.org/the-garrison-group-what-one-top-cia-official-said-about-clay-shaw /.

860 DiEugenio, *Destiny Betrayed*, 270.

861 Ibid., 269.

862 Ibid., 228–231.

863 Ibid., 255, 233.

864 Ibid., 238–239.

865 Saul J. Singer, "The Judaism and Zionism of David Sarnoff," *Jewish Press*, August 24, 2022, https://www.jewishpress.com/sections/features/features-on-jewish-world/the-judaism -and-zionism-of-david-sarnoff/2022/08/24/.

866 DiEugenio, *Destiny Betrayed*, 255–256.

867 Ibid., 235–236.

868 Garrison, *On the Trail of the Assassins*, 230.

869 Ibid., 160.

870 DiEugenio, *Destiny Betrayed*, 287, 305.

871 Ibid., 293.

872 DiEugenio, *Destiny Betrayed*, 294–295.

873 Garrison, *On the Trail of the Assassins*, 235–236.

874 DiEugenio, *Destiny Betrayed*, 295–296.

875 "Clay Shaw Trial Transcripts," Mary Ferrell Foundation, accessed July 10, 2024, https://w ww.maryferrell.org/php/showlist.php?docset=1016.

876 DiEugenio, *Destiny Betrayed*, 302.

877 Ibid., 300.

878 Garrison, *On the Trail of the Assassins*, 243.

879 Ibid., 82.

880 "Clay Shaw Trial Transcript, 25 Feb 1969 (Testimony of Mr. Andrews)," Mary Farrell Foundation, accessed July 10, 2024, https://www.maryferrell.org/showDoc.html?docId= 1302#relPageId=61.

881 James Kirkwood, *American Grotesque* (New York, NY: Harper Perennial, 1992), 555.

882 DiEugenio, *Destiny Betrayed*, 310.

883 James DiEugenio, "The Sins of Robert Blakey," *The Assassinations* (Port Townsend, WA: Feral House, 2003), 52–55.

884 DiEugenio, *Destiny Betrayed*, 339–340.

885 James DiEugenio, "The Sins of Robert Blakey," *The Assassinations*, 52–65.

886 Fonzi, *The Last Investigation*, 6.

887 James DiEugenio, "The Sins of Robert Blakey," 82.

888 DiEugenio, *JFK Revisited*, 55.

889 James DiEugenio, "The Sins of Robert Blakey," *The Assassinations*, 71–72.

890 Fonzi, *The Last Investigation*, 12.

891 Riccardo, "Chomsky on Kennedy Assassination," June 17, 2015, video, https://www.yout ube.com/watch?v=ZSjQOD0I3cM.

892 "Reported Carter Assassination Plot Given Credibility by New Evidence," *New York Times*, May 12, 1979, https://www.nytimes.com/1979/05/12/archives/reported-carterassassin ation-plot-given-credibility-by-new-evidence.html.

893 "Fact Sheet: President Donald J. Trump Orders Declassification of JFK, RFK, and MLK Assassination Files," White House, Briefings and Statements, January 23, 2025, https://w ww.whitehouse.gov/briefings-statements/2025/01/fact-sheet-president-donald-j-trum p-orders-declassification-of-jfk-rfk-and-mlk-assassination-files/.

894 William La Jeunesse, "Hollywood Producer Arnon Milchan Admits Double Life as Israeli Spy," *Fox News*, April 6, 2016, https://www.foxnews.com/entertainment/hollywood-pro ducer-arnon-milchan-admits-double-life-as-israeli-spy.

895 "Vanunu Warns Israel of 'Second Chernobyl' risk," *The Sydney Morning Herald*, July 26, 2004, https://www.smh.com.au/world/vanunu-warns-israel-of-second-chernobyl-risk-20040726-gdjf3x.html.

896 Klaber and Melanson, *Shadow Play*, 305–307.

897 Ibid., 310–311.

898 Pease, *A Lie Too Big to Fail*, 500.

THE SON

899 Steven M. Gillon, *America's Reluctant Prince: The Life of John Kennedy Jr.* (New York, NY: Dutton, 2019), 400.

900 Gillon, *America's Reluctant Prince*, 40–41.

901 Shaw, Maud: Oral History Interview – JFK #1, 4/27/1965, John F. Kennedy Presidential Library and Museum, https://www.jfklibrary.org/asset-viewer/archives/JFKOH/Shaw %2C%20Maud/JFKOH-MS-01/JFKOH-MS-01.

902 Guyénot, *The Unspoken Kennedy Truth*, 111.

903   Rosemarie Terenzio and Liz McNeil, *JFK Jr.: An Intimate Oral Biography*. (New York, NY: Gallery Books, 2024), 28.

904   Ibid., 110.

905   Donald Jeffries, *Hidden History* (New York, NY: Skyhorse Publishing, 2016), 212.

906   Ibid., 212.

907   Guyénot, *The Unspoken Kennedy Truth*, 111.

908   Gillon, *America's Reluctant Prince*, 307.

909   Ibid., 255.

910   Ibid., 309.

911   Guyénot, *The Unspoken Kennedy Truth*, 116.

912   "US Navy Missile hit TWA 800 – Ex-Kennedy Aide", *The Irish Times*, November 8, 1996, https://www.irishtimes.com/news/us-navy-missile-hit-twa-800-ex-kennedy-aide-1.10 3900.

913   Gillon, *America's Reluctant Prince*, 310.

914   Patrick Goodenough, "Kennedy felt connection with Rabin assassination," *CNSNews*, accessed April 26 2022, https://www.cnsnews.com/news/article/kennedy-felt-034conn ection034-rabin-assassination.

915   Leah Rabin, *Rabin: Our Life, His Legacy* (New York, NY: G.P. Putnam's Sons, 1997), 120.

916   William Sylvester Noonan, *My Friendship with John F. Kennedy, Jr.* (New York, NY: Penguin Group, 2006), 189.

917   Oliver Stone, "Our Counterfeit History," *George*, October 1998, https://thesearchersfilm. files.wordpress.com/2016/11/oliver-stone-interview-george-mag-oct-1998.pdf.

918   Guyénot, *The Unspoken Kennedy Truth*, 110.

919   Terenzio and McNeil, *JFK Jr.: An Intimate Oral Biography*, 318.

920   Gillon, *America's Reluctant Prince*, 222.

921   Ibid., 380.

922   Ibid., 382.

923   Guyénot, *The Unspoken Kennedy Truth*, 114.

924   Gillon, *America's Reluctant Prince*, 387.

925   Robert T. Littell, *The Men We Became* (New York, NY: St Martin's Press, 2004), 235.

926   Gillon, *America's Reluctant Prince*, 381–382.

927   Liz McNeil, "Would JFK Jr. Have Run for President? His Best Friends Reveal His Last Days," *People*, July 19, 2016, https://people.com/celebrity/john-f-kennedy-jr-for-preside nt-jfks-sons-political-ambition/.

928   Terenzio and McNeil, *JFK Jr.: An Intimate Oral Biography*, 314.

929 Guyénot, *The Unspoken Kennedy Truth*, 112.

930 Robert F. Kennedy Jr. tweet, December 29, 2023, https://twitter.com/RobertKennedyJr/status/1740784226994167910.

931 NTSB Final Report, Accident Number NYC99MA178, Registration Number N9253N, July 16, 1999, https://heavy.com/wp-content/uploads/2019/01/ntsbreport2.pdf.

932 David Von Pein's JFK Channel, "JFK Jr.'s Plane is Missing (Live Television News Coverage from July 17, 1999)," video, https://www.youtube.com/watch?v=jfO-JX8LsTc and *Dark Legacy II*, directed by John Hankey (John Hankey, 2014), https://www.youtube.com/watch?v=eL6Gn9IkVzU.

933 Jeffries, *Hidden History*, 198–200.

934 Michael Zuckoff and Matthew Brelis, "Plane Fell Fast, Probe Finds," *The Boston Globe*, July 20, 1999, http://archive.boston.com/news/packages/jfkjr/072099_plane_fell.htm and Donald Jeffries, *American Memory Hole: How the Court Historians Promote Disinformation* (New York, NY: Skyhorse Publishing, 2024), 302-304.

935 Jeffries, *Hidden History*, 198, 201.

936 "Visits by Foreign Leaders of Israel," Office of the Historian, U.S. Department of State, https://history.state.gov/departmenthistory/visits/israel.

937 Press Conference by the President and Prime Minister Barak of Israel, Presidential Hall, July 19, 1999, U.S. Department of State, https://1997-2001.state.gov/regions/nea/990719_clinton_barakpress.html.

938 Jon Hilkevitch, "Divers Find Bodies," *Chicago Tribune*, updated August 22, 2021, https://www.chicagotribune.com/news/ct-xpm-1999-07-22-9907220415-story.html and "Crash and Search Timeline," *The Washington Post*, accessed July 10, 2024, https://www.washingtonpost.com/wp-srv/national/longterm/jfkjr/recovery.htm.

939 NTSB Final Report, Accident Number NYC99MA178, Registration Number N9253N, https://heavy.com/wp-content/uploads/2019/01/ntsbreport2.pdf.

940 "Examiner: JFK Jr.'s flying was excellent," *Tampa Bay Times*, July 20, 1999, https://www.tampabay.com/archive/1999/07/20/examiner-jfk-jr-s-flying-was-excellent/#:~:text=McColgan%20said%20Kennedy%20was%20more,me%20for%20his%20flight%20check.%22.

941 "JFK Jr.: The Final Flight," *Hartford Courant*, August 1, 1999, https://www.courant.com/1999/08/01/jfk-jr-the-final-flight/.

942 NTSB Final Report, Accident Number NYC99MA178, Registration Number N9253N, https://heavy.com/wp-content/uploads/2019/01/ntsbreport2.pdf.

943 *Dark Legacy II*, directed by John Hankey (John Hankey, 2014), https://www.youtube.com/watch?v=eL6Gn9IkVzU.

944 Jeffries, *Hidden History*, 198 and David Von Pein's JFK Channel, "JFK Jr.'s Plane is Missing (Live Television News Coverage from July 17, 1999)," video, https://www.youtube.com/watch?v=jfO-JX8LsTc.

945 NTSB Final Report, Accident Number NYC99MA178, Registration Number N9253N, https://heavy.com/wp-content/uploads/2019/01/ntsbreport2.pdf.

946 Laurent Guyénot, "The Broken Presidential Destiny of JFK Jr.," *Aletho News*, February 11, 2019, *https://alethonews.com/2019/02/11/the-broken-presidential-destiny-of-jfk-jr/* and Jeb Burnside, "Revisiting JFK Jr.," *Aviation Safety*, May 16, 2016, https://www.aviationsafet ymagazine.com/features/revisiting-jfk-jr/ and Evan Thomas, "JFK Jr.'s Final Journey," *Newsweek*, August 1, 1999, https://www.newsweek.com/jfk-jrs-final-journey-165688.

947 *Dark Legacy II*, directed by John Hankey (John Hankey, 2014), https://www.youtube.com /watch?v=eL6Gn9IkVzU.

948 Jeffries, *Hidden History*, 202.

949 Joseph E. Burnside, "Revisiting JFK, Jr.," *Aviation Safety*, May 16, 2016, https://www.aviat ionsafetymagazine.com/features/revisiting-jfk-jr/.

950 Ibid.

951 Guyénot, "The Broken Presidential Destiny of JFK Jr."

952 Guyénot, "The Broken Presidential Destiny of JFK Jr." and Zuckoff and Brelis, "Plane Fell Fast, Probe Finds."

953 NTSB Final Report, Accident Number NYC99MA178, Registration Number N9253N, https://heavy.com/wp-content/uploads/2019/01/ntsbreport2.pdf.

954 NTSB Final Report, Accident Number NYC99MA178, Registration Number N9253N, https://heavy.com/wp-content/uploads/2019/01/ntsbreport2.pdf.

955 Ibid.

956 Ibid.

957 Jeffries, *Hidden History*, 201.

958 NTSB Aircraft Accident Brief, Egypt Air Flight 990, October 31, 1999, https://www.ntsb. gov/investigations/AccidentReports/Reports/AAB0201.pdf.

959 Michael Ellison, "Search for Air Crash Survivors Abandoned," *The Guardian*, November 2, 1999, https://www.theguardian.com/world/1999/nov/02/egyptaircrash.usa1.

960 Ibid., 210.

961 "Spatial Disorientation," Federal Aviation Administration, https://www.faa.gov/sites/faa. gov/files/2022-11/spatial_disorientation.pdf.

CONCLUSION

962 Address at Yale University, 11 June 1962, John F. Kennedy Presidential Library and Museum, https://www.jfklibrary.org/asset-viewer/archives/JFKPOF/039/JFKPOF-039 -001.

963 John F. Kennedy, *The Strategy of Peace* (New York, NY: Harper & Brothers, 1960), 162–163.

964 Robert Kennedy, *The Pursuit of Justice* (New York, NY: Harper & Row, 1964), 83.

WHY JFK STILL MATTERS

965 Stacey Flores Chandler, "Did JFK Say It? 'One Person Can Make a Difference and Everyone Should Try,'" The JFK Library Archives, an Inside Look, John F. Kennedy Presidential Library and Museum, October 28, 2019, https://jfk.blogs.archives.gov/2019 /10/28/make-a-difference-quote/.

966 Linda Qui, "Did the U.S. Spend $6 Trillion in Middle East Wars?" October 27, 2016, *PolitiFact*, https://www.politifact.com/factchecks/2016/oct/27/donald-trump/did-us-s pend-6-trillion-middle-east-wars/.

967 Inaugural Address, January 20, 1961, John F. Kennedy Presidential Library and Museum, https://www.jfklibrary.org/learn/about-jfk/historic-speeches/inaugural-address.

968 Ibid.

Index

Aase, Jean, 61
Ace Guard Service, 155. *See also* Cesar, Thane Eugene; Merritt, Jack
Adair, Randolph, 173
Adams, Robert, 65
Adams, Victoria, 93, 130-131
Adoula, Cyrille, 8
AIPAC, 18, 22-24
Algeria, 48-49, 59
Alpha 66, 54
Alsop, Joseph, 126-127
Ambassador Hotel, 141-142, 150, 151-176
American Academy of Forensic Sciences, 119, 165, 187
American Bottlers of Carbonated Beverages, 70, 80
American Israel Public Affairs Committee. *See* AIPAC
American University peace speech, 6, 13, 20
American Zionist Council, 15, 18-19, 23, 127, 143
Amir, Yigal, 213-214
Ancient Mystical Order of Rosy Cross (AMORC), 146
Anderson, George, 12
Andrews, Dean, 56, 108, 196, 201-203
Angleton, James Jesus, 21, 24-25, 36, 44-47, 50-53, 63-64, 78-79, 81, 119, 125-126, 128, 191, 197-199, 203
Arcacha Smith, Sergio, 77
Argonne National Laboratory, 62
Armaments Development Authority, 21
Arnold, Carolyn, 85
ARRB. *See* Assassination Records Review Board

Assassination Records Review Board, 207-208
Attwood, William, 4-5
Aubry, Dick, 171
AZC. *See* American Zionist Council
Azzoni, Meg, 212
B'nai B'rith, 62
Bailey, William, 163
Baker, Barney, 113
Baker, M. L., 94, 130
Ball, George, 23
Banister, Guy, 54-56, 77, 193-195
Barak, Ehud, 219
Barbour, Walworth, 19, 21
Barr, Candy, 113
Bartlett, Charles, 18
Bay of Pigs, 9-10, 14-15, 81
Behn, Gerald, 71, 87
Belgium, 8
Benavides, Domingo, 100, 105
Ben-Gurion, David, 16-17, 19-24, 59, 111, 197. *See also* Israel
Beringer, Thomas, 163
Berlin, 9-11
Berman, Emile, 182
Bethesda Medical Center, 119, 132-1323, 201
Bissel, Richard Jr., 14
Bloom Advertising Agency, 73. *See also* Bloom, Sam
Bloom, Sam, 73-76, 79-80, 86, 95, 108, 115
Bloomfield, Bernard, 59
Bloomfield, Louis Mortimer, 58-59, 62, 203
Blough, Roger, 30
Boggs, Hale, 127-128, 138
Bolden, Abraham, 66-67
Boone, Eugene, 101, 134
Bosch, Juan, 7

Boston Coast Guard, 219
Boswell, J. Thornton, 118
Botting, Laverne, 150
Bowers, Lee, 86, 89
Braden, Jim, 95, 110
Brading, Eugene Hale. See
   Braden, Jim
Brennan, Howard, 96
Bringuier, Carlos, 56
Bronfman, Edgar, 62
Bronfman, Samuel, 62, 70
Bruno, Gerald, 69-72, 74
Bryan, William J., 189
Bucknell, David, 41
Buckner, Everett, 152
Bundy, McGeorge, 125
Bundy, Vernon, 199
Burba, Harold, 171-172
Bureau of Science Liaison, 207
Burgun, Todd, 218. See also
   Boston Coast Guard
Burlet, Bob, 203
Burns, Frank, 157-159, 168-
   169
Burris, Richard, 179
Burroughs, Warren H., 101-103
Butler, David, 164
Byrd, David H., 80
Cabell, Charles, 15, 76
Cabell, Earle, 75-76, 111, 122
Cambodia, 6
Campaign Finance, 18, 24, 33-
   35
CAP. See Civil Air Patrol
Carnegie Endowment for
   International Peace, 16
Carrico, Charles, 97
Carson, Rachel, 31
Carter, Jimmy, 206-207
Carvajal, Jose, 174
Castro, Fidel, 4-5, 9, 53, 55-56,
   63, 81, 110-111, 190-191,
   199-200, 206, 215
CIA. See Central Intelligence
   Agency
Crull, Elgin, 76
Central Intelligence Agency, 2-
   3, 14-15, 21-22, 24-25, 35,

37-38, 44, 51, 54-57, 59-61,
   63-64, 76, 78-80, 91, 110,
   119, 122, 125-126, 128-129,
   136, 143, 155, 178, 189-
   191, 196-198, 203-204, 207
   Bay of Pigs, 9, 12-13
   Congo, 8
   Indonesia, 7-8
   Israel, 21-22
   Oswald, Lee Harvey 45-49,
     52
   Paine, Ruth, 51
   Permendix, 59
   Shaw, Clay, 57, 79
Centro Mondiale Commerciale
   (CMC), 58-59, 62
Cesar, Thane Eugene, 154-
   155, 166-168, 190-192
Chemical Industry, 31
Cheramie, Rose, 74-75
Chicago Assassination Plot,
   65-67
Chomsky, Noam, 206, 231
Church Committee, 55
Civil Air Patrol, 40, 55
Clark, Ramsey, 197, 199
Clinton, Bill, 218
Clinton, Hilary, 215
CMC. See Centro Mondiale
   Commerciale
Cohen, Mickey, 110-112, 115,
   190
Cold War, 3-9, 47, 49, 125, 207
Collier, Charles, 163
Congo, 8-9, 34
Connally, John, 68-73, 77, 90,
   118, 132-133, 135, 161, 205
Cooper, Grant, 182-183, 186,
   190
Cooper, John Sherman, 128,
   138
Crahan, Marcus, 179
Craig, Roger, 96, 103
Craven, Wes, iii
Cronkite, Walter, 6
Cuba, 9, 11, 14, 49, 53-56, 61,
   63-64, 77-78, 81, 110-111,
   114, 116, 128, 195, 215.

See also Bay of Pigs, Cuban Missile Crisis, Cuban exiles
Cuban exiles, 9, 55, 78, 81, 112
Cuban Missile Crisis, 4, 11-12, 49
Cuban Student Directorate (DRE), 56
Cullum, Robert, 70, 74
Cunningham, Cortland, 104, 135
Curry, Jesse, 76, 87, 109, 113-114
Dallas Chamber of Commerce, 69-70, 72, 74
Dallas Citizens Council, 74, 76, 79-80
Dallas Uranium and Oil, 75, 95
Dal-Tex Building, 75, 80, 95, 110
Darshan-Leitner, Nitsana, 214
Davis, Jack, 101
Day, J. C., 134
Delgado, Nelson, 41
Desalvo, Bryan, 189
Diamond, Bernard, 184-185
Dillon, Douglas, 86
DiPierro, Angelo, 160
DiPierro, Vincent, 155, 157, 159-160, 188
Disarmament, 12-13, 20, 64, 124, 228
Dominican Republic, 7, 9
Dougherty, Jack, 84
DRE. *See* Cuban Student Directorate
Duffy, Eselyn, 164
Dulles, Allen, 14-15, 25, 35, 37, 49, 51-52, 59, 128-129, 138, 198, 214
Dymond, Irvin, 200
Edwards, Robert, 92
Egypt, 17, 22, 59, 149, 224-225
Egypt Air 990 plane crash, 224-225
Eisenhower, Dwight, 8-9, 31
Ellsberg, Daniel, 12

Eshkol, Levi, 21-22
Euins, Amos, 92
Evans, Elizabeth, 161, 192
FAA, 217-219, 223
Fair Play for Cuba Committee, 53-54, 56, 61, 63, 114, 116, 195
FBI. *See* Federal Bureau of Investigation
FDA. *See* Federal Drug Administration
Federal Bureau of Investigation, 46, 50, 55, 61, 66, 76, 85-86, 104-106, 108, 110-113, 123, 125-126, 134-138, 149-154, 157, 163, 165, 172, 174-175, 179, 193-195, 197, 202, 204
    Abaraham Feinberg, 24
    Steel Crisis, 30
    Albert Schweitzer College, 42
    Oswald, 44, 48, 52, 54, 56, 65, 67
Federal Bureau of Narcotics, 32-33
Federal Drug Administration, 31-32
Federal Reserve System, 27-28
Feinberg, Abraham, 18, 24-25, 62, 110
Fenner, Nannie Lee, 67-68
Ferrie, David, 40-41, 55-57, 59-61, 77, 95, 194-197, 199-201, 203
Finck, Pierre, 118-119, 201
Fischer, Ronald, 92
Ford, Gerald R., 128, 138
Foreign Agents Registration Act of 1938, 18. *See Also* American Zionist Council
Foreign aid, 4, 35
FPCC. *See* Fair Play For Cuba Committee
Frazier, Buell, 84
Freed, Evan, 173
Freedman, Morty, 75

Fruge, Francis, 77
Gallegos, Rose, 151
Gallivan, Jack, 159
Garner, Dorothy, 93-94, 130-131
Garrison, Jim, 48-50, 53, 55-57, 59, 61-62, 68, 77, 95, 132, 193-204, 207
Gaudet, William, 61
de Gaulle, Charles, 37, 48, 79
Gazit, Mordechai, 15, 17
George, 212-213, 215, 222, 228
Germany, 10, 31
Ghana, 4
Gheesling, Marvin, 65
Givens, Charles, 85, 103
Goldstein, Ira, 160
Gottlieb, Sidney, 91
Graham, Katherine Meyer, 127
Graham, Philip, 126-127
Grammer, Billy, 116
Green, George, 153-154, 172, 174
Green, Stephen, 22-23
Grier, Rosey, 164, 173
Griffin, Booker, 160, 173-174
Gruber, Alexander Philip, 112
Gurvich, William, 198
Habighorst, Aloysius, 196
Haganah, 58, 78, 110-111
Halevy, Efraim, 21
Hamill, Pete, 158
Hargis, Bobby, 90
Harkness, D. V., 95, 114
Harrell, Douglas, 150
Harris, Elizabeth, 73
Harris, Kamala, 209
Helms, Richard, 45, 57, 129, 198
Hendrix, Frank, 155
Henry Schroder Banking Corporation, 59
Hernandez, Enrique "Hank", 178-181, 186
Hilsman, Roger, 5
Hoffa, Jimmy, 112-113
Holland, S. M., 91

Hollinger, Lin, 187
Hoover, J. Edgar, 123, 125-126, 136
Hosty, James, 48, 67, 76, 86, 108
Houghton, Robert A., 178
House Select Committee on Assassinations, 45, 48, 50, 54, 72, 77, 78, 89, 111-112, 136, 198, 204-206
Houston, Richard, 174-175
Howard, John, 177, 192
HSCA. See House Select Committee on Assassinations
Hughes, Howard, 191
Humes, James, 118-119
hypnosis, 173, 184-185, 188-189
Indonesia, 7-9, 35
inflation, 29
International Trade Mart (New Orleans), 57, 59-60, 108, 109, 193, 195
Israel, 2, 15-25, 36-38, 48, 50, 56-58, 60, 64, 68, 70, 75-78, 107-108, 109, 115, 120, 122, 137-140, 143-145, 148, 183, 185-186, 194, 199, 203-204, 209, 215, 229. See also American Zionist Council
Dimona Nuclear Facility, 19-24, 49, 208
Financing of nuclear weapons, 24, 56, 62, 70, 79, 111, 203
Nuclear Materials and Equipment Corporation (NUMEC), 21, 25, 58, 60
Palestinian refugee issue, 15-16, 20, 22, 185-186, 233
Six-Day War, 23, 124, 152
Ivon, Louis, 196
Jarmon, James Jr., 85
Jarvis, James Jr., 88
Jenkins, Walter, 69, 71, 125

JFK film, 207-208
Johnson, Brad, 164
Johnson, Darnell, 155, 174
Johnson, Guy, 77
Johnson, Joseph E., 16
Johnson, Lyndon, 6-8, 12, 22-
    25, 38, 68-69, 73, 79, 89,
    107, 119, 122-124, 126-127,
    129, 140-141, 144, 207
Johnson, Rafer, 159, 163, 171,
    173, 176
Jones, Howard, 7
Jonnson, J. Eric, 70, 74
Katzenbach, Nicholas, 123,
    125-126, 138
Kefauver Committee, 112
Keir, Katie, 175
Kelsey, Frances, 31
Kenen, Isaiah L., 18, 22, 24-25
Kennedy, Jackie, 6, 9, 52, 64,
    90, 117-118, 121, 140-141,
    212-213,232
Kennedy, John F. *See* all other
    index items
Kennedy, John F. Jr., iv, 210-
    227
Kennedy, Joseph, 24, 89
Kennedy, Robert F., iv, , 2, 4,
    18, 24, 30, 32-35, 64, 113,
    123, 126-127, 140-192, 204,
    206, 208-211, 230-231
Kennedy, Robert F. Jr.,
    209,216
KGB, 44, 63, 128
Khrushchev, Nikita, 10-11
Kilduff, Malcolm, 97
Kimble, Jules, 59
Klein, Joseph, 168
Klein's Sporting Goods, 62,
    107
Komer, R. W., 17, 20
Kostikov, Valery, 63, 128
Krock, Arthur, 64
LaBeau, Albert, 149-150
LaHive, Joe, 164
LAKAM. *See* Bureau of
    Science Liason
Lamoreaux, Al, 163

Lane, Mark, 41
de Lannurien, Georges, 78
Lansky, Meyer, 110, 112, 119,
    125-126
Laos, 5-6, 9-10
LAPD. *See* Los Angeles Police
    Department
Latona, Sebastian Frances,
    106, 134
Lawson, Winston, 73-74
LeMay, Curtis, 11-12, 119
Leven, Gustave, 70
Littell, Robert, 211, 215
Lockheed, 41, 154
Long, Russell, 193, 196
Lorenz, Marita, 78
Los Angeles Police
    Department, 149-150, 154,
    157, 162-163, 168, 172,
    177-178, 186, 190
Lovelady, Bill, 85, 130-131
Lowe, Jacques, 214
Lowenstein, Allard, 144
Lubic, Richard, 166, 168, 171-
    172
Lubic, Robert, 158
Lumumba, Patrice, 8
MacArthur, J. R., 163
Maheu, Robert, 190-191
Mankiewicz, Frank, 154
Marchman, Eara, 154
Marilyn-Belt Manufacturing, 75,
    95
Martel, Ned, 212
Martin, B. J., 86
Martin, Consuela, 55
Martin, Jack, 55, 193-194
Mattei, Enrico, 59
McBroom, Marcus, 168
McClelland, Robert, 97-98
McCloy, John J., 128-129, 131,
    134, 138
McColgan, John, 220-221
McCone, John, 22
McCord, James, 54
McNamara, Robert, 5, 10, 30
McWillie, Lewis, 112-113
Meir, Golda, 17, 19

Meltzer, Harold, 110, 112
de Menil, Jean, 48, 49, 55, 57
Mercer, Julia Ann, 84-85, 87, 90
Merritt, Jack, 173
Meyer, Edward, 222
Meyers, Lawrence V., 61-62, 95
Milchan, Arnon, 207-209
Mobutu, Joseph, 8-9
de Mohrenschildt, George, 48-52, 55
Mooney, Luke, 98, 101
Moore, J. Walton, 49-50
Mossad, 21, 49, 59, 79, 189
Moyers, Bill, 123, 125
Moynihan, Daniel Patrick, 215
Nasser, Gamal Abdel, 16-17, 23, 149
National Crime Syndicate, 110, 119, 125
National Photographic Intelligence Center, 136
National Transportation Safety Board, 213, 217, 219, 221-226
Nightmare on Elm Street, iii
Noguchi, Thomas, 156, 161-62, 183, 187
Non-Aligned Movement, 7
Noonan, Billy, 215
Norman, Harold, 88, 93
Novel, Gordon, 198
NPIC. See National Photographic Intelligence Center
NTSB. See National Transportation Safety Board
Nuclear Materials and Equipment Corporation, 21, 25, 58, 60
NUMEC, See Nuclear Materials and Equipment Corporation
O'Donnell, Kenny, 71-72, 117-118
Office of Naval Intelligence, 54, 77, 110, 119, 198

Office of Strategic Services, 110, 198
ONI. See Office of Naval Intelligence
Operation Underworld, 110
Organized crime, 2, 38, 110-112, 115, 143, 190-194, 204
OSS. See Office of Strategic Services
Oswald, Lee Harvey, 40-68, 71, 74-110, 111, 113-117, 119-121, 122-123, 125, 128, 130, 132, 133-138, 193-196, 199-203, 205-206, 211, 230-231
    Albert Schweitzer College, 42-43
    Arrest, 56, 60, 101-108
    Atsugi, Japan, 41
    Espionage watch list, 65
    FBI, 44, 48, 52, 54, 56, 65, 67
    Government files, 45-46
    Marines, 40-42
    Marksmanship, 42
    Mexico City, 62-65, 129
    Murder of, 107, 113-115
    New Orleans, 53-61
    Return to U.S., 47-48
    State Department, 45-47, 63
    Suicide attempt, 44
    Texas School Book Depository, 65, 82-84, 87-88, 92-94, 96-98
    Tippet shooting, 99-100
    US Embassy, 44
    Voter registration event, 56-57, 198
Oswald, Marina, 46-48, 53-54, 61, 67, 84, 136
Oswald, Robert, 40, 67
Pack, Dean, 152
Paine, Michael, 50-52
Paine, Ruth, 50-53, 61, 65, 67, 79, 103
Palencia, Arthur, 76

Palestinians, 15-16, 23, 185-186, 213, 233. *See also* Sirhan Bashira Sirahn

Panda, Ronald, 169, 172

Parkland Memorial Hospital, 96, 117, 131-132, 135

Parsons, Russell, 190

Patrusky, Martin, 155,159

Pena, Manuel, 178

Pentagon Papers, 12

Pepper, William, 188

Peres, Shimon, 207-208

Perez, Jesus, 154-155

Permindex, 49, 55, 58-59, 62, 79, 203, 207

Perry, Malcolm, 97, 132

Pharmaceutical industry, 31

Phillips, David Atlee, 15, 54

Pitts, Elnora, 114

Plimpton, Freddy, 159, 169, 173

Plimpton, George, 173

Postal, Julia, 101, 108

Price, J. C., 90

Pruszynski, Stanislaw, 164-165

Rabin, Yitzhak, 213-214

RAFAEL. *See* Armaments Development Authority

Reilly Coffee Company, 54

Rhodes, Nina, 164, 172

Roberts, Delphine, 55

Roberts, Earlene, 99, 101

Roberts, Emory, 86-87, 89

Rocca, Ray, 197, 203

Rockefellers, 35, 49, 130, 199

Rolon, Raymond, 163

Romero, Juan, 151, 155, 157-159, 171

Roselli, Johnny, 190

Ross, Karen, 151

Rostow, Eugene, 123-127

de Rothschild, Edmond, 58

Rowland, Arnold, 87-88

Rozzi, Robert, 163

Russell, Richard B., 128, 138

Russo, Perry, 200

Salinger, Pierre, 209-214, 215

Sarnoff, David, 198

Sarnoff, Robert, 198

Saxon, James, 27-28

Schepps, Julius, 70

Schlei, Norbert, 171

Schlesinger, Arthur Jr., 12-14, 127

Schlumberger Corporation, 48, 55-57, 77

Schneid, William, 149

Schrade, Paul, 162, 191, 209

Schulman, Don, 166-168

SDECE, 78-79

Secret Service, 31, 55, 66-67, 71-73, 76, 80, 86-87, 89, 91-92, 95, 98, 106, 116-117, 132, 136, 197, 213

Serrano, Sandra, 149-150, 171, 174-177, 182

Seven Days in May, 64

Shalit, Binyamin, 190

Shanklin, Gordon, 68

Sharaga, Paul, 174-176

Shaw, Clay, 49, 56-57, 59-60, 77, 79, 108, 109, 193, 195-203, 207

Shelley, William, 85, 130-131

Sheridan, Walter, 198

Shirkova, Rimma, 44

Silent Spring, 31

Sirhan, Adel, 178

Sirhan, Sirhan Bishara, 140-192, 208-209, 230

Smith, J. M., 91

Soviet Union, 3-4, 6, 8-13, 16, 37, 41, 43-49, 59, 63-64, 67, 102, 124, 128, 136, 148, 198

Special Unit Senator, 178, 190

Spiegel, Herbert, 185

Spiesel, Charles, 200-201

Standard Oil, 49

Starnes, Richard, 64

Statler Hilton, 70-71, 73, 80

Steel crisis, 29-31

Stern, Edgar B. Sr., 60-61, 80, 109, 120

Stern, Edgar Bloom Jr., 60-61, 80, 109, 120

Stevenson, Adlai, 8-9
Sturgis, Frank, 78
Styles, Sandra, 93, 130-131
Suharto, 7-8
Sukarno, 8, 35
SUS. *See* Special Unit Senator
Taxation, 26-29, 32-33, 35
Taylor, Maxwell, 5, 10
Terenzio, RoseMarie, 216
Texas School Book Depository,
  65-66, 68-69, 72, 74-76, 80,
  84, 86-88, 92-93, 95, 98-99,
  101-105, 136
Texas Theater, 100-103
The Manchurian Candidate,
  142, 207
Thornley, Kerry, 41
Tippit, J. D., 96, 99-102, 104-
  105, 134-135, 137
Trade Mart (Dallas), 69-74, 76
Truck, Dick, 170
Truly, Roy, 93-94
Truman, Harry, 122, 127
TSBD. *See* Texas School Book
  Depository
Turkey, 11
TWA flight 800, 212
U-2, 41, 45, 49, 66, 156
Uecker, Karl, 142, 155-159,
  164, 168, 171
Umbrella man, 88-89
United Nations, 6, 9, 16, 186
Urso, Lisa, 158-159, 166, 168
USS *Liberty*, 23, 119
Vallee, Thomas Arthur, 66-67
Vallero, Ernest, 149
Van Praag, Philip, 164
Vanunu, Mordechai, 208
Veciana, Antonio, 54
Vietnam, 5-10, 14, 37, 64, 66,
  126, 140, 207
Warren Commission, 41, 49-
  50, 56, 61, 68, 72, 84, 92,
  95, 96, 98-100, 103, 105,
  107-108, 123, 128-133, 136-
  138, 194, 195, 197-199,
  201-202, 204-205
WDSU, 60

Webster, Robert, 46
Weitzman, Seymour, 91, 101,
  134
Wiegers, Mary Ann, 175
Wilcott, James A., 48
Williams, Bonnie Ray, 85, 88,
  98
Witt, Steven, 89
Wolfer, DeWayne, 161-163,
  186-187
Women's Building, 71-73, 87
Woodward, Mary, 87
World War II, 10, 24, 43, 48,
  54, 89, 106, 110, 128, 198
Worrell, James, 92
Wright, Charles, 163
Yarborough, Ralph, 69
Zapruder film, iii, 121, 133,
  136, 204